Teaching Mathematics in Diverse Classrooms
for Grades 5-8

Teaching Mathematics in Diverse Classrooms for Grades 5-8

PRACTICAL STRATEGIES AND ACTIVITIES THAT PROMOTE UNDERSTANDING AND PROBLEM SOLVING ABILITY

Volume 2

Benny F. Tucker
UNION UNIVERSITY

Ann H. Singleton
UNION UNIVERSITY

Terry L. Weaver
UNION UNIVERSITY

PEARSON

Boston   Columbus   Indianapolis   New York   San Francisco   Upper Saddle River
Amsterdam   Cape Town   Dubai   London   Madrid   Milan   Munich   Paris   Montréal   Toronto
Delhi   Mexico City   São Paulo   Sydney   Hong Kong   Seoul   Singapore   Taipei   Tokyo

Executive Editor and Publisher: Stephen D. Dragin
Editorial Assistant: Katherine Wiley
Marketing Manager: Joanna Sabella
Production Editor: Paula Carroll
Editorial Production Service: Element LLC
Manufacturing Buyer: Megan Cochran
Electronic Composition: Element LLC
Cover Designer: Jennifer Hart

Credits and acknowledgments borrowed from other sources and reproduced, with permission, in this textbook appear on the appropriate page within text.

Photo Credits

Page 2: Barbara Schwartz/Merrill. **Page 3:** Barbara Schwartz/Merrill. **Page 13:** Annie Pickert Fuller. **Page 17:** Susan Van Etten/PhotoEdit. **Page 31:** Silver Burdett Ginn Needham. **Page 49:** Jim West/Alamy. **Page 69:** Bob Daemmrich/Alamy. **Page 107:** Barbara Schwartz/Merrill. **Page 133:** Silver Burdett Ginn. **Page 148:** Todd Yarrington/Merrill. **Page 154:** Bill Aron/PhotoEdit. **Page 177:** Todd Yarrington/Merrill. **Pages 222:** Silver Burdett Ginn. **Page 234:** Temple Daily Telegram, Andrew Nenque/AP Images. **Page 268:** Michael Newman/PhotoEdit. **Page 275:** Todd Yarrington/Merrill.

Previous editions were published under the title *Teaching Mathematics to All Children: Designing and Adapting Instruction to Meet the Needs of Diverse Learners, Second Edition* © 2006, 2002.

Many of the designations by manufacturers and sellers to distinguish their products are claimed as trademarks. Where those designations appear in this book, and the publisher was aware of a trademark claim, the designations have been printed in initial caps or all caps.

Library of Congress Cataloging-in-Publication Data

CIP data not ready at press time but is on file.

10 9 8 7 6 5 4 3 2 1

www.pearsonhighered.com

ISBN 10: 0-13-290729-1
ISBN 13: 978-0-13-290729-3

brief contents

contents

about the authors

Benny F. Tucker earned his Ph.D. at the University of Illinois in 1975. He has authored or co-authored more than 50 books, on topics ranging from teaching methods for elementary school mathematics to the use of instructional activities in the mathematics classroom. He has authored or co-authored more than 20 articles in professional journals and has made more than 30 presentations at professional conferences.

Ann Haltom Singleton is Associate Dean of the School of Education at Union University in Jackson Tennessee. She earned her Ed.D in Special Education from the University of Memphis. Her research areas include leadership development and mathematics instruction, especially in inclusive settings. She has contributed to numerous articles and has made over 30 national presentations. She was recognized as the Union University 2003 Faculty of the Year.

Terry L. Weaver honed his teaching skills in the Miami-Dade County School System. He received his Ph.D. in Special Education from George Peabody College for Teachers at Vanderbilt University. Dr. Weaver then shared his teaching skills at Carson-Newman College and Union University where he continues to teach. Dr. Weaver has served as an item writer for and participated in the revalidation of the Praxis II Specialty Area Test in SE (Core Knowledge). He is a co-author of *Teaching Mathematics to All Children: Designing and Adapting Instruction to Meet the Needs of Diverse Learners*, has presented on differentiated instruction and assessment, universal design, inclusion, and adapting instruction for diverse learners, and recently lead the revision of a chapter on mathematics in Vaughn's and Bos's *Strategies for Teaching Students with Learning and Behavior Problems*.

preface

Why This Book?

The student diversity found in middle-grade classrooms is extensive. The students in a typical classroom are diverse in gender, diverse in race and ethnicity, and diverse in religion and culture. Students are diverse in ability and interest, and diverse in preferred learning styles. They are diverse in family background, and diverse with respect to resources in the home such as books and technology. They are diverse in intellectual strengths and weaknesses. In the face of such diversity, how can the teacher expect to plan for effective instruction?

Although teachers must certainly be aware of student diversity and the need to accommodate that diversity, it is perhaps more important for middle-grade teachers to be aware of the ways in which their students are alike. For example, almost universally, young people are kinesthetic learners. It is natural for them to get up and move around. They enjoy classroom activities that allow (even require) them to get up and move about. Young people are naturally inquisitive. They are interested in what, why, and how. It is their nature to talk about things. They like to talk to one another. They like to talk about the things that they are experiencing and learning. Young people are concrete learners. They like to see and show how things are related. They like it when meaningful experiences come together in a sensible way. They like to understand.

In this text, we provide an approach to the planning and teaching of middle-grade mathematics that is based on the nature of middle-grade students. We encourage the planning of lessons that

- require students to get out of their seats and move about as the concepts and skills are being developed,
- require verbal discourse among the students,
- use physical and pictorial models that help the students see and understand the big ideas and relationships that comprise mathematics.

We understand that teachers are responsible for knowing how well their students are learning and what their students are not learning. Therefore, we encourage teachers to plan lessons that include opportunities for continual monitoring of student learning.

Structure of the Book

The text begins with three introductory chapters that provide a basic understanding of instructional activities and lesson planning. Then there are seven chapters devoted to teaching the content that most commonly appears in mathematics textbooks for grades 5-8. We have not attempted to provide comprehensive coverage of every topic that might appear in a 5-8 textbook. Rather, our intent has been to emphasize a way of planning and teaching effectively that will result in learning, understanding, and retention of important concepts and skills that lead to the ability to apply those concepts and skills to solve problems. Important to that way of teaching is effective planning. Therefore, we have made planning for effective teaching an important part of this text. We also have included some material that appears in earlier grades with particular attention diagnosis and remediation.

Emphasis on Concept and Skill Development

On the basis of findings of educational research that support a more thorough development of concepts and skills as well as our personal experiences, we have chosen to make more effective development of mathematical concepts and skills a major emphasis. As a result of that emphasis, virtually all activities suggested in the chapters are developmental activities (activities that develop specific concepts and skills in those chapters). Since we made a conscious choice not to include practice activities in those chapters, the final chapter is devoted to effective practice. In that chapter, we present a selection of practice activities that can be used after the concepts or skills have been developed.

Basic Philosophy

We believe that successful teaching results in understanding, that understanding provides the soundest basis for skill development, and that understanding results in better retention of what is learned. We believe that the best way to help students understand mathematical ideas is to lead them to connect those ideas to other ideas that they already understand. We believe that, for middle-grade students, understanding of mathematical concepts and skills depends on the development of appropriate mental imagery for those concepts and skills. And, we believe that *all students* should be given the opportunity to develop that kind of understanding of mathematics.

Acknowledgments

This book evolved from informal conversations with many colleagues about how teachers could plan to teach more effectively, from preservice and in-service teachers who responded to our ideas before they were fully formed, and from experiences of young people who demonstrated that the more fully evolved teaching methods really worked. And, of course, invaluable assistance was provided by these professionals, whose reviews of the preliminary manuscript helped to direct the text into its final form: Jim Burns, The College of St. Rose; Linda K. Elksnin, The Citadel; and Daniel C. Orey, California State University, Sacramento. Finally, we wish to thank the preservice and in-service undergraduate and graduate students who provided suggestions for clarification of this text.

Benny F. Tucker
Ann H. Singleton
Terry L. Weaver

Teaching Mathematics in Diverse Classrooms
for Grades 5-8

one

INSTRUCTIONAL ACTIVITIES
The Building Blocks for Effective Instruction

CHAPTER OUTLINE

Instructional Activities

Developmental Activities

    Exploratory Developmental Activities

    Consolidating Developmental Activities

Practice Activities

    Think-Time Practice Activities

    Speed-Drill Practice Activities

Application Activities

    Classroom Applications

    Real-World Problems

Assessment Activities

Flexible Use of Activities and Materials

Exercises and Activities

Instructional Activities

A common pitfall for teachers who use an activity-based program of instruction is to focus on the procedures of the activity and to judge its instructional value primarily on how fun it is, on how much the students like it, or on how "cool" it is. Certainly, we want learning to be fun. We want our students to like learning, and we want to do things with them that are "really cool." However, really cool isn't enough. The primary criterion for judging an instructional activity should be: *What are the students learning during the activity?* It follows, then, that the first step in selection of an instructional activity must be identification of the learning objective. The type of activity that is appropriate depends on the nature of the objective. The kind of activity that should be used depends on whether the objective is for students to learn something new, to become proficient with something that they have already learned, or to be able to use what they have already learned to solve problems, or whether the objective is for the teacher to find out what level of mastery the student has achieved. For our purposes in this book, we will classify activities into four types:

1. Developmental (for new learning)
2. Practice (for development of proficiency with material already learned)
3. Application (for problem solving using concepts and skills already learned)
4. Assessment (for demonstration of level of learning)

Developmental Activities

Developmental activities are activities that teach something new. If students have to already know the target concept or skill in order to do the activity, then the activity is not developmental. There are two distinct levels of developmental activities: *exploratory* and *consolidating*.

Exploratory Developmental Activities

The purpose of exploratory developmental activities is to provide a core of experiences that will form the basis for generalization of concepts or skills. Sometimes the students' previous life experiences are an adequate basis for the needed generalizations. But, more frequently, it is necessary to create opportunities for students (at least some of them) to have the needed experiences. This necessity arises out of the obvious fact that before students' experiences can be used by the teacher to develop a new idea, the students must have had those experiences.

Consolidating Developmental Activities

The purpose of consolidating developmental activities is to help students to identify patterns and recognize relationships, to hypothesize and test those relationships, to clarify concepts, to develop procedures, and to learn terminology and notation with which to communicate about those patterns, relationships, concepts, and procedures.

Practice Activities

Practice activities are activities that help students to become proficient in the use of concepts and skills that have already been developed. Whereas the emphasis of developmental activities is to develop comprehension or understanding, the emphasis of practice activities is to develop skill. As a general rule, students do not learn new things from practice. However, through practice, they may very well become more proficient with what they have already learned. Appropriate practice may also help to add more permanence to that learning. As is true with developmental activities, there are two distinct types of practice activities: *think time* and *speed drill*.

Think-Time Practice Activities

Think-time practice activities place the emphasis on accuracy. Students have adequate time to think carefully about concepts and connections, and plenty of time to think carefully through each step of a procedure. They may even be allowed time to look up things that need clarification. Students are told, "There is no hurry, but be sure you are right."

Speed-Drill Practice Activities

Speed-drill practice activities place the emphasis on quick answers. Some teachers believe that speed drill can contribute to memorization and to the ability to habituate procedures. Other teachers point out that, under speed-drill conditions, answers come from only the children who already have quick recall of the facts or those who can already quickly apply the procedure. These are, of course, certainly the students who do not need this practice. On the other hand, those who cannot respond quickly are encouraged to make a wild guess or simply say "I don't know" and then stop thinking about it.

We must seriously consider whether the overall effect of speed drill is negative rather than positive. Indeed, with very few exceptions, very little is accomplished with speed-drill practice that would not be accomplished more effectively with appropriate think-time practice. Speed-drill practice activities will, therefore, receive limited attention in this book.

Application Activities

Application activities are activities that help students learn to use concepts and skills in settings that are different from the settings in which those concepts and skills were learned. Application activities allow students to solve a variety of problems by using the concepts and skills that they understand and at which they are proficient. Application activities can be categorized into two groups: *classroom applications* and *real-world problems.*

Classroom Applications

Classroom applications include instructional activities that require students to build on already learned concepts and skills by using them to develop new ones. Since an activity may involve application of old ideas to develop new ones, it follows that a single activity could be application with respect to one topic and also developmental with respect to another topic. Classroom applications also include contrived examples, such as textbook problems, that require students to use recently learned concepts and skills. A thin line separates this kind of classroom application from practice. The difference is that practice typically requires students to use the new concept or skill more or less as they used it when it was being learned. On the other hand, contrived examples used as classroom application typically require students to use the new concept or skill in ways that are, to some degree, different from the ways the concept or skill was used when it was being learned.

Real-World Problems

Real-world problems are problems that students will encounter outside the classroom. To devise a real-world problem that applies a particular concept or skill, the teacher must first determine how that concept or skill is used outside the classroom (that is, in the real world). The next step is to create an activity that will require the students to use the concept or skill in exactly that way.

Assessment Activities

Assessment activities are activities that require students to demonstrate, in an observable way, their depth of learning of concepts and skills. Assessment nearly always consists of having students complete a task or several tasks that are indicators of their learning. For example, the teacher might ask students to complete a chapter test, to complete homework consisting of a set of exercises, or perhaps simply to answer a straightforward question. Unfortunately, assessment is often superficial because the assessment task is incomplete.

The old story about six blind men describing an elephant illustrates such an incomplete assessment. One blind man felt the side of the elephant and concluded that an elephant is like a wall. A second blind man felt the elephant's leg and decided that an elephant is like a tree. A third blind man felt the elephant's trunk and believed that an elephant is like a large squirming snake. A fourth blind man felt the elephant's tusk and decided that an elephant is like a large sword. A fifth blind man felt the elephant's ear and decided that an elephant is like a fan. The sixth and last blind man felt the elephant's tail and concluded that an elephant is like a rope.

Of course, all the blind men were correct, but each of their descriptions was based on a biased perspective. Their descriptions of the elephant were correct but incomplete. Similarly, our assessment of student learning is often incomplete because, like the blind men, we rely on limited information. Instead of basing our assessment on a single assessment task, we can get a more complete, a more reliable, a more useful assessment of student learning if we get our information from various of sources.

People normally think of assessment as a formal process such as giving a test or quiz, usually after the teacher has completed instruction. Such assessment can determine whether the students have learned the material that was taught, it can determine what material was not learned, and it can even determine how effective the teacher was. This assessment information can inform the planning of future lessons. However, there is another approach to assessment that has many additional benefits.

A typical lesson would include a variety of instructional activities. For example, a short practice activity may be used to review previously learned material. A series of developmental activities may be used to teach a new concept or skill. There might be an application activity that illustrates how the new material can be used. Each of these different parts of the lesson is an opportunity for the teacher to *monitor* student *understanding* and gather assessment information.

The significant characteristic that allows traditional instructional activities to produce assessment information is that *the teacher is paying attention*. The teacher must carefully monitor the students during every instructional activity. He or she must take note of what the students know and what they do not know, and focus on the contexts in which each student can do what is required as well as those in which the student cannot do what is required. This information can provide a clearer understanding of each student's level of learning. If the teacher is observing and gathering information (monitoring), then *every developmental, practice, or application activity can also be an assessment activity.*

Monitoring student learning should be an essential and integral part of every instructional activity. By continually observing their work, the teacher is able to make adjustments during the lesson for those students who are having difficulties. For example, the teacher might realize that other examples are needed. She or he might refer to prior knowledge that is the basis for the new lesson, or perhaps assign a practice activity, allowing students to work with partners while the teacher works with individuals who are having difficulty.

Flexible Use of Activities and Materials

In order to develop an activity-based system of instruction, the teacher must identify content topics and then develop a variety of instructional activities for those topics. Activities for each topic should focus on development, practice, application, and assessment. Pencil-and-paper activities, physically active activities, whole-class activities, small-group activities, or individual or partner activities should be included. The teacher's work can be reduced substantially if the teacher considers the ways that those activities can be used flexibly. Since virtually any effective instructional activity or game can be adapted and used in other content areas and at other levels, a game or an activity that works well with one content topic should be adapted for use with a variety of content topics. When a teacher has found a particularly nice set of materials or has spent time and effort to develop such a set of materials, it is always useful to consider the many ways that those materials might be used. In this way, a single set of materials can be adapted to meet a variety of instructional needs.

Exercises and Activities

1. Suppose you are preparing to teach first-grade children to add two- and three-digit numbers with regrouping (renaming, carrying). Describe an exploratory developmental activity that will give the children preliminary experience with regrouping outside the context of addition. To build mental imagery for the regrouping process, use bundled sticks in the activity.

   For example, the number represented here

   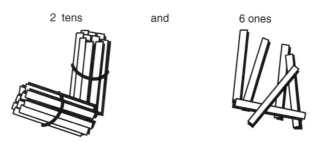

   | 2 tens | and | 6 ones |

   is the same as the number represented here

   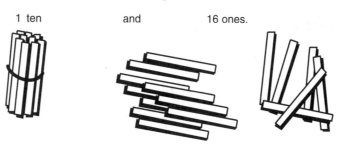

   | 1 ten | and | 16 ones. |

2. Suppose you are preparing to teach a measurement lesson to third-grade students on the customary units of length (inches, feet, and yards). Before teaching the lesson, you want to establish the need for standard units. Describe an exploratory developmental activity that will give the children an understanding of why we need standard units of length.

3. Consider the following instructional activity for teaching how to find the area of rectangles. Decide whether the activity is a developmental activity or a practice activity. Explain your reasons.

   Display, on the walls of the classroom, about 20 trapezoids cut from colored construction paper. Write the length and width in inches on each trapezoid. Have the children work with partners. Each pair of partners should choose and find the areas of 2 trapezoids.

4. It has been said that whenever teachers evaluate the work of their students, they are also evaluating the work of their students' teacher. Explain what you think this statement means. If this statement is true, why is it important to include assessment activities in your lessons?

5. Choose any lesson from a commercially published elementary school mathematics textbook. Analyze the lesson plan that is presented in the teacher's guide. With respect to its contribution to learning of the stated lesson objective, identify and label each part of the suggested lesson plan as developmental, practice, application, or assessment.

6. This game is a practice activity for *hard basic multiplication facts:*

   Prepare a set of 24 cards, each showing a hard basic multiplication fact with the answer missing. Give the cards to two children and have them play this game: After the cards are shuffled, the dealer gives each player 4 cards, facedown. When the dealer says "Start," the players race to arrange their cards in order, from smallest answer to largest answer. If the first player to finish is correct, that player gets 1 point. If the other player challenges the result, the first player must prove the answers. The players repeat the process until all the cards have been played. The player who scored the most points is the winner.

   Adapt this game for the topic *area of parallelograms.*

7. This activity is a developmental activity for teaching *parallelograms:*

   Display about five parallelograms, all with different shapes. Explain that these shapes are all parallelograms. Ask the children to tell you what is the same for all parallelograms. (Answers may vary. For example, the children may point out that all the parallelograms have four sides. Or, they may say that all the parallelograms have straight sides. Or, they may notice that all the shapes are closed figures.) If they indicate that all the parallelograms have three sides, agree with them that all parallelograms have four sides, then draw a counterexample like the one on the right. Ask if this is a parallelogram. Ask why not. Repeat this process with counterexamples that do not have other required characteristics of parallelograms.

   Adapt this activity for teaching *trapezoids.*

8. Find an article that describes a learning activity or game. Analyze the activity or game and decide whether it is developmental, practice, application, or assessment.

References and Related Readings

Baker, J. M., & Zigmond, N. (1990). Are regular education classes equipped to accommodate students with learning disabilities? *Exceptional Children, 56,* 515–526.

Bransford, J. D., Brown, A. L., & Cocking, R. R. (1999). *How people learn: Brain, mind, experience, and school.* Washington, DC: National Academy Press.

Csikszentmihalyi, M. (1990). *Flow: The psychology of optimal experience.* New York: Harper and Row.

National Council of Teachers of Mathematics. (1989). *Curriculum and evaluation standards for school mathematics.* Reston, VA: Author.

National Council of Teachers of Mathematics. (1991). *Professional standards for teaching mathematics.* Reston, VA: Author.

National Council of Teachers of Mathematics. (2000). *Principles and standards for school mathematics.* Reston, VA: Author.

Websites

www.2ed.gov/pubs/EarlyMath/index.html
A site targeted at parents. Good parental involvement ideas.

www.2ed.gov/pubs/parents/Math/index.html
What parents can do at home.

www.sedl.org/pubs/classroom-compass/
Instructional ideas in math.

http://mathforum.org/mathed/assessment.html
Links to articles.

www.nap.edu/catalog.php?record_id=2235
Measuring what counts.

www.learner.org/exhibits/dailymath/
Applications of math in daily life.

PRIOR STUDENT KNOWLEDGE

The Basis for Learning and Instruction

CHAPTER OUTLINE

Building on Prior Knowledge
   Assessing Prior Knowledge
   Remediation of Prerequisite Knowledge

Additional Classroom Scenarios
Exercises and Activities

Building on Prior Knowledge

When planning to teach mathematics in grades 5 through 8 (or at any grade), it is important to understand that the students already have a broad base of knowledge from which the new learning can be developed. Some things that they learned earlier are clearly understood. On the other hand, some things will be misunderstood. Some of their previously learned mathematical concepts and skills are logically connected to a rich network of other concepts and skills. But some things will have been learned as isolated unrelated facts. Some of the students' prior mathematical knowledge will have been based on big ideas that are easily transferred to new settings. However, some of their knowledge will have been learned by rote and will be difficult to remember. Sometimes, a student's math knowledge will be so well understood that he or she will easily recognize settings in which the concepts and skills can be used to solve problems. Unfortunately, sometimes a student will be unable to recognize particular concepts or skills that are related to a problem setting.

In any mathematics textbook series, the content at each grade level is developed from the content learned in the earlier grades. Although there are some lessons in which content from previous grades is retaught, it is generally assumed that the students have already learned those prior concepts and skills, but often that assumption is incorrect. Therefore, when you (the teacher) plan your lesson, it is good to consider first what background knowledge the students know in order to successfully learn the new content.

A wise teacher will often begin the lesson with an activity that provides a brief review of the prerequisite knowledge and skills. The purpose of the review activity is twofold. First, it refreshes the students' memories of the required knowledge. This will make the entire lesson progress more smoothly. Second, the review activity can identify content that students need to know but do not. What does the teacher do when the students do not know something that they are supposed to already know? The teacher needs to reteach that needed content.

Teachers often are reluctant to take the time to reteach content that students should already know, but if that content is truly prerequisite, then the lesson will not be successful unless that content is retaught. The reteaching (*remediation*) of prerequisite content that has been forgotten or not already learned may take place in a variety of settings. You may need to reteach the material to the entire class, to a small group of students, or to one or two individuals. In each of these settings, you should do a more thorough diagnosis of what is already known by the students and what is not. Remember, whether you are teaching new material or remediating material that has been previously taught, you must start with concepts and skills that students have already learned. It is on those concepts and skills that you build new skills and understanding of new concepts. Consider the following examples.

Assessing Prior Knowledge

Early in the school year, a fifth-grade teacher prepared to teach a lesson on multiplication by multiples of ten and multiples of one hundred. The objective is for the students to be able to correctly complete multiplication examples like these:

$$\begin{array}{cccc} 34 & 241 & 45 & 724 \\ \times 40 & \times 70 & \times 200 & \times 300 \end{array}$$

The teacher understood that the students would not be successful with multiplication by multiples of 10 and 100 unless they had already mastered the basic multiplication facts. So to check for that mastery, the teacher opened the lesson with Activity 2.1.

Activity 2.1   Match Me

Prepare a set of cards with basic multiplication facts without answers and a second set of cards with the answers. Limit the facts to ones that involve multiplication by 4, 6, 7, 8, and 9 because they are most difficult for students.

Shuffle the cards together and pass them out to the students. Explain that some have problems and some have answers. Those with problems are to find partners with answers to their problems. Those with answers are to find partners who have problems that match their answers. If all the cards are not used, there may be some problems or some answers without matches. If there is an unmatched answer, ask the students to suggest a problem that matches that answer. If there is an unmatched problem, have the class suggest a correct answer.

After observing the students and listening to their discussions, the teacher was confident that the class had no serious difficulties with basic multiplication facts. So, the teacher proceeded with the planned lesson. *Note that the teacher's careful observation turned what was essentially a practice activity into an assessment activity.*

Remediation of Prerequisite Knowledge

A seventh-grade math teacher was preparing to teach a lesson on area of composite shapes. The objective of the lesson was for students to be able to find areas of shapes like these:

The teacher understood that before the students would be able to compute areas of the composite shapes, they needed to be able to compute the areas of the simple shapes that are combined to form the composite shapes. The teacher started the lesson with a review of area formulas for rectangles, parallelograms, triangles, trapezoids, and circles. During that review, it became apparent that many of the students were unable to find the areas of trapezoids or circles.

The teacher used the rest of the class time reteaching the area formulas for trapezoids and circles. The lesson on area of composite shapes was taught the next day. The teacher had prepared cutouts of composite shapes and had students cut the composite shapes into shapes for which they knew area formulas. The teacher kept emphasizing that when you have an unfamiliar shape, try to cut it into familiar shapes.

The seventh graders found the lesson to be interesting and challenging. The teacher assigned a practice page and allowed the students to work with partners. They were able find areas of all the composite shapes.

Additional Classroom Scenarios

An eighth-grade mathematics teacher was preparing to teach a lesson on addition and subtraction of irrational numbers. The objective was for students to be able to complete examples like these:

$$4\sqrt{3} + 2\sqrt{2} + 3\sqrt{2} \qquad 8\sqrt{5} - 6\sqrt{5} \qquad 5\sqrt{3} + 4\sqrt{2} + 3\sqrt{2} - 3\sqrt{3}$$

The teacher, who decided to show a lot of examples that would illustrate the big idea of addition and subtraction, reminded the class, "We always add or subtract like units." (In algebra, this same big idea would be, "We always add or subtract *like terms*.") The teacher planned to begin with Activity 2.2, which relates addition and subtraction of irrational numbers to the students' prior knowledge.

Activity 2.2   *Adding and Subtracting Like Units*

Begin by writing this example on the board: $251 + 43$

Ask a student to do the addition. Then ask why the 5 and the 4 were added. Ask why the 1 and the 3 were added. Ask why nothing was added to the 2. [Because you add ones to ones, tens to tens, and hundreds to hundreds. We add like units.]

Next, write these examples on the board: $\frac{4}{5} - \frac{1}{5}$ $\frac{2}{5} + \frac{3}{7}$

Ask which example would be easiest. [The first example.] Then why would the second example be more difficult. [Because you need a common denominator.] Explain that when they add or subtract fractions, they always add or subtract like units.

Write this example on the board: 7 feet 5 inches + 2 feet 3 inches

Have a student write the answer. Ask why the 7 feet were added to the 2 feet and why the 5 inches were added to the 3 inches. [We always add like units.]

After completing the activity on adding and subtracting like units, the teacher planned to write the following radical expressions on the board:

$$2\sqrt{7} \qquad 4\sqrt{7}$$

The students would be asked how many square roots of 7 are in the first expression. [2] And how many square roots of 7 are in the second expression. [4] Then the teacher would place a plus sign between the two expressions and ask, "If we add, how many square roots of 7 do we have altogether?" The teacher would point out, "We could do the addition because we added like units. The teacher planned to generalize addition and subtraction or irrational numbers by leading the class through the following examples:

$$6\sqrt{2} - 3\sqrt{2} \qquad 3\sqrt{5} + 4\sqrt{7} + 6\sqrt{5} \qquad 7\sqrt{11} + 5\sqrt{3} - 2\sqrt{11}$$

A sixth-grade teacher was planning a lesson on addition of fractions. The textbook directed the students to reduce answers to lowest terms. The teacher knew from past experience that nearly all the difficulties that the students would have with this lesson would not be related to adding fractions. Rather, the difficulties would be related to reducing the answers to lowest terms. Therefore, the teacher decided to teach an entire lesson on reducing fractions before attempting to teach the lesson on addition of fractions, requiring students to reduce answers to lowest terms.

A seventh-grade teacher was planning a lesson on solving proportions. The teacher realized that since a proportion is a statement that two ratios are equal, solving proportions is similar to finding equivalent fractions. The teacher decided to open the lesson with a review of equivalent fractions.

A fifth-grade teacher was planning a lesson on comparing and ordering fractions. The teacher wanted to use the big idea of comparison: *Always compare like units.* And so the teacher planned to begin the lesson with comparisons that emphasize that big idea.

The following examples were included at the beginning of the lesson plan:

Which is longer, 2 hours and 72 minutes or 1 hour and 93 minutes?

Convert both times to minutes. Then the comparison is easy. This is why *we always compare like units.*

Which is more, 22 quarters or 47 dimes?

Convert both amounts to cents. Then the comparison is easy because *we are comparing like units.*

Which length is longer, 3 feet and 42 inches or 4 feet and 17 inches?

Convert both lengths to inches. Then the comparison is easy because *we are comparing like units.*

Which is more, $\frac{3}{5}$ or $\frac{5}{7}$?

Rewrite the fractions with the same fractional unit (common denominator). Then the comparison is easy. Remember that *we always compare like units*

An eighth-grade math teacher was planning a lesson on evaluation of algebraic expressions. The teacher knew that the students would need to be proficient with the order of operations in order to evaluate algebraic expressions, so a review of order of operations was planned as a lesson opener.

Exercises and Activities

1. Choose a lesson from a published textbook series from each grade, 5 through 8. For each lesson, identify at least one item of prior knowledge—a concept or a skill—that students would need in order to be successful in your chosen lesson.

2. Jake is a seventh grader who is having trouble solving equations. His incorrect work is shown in the following three incorrect examples:

$$
\begin{array}{lll}
2(3 + X) = 8 & 5X = 3(X + 6) & 6(X + 1) = 4(X - 3) \\
6 + X = 8 & 5X = 3X + 6 & 6X + 1 = 4X - 3 \\
X = 2 & 2X = 6 & 2X + 1 = -3 \\
& X = 3 & 2X = 4 \\
& & X = -2
\end{array}
$$

a. What are the correct answers?

b. What is Jake doing wrong?

c. What important prior knowledge does Jake seem to have missed?

d. Plan a short remediation lesson that would supply Jake's missing prior knowledge.

LESSON DESIGN

Planning for Effective Instruction and Maximum Learning

CHAPTER OUTLINE

Combining Activities into a Lesson

What Is a Lesson?

A *lesson* is a related set of instructional and learning activities organized in a coherent manner. A lesson is generally organized in parts, each of which is designed to accomplish some part of the process needed to meet the learning objectives. For our purposes, we will organize our lessons to include the following parts. Although other components may also be included, most lessons would include the lesson opener, development, monitoring learning, practice, and the lesson closer.

Lesson Opener.   The lesson opener should provide context for the concept or skill being developed. It draws the attention of the student and smoothly leads into the lesson.

Development.   This part of the lesson provides the experiences that help the student learn the new concept or skill. Development should smoothly build on what the student already knows. Students progress from not knowing to knowing the new material. Development leads to their being able to do the independent practice exercises.

Monitoring Learning.   Ideally, this part of the lesson is not separated from the other parts. When learning is constantly monitored, the teacher will be aware of who

understands and who does not, of when teaching is being understood and when it is not, and of what needs to be retaught and what needs to be taught differently. Some teachers mistakenly think they are monitoring learning by walking around the classroom making sure students are on task. However, monitoring learning involves teachers stopping and listening to student dialogue and even inserting themselves into conversations.

Practice. Practice provides reinforcement of what has been learned in the development part of the lesson and should not begin until the teacher is sure that understanding of the concept or skill has been accomplished. If the students do not yet understand, then more development is needed before the practice.

Lesson Closure. This part of the lesson allows students to think about what was learned during the lesson and to reflect on the importance of this new information. During closure, students are often asked to verbalize their understanding of the concept/ skill presented and are given the opportunity to demonstrate their learning by solving one more problem from the current lesson.

A Traditional Lesson Plan

We begin by examining a plan for a mathematics lesson that was developed by following the kind of suggestions that are typically provided in the teacher's guide. This lesson plan is very traditional. It calls for the teacher to teach the textbook pages in the way that most teachers would teach them. The lesson plan is actually a fairly good one.

LESSON OBJECTIVE

The student will recognize symmetric shapes and lines of symmetry.

Lesson Opener

State the following: "We have already learned to recognize congruent figures. Today, we will learn to identify figures that are symmetric."

Development

Begin by showing half of each of the following shapes: circle, heart, star. Have students identify the shapes by looking at the half shapes:

Next, direct students' attention to the first teaching example in the student book. Ask students how they could check to be sure that the two halves of the triangle are congruent Point out that if the triangle were folded along the dotted line, the two halves of the triangle would match exactly. They would be congruent.

Tell the students that when a shape can be folded in half like this so that the two halves match exactly, then the shape is *symmetric*. We call the line along which the shape was folded the *line of symmetry*.

Tell the students that some shapes have more than one line of symmetry. Direct their attention to the second shape on the page. This shape could be folded in two ways so that the two halves match exactly. This shape has *two* lines of symmetry.

Monitoring Learning

Lead students through the *Check Understanding* examples in the student book. On the basis of student responses to the *Check Understanding* examples, identify those students who have difficulty understanding.

Practice

Assign the *Reteaching Worksheet* to those who would benefit from reteaching. Assign the practice exercises from the student book to the rest of the students.

Closure

As math time is ending, remind the children that:

1. A *symmetric* shape is one that can be folded so that the two halves match exactly.
2. The fold line for symmetric shapes is called the *line of symmetry*.

The Nature of Standard Traditional Lessons

As mentioned earlier, traditional lessons that follow suggestions in the teacher's edition are usually good lessons. Traditional lessons normally have two common characteristics. First, they are designed to teach the textbook pages. Second, they are aimed at the average students. On the average, they serve their purpose well. The difficulty, of course, is that very few students fit that "average" mold. Such lessons do not usually allow for diverse learning preferences. Moreover, such lessons typically do not take into consideration the diverse learning needs of most students.

Adapting Lessons for Diverse Learning Needs

Rather than attempting to provide separate adaptations of these lessons for every student's learning needs, we will adapt the lessons by expanding the types of activity that appeal to most learning-style preferences and that provide for most learning needs. It is understood, of course, that even after these suggested changes are made, additional adaptations may very well be needed to provide for some students. Traditional lesson plans will be adapted in the following five ways.

First, the developmental part of the lessons will be expanded. This is the most important thing that can be done to make lessons more effective—if we equate effectiveness with students' learning of concepts and skills. More thorough development of concepts and skills can be accomplished in several ways. Understanding must develop out of personal experiences with real things. Those experiences should be designed to allow the students to "see" important relationships and procedures. The nature of what we help them see should provide them with useful mental imagery for the concepts and skills being learned.

Understanding must be developed by helping the students see and understand how what is being learned is related to other things that they already know (Carpenter, 1986; Ginsburg, 1989). These interrelationships should have an almost-constant emphasis. Whenever a teacher is trying to help a student understand something new, a common approach should be "Let's think about what we already know that can help us here." This will tap into the student's previous learning and encourage many more natural interconnections that enhance memory and recall.

In the development of concepts, a wide variety of examples and nonexamples should be examined. For every example of the concept, the students should discuss why it is an example. For every nonexample that is identified, the students should discuss why it is not an example. The why and why-not questions keep a constant focus on the essential characteristics of the concepts being learned.

The students should continually search for patterns and learn to generalize concepts and procedures from those patterns. Their ability to test those generalizations by trying them out to verify whether or not the generalization is correct helps develop students' confidence.

An excellent developmental teaching method is one called the *laboratory approach*, in which the students are led through a series of steps:

1. **Explore (or experiment).** In this step, the student explores the topic under the guidance of the teacher, using a physical or pictorial model. Usually, the student is led to use the model to find a variety of results (answers). If the process is modeled effectively, the student will believe that the results are correct. Since he or she can see where the answer came from, common sense will tell the student whether the answer is correct.

2. **Keep an organized record of results.** The teacher leads the student to record the results achieved with the model. The recording is done in a way that will facilitate recognition of the patterns that the teacher wants the student to notice.

3. **Identify patterns.** The patterns should be stated in the language of the student. "Every time we did this, the answer turned out to be. . . ." The patterns will suggest ways to get the result (answer) without using the model.

4. **Hypothesize (or generalize) how to get results without the model.** "We can get the answer by. . . ."

5. **Test the hypothesis (the generalization).** Complete an example using the hypothesized procedure. Then redo the example using the model to verify that the result is correct.

This instructional process, which is an *inductive* process, is utterly convincing to students. Students have discovered a way to get answers that are believable because they can literally see where those answers come from. Students will believe that the procedure is correct because they have seen the procedure working.

There is, however, one real danger in the use of inductive teaching. The results are derived from experience with a series of examples. If the examples are not sufficiently varied and are examples of only some special case, it may be possible to find a pattern that is consistent for the examples used but not consistent for all examples. It is possible for patterns drawn from special cases to lead to procedures that are true of those special cases but not true in general. For example, suppose you used a model to discover that:

$$\frac{1}{3} + \frac{1}{5} = \frac{8}{15}, \quad \frac{1}{3} + \frac{1}{6} = \frac{9}{18}, \quad \frac{1}{2} + \frac{1}{3} = \frac{5}{6}, \quad \frac{1}{4} + \frac{1}{3} = \frac{7}{12}, \quad \text{and} \quad \frac{1}{5} + \frac{1}{2} = \frac{7}{10}.$$

The students might see that, in every case, the numerator of the answer is the *sum of the denominators* of the fractions being added, and the denominator is the *product of the denominators* of the fractions being added. Although this "rule" is true whenever you are adding unit fractions, it is not true when you are adding other kinds of fractions. During instruction, the teacher should avoid making generalizations based on special cases, because children tend to apply those generalizations in settings for which they are not appropriate.

More thorough development of concepts and skills accomplishes several important things. Development results in more complete understanding, a common result when interconnections with other things that students know are emphasized. Because of those interconnections, retention of what is learned is better. Because of improved retention, much less time needs to be spent on review and practice. Because of the interconnections and better understanding, students are better able to apply what they have learned to solve problems.

Second, the lessons will be adapted to provide more visual input. In most lessons, there is more than enough auditory information; however, students nearly always need more visual information. Procedures are described, but students need to have them demonstrated. Teachers explain rules and directions, but students need to see them written down and demonstrated. Teachers define what a trapezoid is, but students need to be shown. Teachers explain how to borrow in subtraction, but students need to see a tenth being traded for 10 hundredths.

Third, the lessons will be adapted to include more kinesthetic activity. Young people are not passive creatures. Motion is an integral part of what they are. They fidget, wiggle, and squirm. They like to interact actively with things. They like to try things and do things. Teachers can wear themselves out trying to make students sit still. Lessons that place a high premium on sitting still and listening go against the nature of young people. Kinesthetic learning activities, on the other hand, encourage youths to move. They use the youths' natural tendency toward movement for learning. Fewer behavior problems result because the young people are able to do what is natural without getting into trouble. Because they are involved both physically and cognitively in the learning activity, attention problems are reduced. It should be noted that kinesthetic learning activities are particularly effective for students with attention deficit disorder (ADD) or attention-deficit/hyperactivity disorder (ADHD).

Fourth, the lessons will be adapted to encourage more communication from and among the students. The classroom should be viewed as a community of learning. All members of that community should be a part of an intellectual exchange about mathematics (Baroody, 1996). Together, they should explore ideas, gather information, look for patterns, generalize concepts and procedures, and try out those generalizations and adjust them on the basis of their experiences. Unfortunately, teachers may not feel confident in discussing mathematics in this way. Many teachers come to math classrooms with little experience in articulating their understanding. Some strategies to facilitate communication from

and among students include (1) asking a student to explain or summarize a classmate's response, (2) asking a student to give an alternative way of solving the problem, (3) asking a student how a problem is similar to a previous type of problem, (4) asking a student how a problem is different from a previous type of problem, (5) asking a student how a problem demonstrates a key concept, and (6) asking a student how understanding the problems solved during a lesson can be used in everyday life. All of this requires constant communication within the learning community. One benefit of increased communication is a deeper sense of involvement on the students' part. Learning activities should be planned that encourage—and even require—communication from and among the students, as well as from the students to the parents (Escalante & Dirmann, 1990).

Fifth, the lessons will be adapted to make monitoring of learning more continuous throughout the lesson. Too often, learning is monitored only after the lesson has been taught. An after-the-fact check on learning can inform the teacher whether or not the lesson has been effective. However, if the lesson has failed with the whole class, or even with individual students, the teacher must wait until next time to clarify unclear ideas, correct skills that are full of errors, or straighten out misconceptions. By then, those unclear ideas, error-filled skills, and misconceptions will have been practiced and will be more difficult to undo. Rather, the teacher must monitor learning while it is happening. In the midst of the lesson, understanding must constantly be checked so the teacher has a strong sense of what is understood and what is not, of what the students can and cannot do, and of who is learning and who is not. The teacher should know when the teaching is effective and when it is not, when another teaching example is needed, when a different approach is needed, when students are interested and when they are not, and when instruction is working and when it needs to be changed.

In summary, lesson planning that is more likely to be appropriate for all students in a diverse classroom includes accomplishing the following:

Expanded development using
  Increased visual imagery
  Increased kinesthetic activity
  Increased student communication while
  Continually monitoring learning

Adapting a lesson in this way makes it appropriate for a diverse group of students. However, you should also bear in mind that further adaptations may still be necessary to provide for the specific needs of some students.

A Lesson Adapted for Diverse Learners

On the following pages is a lesson plan adapted from the traditional lesson plan on symmetry that we have already seen. As you consider this adapted plan, note how much more time is devoted to development. Also note how visual input has been increased, how kinesthetic activity has been added, how more opportunities for student communication are included, and how learning is monitored during all the major activities of the lesson.

LESSON OBJECTIVE

The learner will recognize symmetric shapes and lines of symmetry.

Lesson Opener

Cut symmetric figures in half along their lines of symmetry and pass out the picture halves to the students.

Explain that you have cut some pictures in half and each person has half of a picture. Have each student find the other student who has the matching half of their picture. Ask the children what they can say about the two halves of a picture when the halves are an exact match. (Remind them if necessary of previous learning. They are congruent.) **Monitor understanding**. Identify students who do not understand or who are having difficulty. Provide assistance to them.

State the following: "We already know what congruent figures are. Today, we will learn to identify symmetric figures."

Development

Prepare eight sheets of tracing paper with large letters on them. Make two copies of the letters *F*, *O*, *S*, and *Y*. Show the letters to the students:

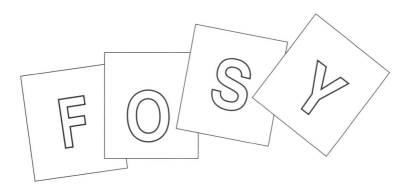

Ask which of the letters could be cut into halves so that the two halves would be an exact match. Allow the children to come to the front and cut the sheets.

Ask how we could check to make sure before cutting. [We could fold the paper.] Fold the *Y* to see if the two parts will be an exact match. Have the students come to the front to see if they can fold the other letters to get an exact match.

Group the students with partners. Hand out to each pair of partners a shape that has been cut from paper. Some shapes should be symmetric and others should not be symmetric.

Give simpler shapes like the following ones to students with low cognitive functioning:

Tell the students to work with their partners to try to fold the shape so that the two parts are an exact match. When everyone is finished, have them show what they found out. **Monitor learning**. Identify students who are having difficulty and provide assistance.

Tell the children that when a shape can be folded in half like this so that the two halves match exactly, the shape is *symmetric*. Write *symmetric* on the board. Explain that the line along which the shape is folded is the *line of symmetry*. Write *line of symmetry* on the board.

Have everyone with a symmetric shape hold it up for the class to see. Have those with shapes that are not symmetric hold them up for the class to see. **Monitor learning**. Identify students who do not understand and, at the first opportunity, provide assistance.

Next, direct students' attention to the first teaching example in the student book. Point out that if the triangle were folded along the dotted line, the two halves of the triangle would match exactly. The shape is *symmetric*. The dotted line is the *line of symmetry*.

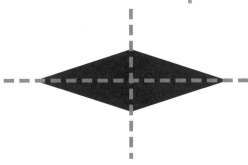

Tell the students that some shapes have more than one line of symmetry. Direct their attention to the second shape on the page. This shape could be folded in two ways so that the two halves match exactly. This shape has *two* lines of symmetry.

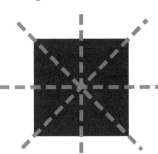

Hold up a square. Tell the students that a square also has several lines of symmetry. Have a student come to the front and fold the square to show one line of symmetry. Have another try to fold the square to show a different line of symmetry. Continue until all four lines of symmetry have been found.

Show the students a shape like the one pictured at the right. Have the students come forward and fold the shape to find lines of symmetry. Ask how many lines of symmetry the shape has. [3]

Use the third example on the student page to demonstrate how to use scissors to cut a symmetric shape from a folded sheet of paper. Have two students come to the front and cut out other symmetric shapes.

Lead the children through the *Check Understanding* examples in the student book. **Monitor learning**. On the basis of student responses to the *Check Understanding* examples, identify those students who are having difficulty understanding.

Practice

Group the students with partners. Have them work with their partners to complete the practice examples in the student book. **Monitor learning**. Pay extra attention to the students who have been experiencing difficulty and their partners. If their difficulties continue, provide help or reteaching.

Closure

As math time is ending, ask what kind of shapes we have learned about today. [Symmetric shapes.] Ask how we can tell if a shape is symmetric. [Symmetric shapes can be folded so that the two halves match exactly.] Ask what we call the fold line in a symmetric shape. [The fold line is the line of symmetry.]

Follow-Up

Tell the children to explain to their parents what a symmetric shape is. Have them, with the help of their parents, make a list of symmetric things that they see at home.

The Planning Process and "Official" Lesson Plans

When adapting the preceding lesson plan as well as lesson plans in later chapters, we use a format that includes certain lesson components. We understand, however, that practicing teachers are often required to complete lesson plans by using a required format that may include components that are different from those used in this text. Teachers may be required to have lesson plans available for the use of a substitute teacher when the regular teacher is absent. The plans may play a role in the teacher evaluation process. In either case, a consistent format is useful and, of course, teachers should comply with the lesson plan requirements.

We emphasize making five adaptations that will increase the thoroughness of the developmental part of the lesson, increase the use of visual imagery, include more kinesthetic activity, encourage (even require) more student communication, and provide for continual monitoring of learning. We believe that these five things are important when lessons are being planned or when lessons are being adapted to make them more effective for diverse students. It is this planning *process* that is important rather than any particular lesson format. However, for consistency—so that the reader can easily see how we have emphasized these five adaptations—we will use the same lesson format throughout the text.

The Planning Process and Teaching Notes

Note that the adapted lesson plans are very long and detailed. Again, we believe that the planning process should be complete. Thorough planning includes planning every teaching example so that the students are able to recognize the patterns that can be generalized into the concepts and skills that are being taught. Thorough planning includes anticipation of questions that might arise and what responses are appropriate. It includes deciding what materials are needed and exactly how they will be used, determining what questions you will ask and what you will ask students to do. Thorough planning will also include what you will look for so that you know who is learning what and how well he or she is learning it. Thorough planning includes all these things and more; so, when a teacher writes down what he or she has thoroughly planned to do, the teacher will have a very long and detailed lesson plan.

A teacher who attempts to teach from such a plan will often get lost in the detail and end up focusing on the written lesson plan instead of on the students. When the focus of the teacher is not on the students, many undesirable results may occur, ranging from unawareness that students do not understand to serious student behavior problems. Therefore, after a lesson has been thoroughly planned, the teacher could translate the plan into brief teaching notes that are sufficient to guide the lesson but are not so detailed that they will distract the teacher's attention from the students.

Exercises and Activities

1. Read the discussion of "Standard 3: Knowing Students as Learners of Mathematics," on pages 144–150 of *Professional Standards for Teaching Mathematics*, published by the NCTM in 1991. Compare and contrast the recommendations in this chapter with those included in the discussion of this standard.
2. Choose a lesson from any published elementary school mathematics program.
   a. Identify procedures that the authors suggest that provide information to the students visually. Describe ways that additional visual input could be provided.
   b. Identify the developmental part of the lesson. Describe how to expand the developmental part of the lesson.
   c. Identify the ways that the children are involved. Describe how you could involve the children in more kinesthetic activity.

d. Describe how you could provide more opportunities for the children to communicate among themselves and to the teacher about the concepts or skills being learned.

e. Identify the parts of the lesson in which the teacher should monitor learning. In each case, what should the teacher be looking for?

3. Choose a lesson from any published elementary school mathematics program. Adapt the lesson by expanding the developmental part of the lesson, providing for more visual input, adding more kinesthetic activity, increasing opportunities for student communication, and calling for continual monitoring of learning.

4. Read Assumption 1 on page 17 of *Curriculum and Evaluation Standards for School Mathematics*, published in 1989 by the NCTM. How does this assumption relate to the recommendation in this chapter that the developmental part of lessons be expanded?

5. Read the discussion of "Standard 2: Mathematics as Communication," on pages 26–28 of *Curriculum and Evaluation Standards for School Mathematics*, published by the NCTM in 1989. How does this standard relate to the recommendation in this chapter that the lessons should include more communication from and among children?

References and Related Readings

Baroody, A. J. (1996). An investigative approach to the mathematics instruction of children classified as learning disabled. In D. K. Reid, W. P. Hresko, & H. L. Swanson (Eds.), *Cognitive approaches to learning disabilities* (pp. 545–615). Austin, TX: PRO-ED.

Carpenter, T. P. (1986). Conceptual knowledge as a foundation for procedural knowledge: Implications from research in the initial learning of arithmetic. In J. Hiebert (Ed.), *Conceptual and procedural knowledge: The ease of mathematics* (pp. 113–132). Hillsdale, NJ: Erlbaum.

Escalante, J., & Dirmann, J. (1990). *The Jaime Escalante Math Program*. Washington, DC: National Education Association.

Ginsburg, H. P. (1989). *Children's arithmetic* (2nd ed.). Austin, TX: PRO-ED.

National Council of Teachers of Mathematics. (1989). *Curriculum and evaluation standards for school mathematics*. Reston, VA: Author.

National Council of Teachers of Mathematics. (2000). *Principles and standards for school mathematics*. Reston, VA: Author.

Whitin, P., & Whitin, D. J. (2002). Promoting communication in the mathematics classroom. *Teaching Children Mathematics*, 9, 205–211.

Websites

www.corestandards.org/the-standards/mathematics
The Common Core State Standards for Mathematics can be found at this site.

www.Idonline.Org/indepth/adhd
Links to resources on ADHD.

www.nctm.org/standards/
Principles and standards for school mathematics.

http://nctm.org/about/
About NCTM.

www.mcrel.org/compendium/SubjectTopics.asp?subjectID=1
Math standards and topics.

www.nwrd.org/psc/bestofnw/singleprac.asp?id=74&phrase=mathematics
Report on an exemplary school program that used a visual, hands-on approach.

http://teachers.net/lessons/
Lesson plans from teachers.

www.proteacher.com/100000.shtml
Lesson plans for content areas.

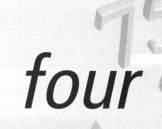

four

COMPUTATION WITH WHOLE NUMBERS

A Review of Addition and Subtraction

CHAPTER OUTLINE

Three Important Considerations

Number Sense

The Standards of the National Council of Teachers of Mathematics (NCTM, 1989, 2000) emphasize the importance of the development of *number sense*. This text includes, throughout the chapters, activities that can result in the development of number sense with whole numbers, fractions, decimals, rational numbers, and real numbers. Those activities include building on what students already know, developing mental imagery for numbers and operations on numbers, seeing relationships among numbers and among different kinds of numbers, and estimation of quantities.

To help you recognize that the development of number sense takes place within a variety of mathematical topics and at a variety of ages, we will use the symbol shown in the left margin to indicate instruction that will contribute to the development of number sense. *Remember, when you see that symbol, the discussion is developing number sense.*

Foundations of Algebra

This text includes a separate chapter on the *foundations of algebra*. However, in this chapter and in several other chapters, topics are introduced that help to develop of foundations of algebra. To alert you that a topic being studied also contributes to development of foundations of algebra, we will use the symbol shown in the left margin. *Remember, when you see that symbol, the discussion is also developing foundations of algebra.*

Basic Concepts and Skills

Basic concepts and skills are prerequisites for learning other concepts and skills. In mathematics, some concepts and skills are so basic that they form the basis for almost everything else. For example, consider basic addition facts. If the student has not learned the basic addition facts, she or he will be unable to do multidigit addition, multiplication, addition of measurements or finding areas, study statistics, and so on. It follows, then, that math teachers need to, first and foremost, assure that basic addition facts have been mastered before attempting to teach the other things.

Similarly, the basic subtraction facts are also the basis for much of the mathematics curriculum. You cannot expect your students to be successful in mathematics if they have not mastered basic addition and subtraction facts. It follows, then, that middle grade teachers must be ready to remediate deficiencies in their students' learning of basic addition and subtraction facts.

An Overview of the Development of Computation

When teaching any operation on whole numbers, the teacher must complete three distinct instructional tasks: Develop the meaning of the operation, develop the basic facts, and develop the algorithm(s). A closer examination of these instructional tasks yields a clear pattern of development.

The Meaning of the Operation

When teaching the meaning of the operation, teachers need to lead the child to accomplish two things. First, the child must associate the arithmetic operation with some physical operation. This association provides a basis for modeling the operation and establishes mental imagery for the operation. Second, the child must learn to use some already-available skill to figure out the answer. When established in this way, the meaning of the operation provides the student with a way to discover answers to specific examples.

The Basic Facts

Some facts are committed to memory, whereas others are "figured out" by using a step-by-step procedure. Basic facts are those needed to figure out the others. Basic facts serve as the basis for the rest of the facts. Normally, students are initially taught a body of easy basic facts for an operation, and then later they are taught the harder basic facts for that operation. However, for both the easy basic facts and the hard basic facts, there are three things that the students should be led to do.

First, the students should discover the answers for themselves. The meaning of the operation is applied to find answers to the easy facts. However, as the numbers get larger, the skills used in the application of the meaning are too inefficient. So, more efficient thinking strategies need to be developed for finding answers to the hard basic facts.

Second, the students should recognize relationships that exist among the facts. There are two major benefits of this emphasis on relationships. The emphasis on relationships improves retention, because it is easier to remember things that are related to other things that we already know. Also, recognition of those relationships drastically reduces the amount of memorization needed.

Third, the students should commit the facts to memory. Of course, if the meaning of the operation has been effectively taught, the students can figure out the answers to basic facts. So, why is it important that facts be memorized? Remember that the basic facts are used to find computation answers. If the basic facts are not memorized, the computation process becomes so slow and tedious that mathematics learning grinds nearly to a stop. If the basic facts are not memorized, children develop a sense of "can't do."

The Algorithm(s)

The algorithms are the step-by-step computation procedures that are followed to complete multidigit examples. Since the algorithms are procedures, it is tempting to resort to teaching a series of rote rules that describe the procedures. Memorization of rote rules has traditionally been the predominant method for learning algorithms for arithmetic operations. Rules are generalizations, usually important ones. However, effective teachers deemphasize rote rules. The problem with this method of learning is that rote rules are meaningless rules. The word *rote* literally means "mechanically and without intelligent attention."

Rote rules are also confusing. Children often learn them slightly wrong. Rote rules are often only slightly different from other rote rules, and students mix them up. They tend to use them in the wrong context. Retention is also poor. Although the teacher may get what appears to be quick mastery after intense practice of a rote rule, that so-called mastery often goes away as soon as the practice stops. A weekend away from practice will have a devastating effect on retention. And, if we carefully consider the content of rote rules as they are taught, most of them are not even true. Every rote rule that is commonly taught is true only within some very narrow context. Eventually, as the setting changes, the rule has to be corrected with a new rule. This adds to the confusion. The student's dilemma becomes: When do I use that rule? When do I use this rule? Is either rule the right one?

Instead of teaching rote rules, the teacher should emphasize big ideas that explain the process (Thornton, Tucker, Dossey, & Bazik, 1983). *Big ideas* are ideas that are constantly recurring. Each recurrence of a big idea becomes an extension of something already learned. The algorithms should be taught with effective physical or pictorial models. Modeling a concept or skill lets the children see what the concept or skill looks like and helps the students develop clear mental imagery. Modeling gives meaning to the algorithms. Note that we are not contending that students should not learn rules in mathematics. Indeed, with meaningful teaching, *the students still learn rules*. However, the *rules arise out of patterns observed by the students* as they use appropriate models that allow them to visualize the mathematical procedures. Rules are simply *statements of helpful ways to do the work*. Meaningful rules *make sense to the children* and are not "what we do because the teacher told us to."

Review and Remediation of Whole Number Addition

Relationships among the Addition Facts

Once the children have found answers for a body of easy basic addition facts, the teacher should lead the class through the process of accumulating these facts into an organized list. The facts should be organized in many different ways to help the students see patterns. The patterns that they see help them remember relationships that exist among the facts.

For example, we might have the students make a list of all the facts where 1 is being added. The students could then see that when we add 1 to a number, we get the next number (next in the counting sequence). When listing all the facts where 0 is being added, the children can easily see and remember that whenever 0 is added, we get the same number. If the teacher points out $2 + 3 = 5$ and $3 + 2 = 5$, $5 + 1 = 6$ and $1 + 5 = 6$, $5 + 3 = 8$ and $3 + 5 = 8$, and other similar pairs, the children can see and remember that rearranging the numbers does not change the answer. If the students are led to organize the facts so that facts with the same answer are together, they can discover and remember that there are many different ways to name a number. For example, $6 + 1$, $4 + 3$, $1 + 6$, $2 + 5$, $0 + 7$, $5 + 2$, $3 + 4$, and $7 + 0$ are all names for the same number, 7.

The emphasis on relationships provides two benefits. First, the interrelationships among the facts make them easier to remember. And, once the facts have been memorized, the interrelationships will improve retention. *It is always easier to remember things that are related to other things that we know.*

Second, the emphasis on relationships substantially reduces the quantity of information to be learned. Suppose we consider the addition facts with sums of 10 or less to be easy basic addition facts. These facts are displayed in the following table. Note that there is a total of 64 easy facts. That's a lot to have to learn.

+	0	1	2	3	4	5	6	7	8	9
0	0	1	2	3	4	5	6	7	8	9
1	1	2	3	4	5	6	7	8	9	10
2	2	3	4	5	6	7	8	9	10	
3	3	4	5	6	7	8	9	10		
4	4	5	6	7	8	9	10			
5	5	6	7	8	9	10				
6	6	7	8	9	10					
7	7	8	9	10						
8	8	9	10							
9	9	10								

Notice that there are 19 facts that involve the addition of 0. But when we study relationships among the facts, we find that when adding 0, we always get the other number. That is only 1 thing to learn instead of 19 things:

+	0	1	2	3	4	5	6	7	8	9
0	0	1	2	3	4	5	6	7	8	9
1	1	2	3	4	5	6	7	8	9	10
2	2	3	4	5	6	7	8	9	10	
3	3	4	5	6	7	8	9	10		
4	4	5	6	7	8	9	10			
5	5	6	7	8	9	10				
6	6	7	8	9	10					
7	7	8	9	10						
8	8	9	10							
9	9	10								

19 facts, but only one thing to learn.

The facts 1 + 0 and 0 + 1 were included in the preceding table. There are 17 other facts where 1 is being added. In the exploration of patterns and relationships, the students have already seen that when we add 1, we get the next number in the counting sequence. So, instead of needing to learn these 17 facts as separate things, the students have only one thing to learn:

+	0	1	2	3	4	5	6	7	8	9
0	0	1	2	3	4	5	6	7	8	9
1	1	2	3	4	5	6	7	8	9	10
2	2	3	4	5	6	7	8	9	10	
3	3	4	5	6	7	8	9	10		
4	4	5	6	7	8	9	10			
5	5	6	7	8	9	10				
6	6	7	8	9	10					
7	7	8	9	10						
8	8	9	10							
9	9	10								

17 facts, but only one thing to learn.

Now, if the children have seen that rearranging the numbers does not change the answer, 6 + 3 and 3 + 6 can be learned together, not as 2 things to learn, but as 1 thing. This is, of course, what mathematicians call the *commutative property of addition*. Similarly, 2 + 8 and 8 + 2 become 1 thing to learn. In the 64 easy basic facts that we are considering, there are 12 of these commutative pairs. That is, 24 facts, but only 12 things to learn and remember:

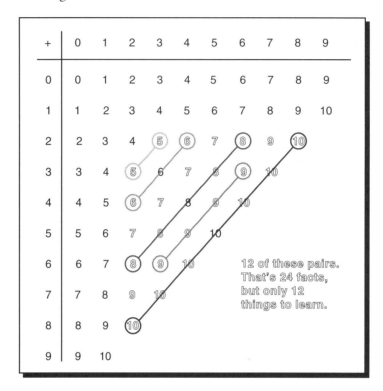

We have now reviewed all but four of the easy basic addition facts. These are the doubles: 2 + 2, 3 + 3, 4 + 4, and 5 + 5. They must be learned as separate facts, but students generally find them relatively easy to learn and remember. Let's review how these few relationships reduce the amount of memorization that is necessary:

Group of Facts	Number of Facts	Things to Learn
Adding 0	19	1
Adding 1	17	1
Commutative pairs	24	12
Doubles	4	4
All easy facts	64	18

Remediation of the Easy Basic Addition Facts

If remediation of the easy basic addition facts is needed, eight principles should be kept in mind:

1. Students should be aware that the objective is to memorize the facts. They should be told to remember. (Surprisingly, children are often not told to remember the facts.)
2. The activities should use an interesting and fun format.
3. The activities should have a high level of involvement. Minimize time spent waiting. Maximize time spent thinking about the facts.

4. The activities should focus on a small number of unmemorized facts at any given time.

5. Some already memorized facts should be mixed in with the target unmemorized facts. This will improve retention.

6. If a child does not know an answer, then he or she should be required to figure it out. This implies that the child will have time to figure it out. Discourage guessing by asking, "How did you figure that out?"

7. To figure out an answer, the student should think about what he or she already knows that will help find the answer. What other already known facts will help? What already known relationship will help? Counting should be used only as a last resort.

8. Emphasize accuracy, not speed. Accuracy is of great importance. Speed is of little importance. Speed will come after accuracy and confidence.

Remediation of the Hard Basic Addition Facts

A Thinking Strategy for Hard Basic Addition Facts. When developing the hard basic addition facts (sums of 11 through 18), children can still find answers by counting. However, with the larger numbers, counting is inefficient and consequently very slow. So, at this point in the development, more-efficient strategies are needed to allow the student to find answers quickly and accurately (Thornton et al., 1983). A wide variety of fact strategies are taught to students. The objective is to commit these facts to memory. Some fact strategies seem to lead to memorization, while others do not. The strategies that successfully lead to memorization have two common characteristics.

First, *successful fact strategies are mental strategies.* They consist of a series of quick, easy mental procedures. They are not pencil-and-paper strategies, though they can be recorded by using mathematical notation. They are not mechanical strategies. They are not performed by manipulating fingers or other objects, although the fingers or other physical materials could be used to establish mental imagery for the strategies.

Second, *successful fact strategies require the student to use facts that are already memorized to figure out the facts that are not yet memorized.* The students should be constantly thinking about what they already know that can help them figure out what they do not know. They should have a sense of building on what is already known. New knowledge is closely related to existing knowledge, and it is always easier to remember things that are related to other things that are known.

Make Ten A strategy that has been shown to be most effective is the make-10 strategy. It is based on the understanding that basic addition facts with sums of 10 are typically learned before the basic addition facts with sums greater than 10. In this strategy, the purpose is to mentally rearrange the quantities being combined to form a group of 10 and some leftovers. The strategy is taught easily when some device such as a 10-frame is used to provide mental imagery for the process:

To find 8 + 6, place the larger number in the 10-frame and place the other number outside the 10-frame.

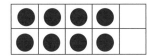

Use some of the smaller number (the 6) to fill the 10-frame.

You can see that the answer is 10 + 4. So, 8 + 6 = 14.

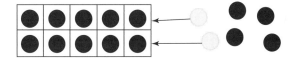

To find 3 + 9, place 9 in the 10-frame and place 3 outside the 10-frame.

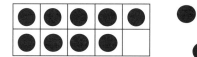

You need to move 1 to fill the 10-frame. That leaves 2 outside the 10-frame. The answer is 12. So, 3 + 9 = 12.

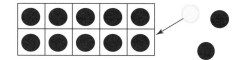

The children should practice using the 10-frame to find answers until mental imagery for the process is established. Then they are able to get answers by just thinking about how they would use the 10-frame. For example, finding the answer to 8 + 7 requires the following series of mental steps:

8 + 7

Place 8 inside the 10-frame.

Move 2 to fill the 10-frame.

That leaves 5 outside the 10-frame.

The answer is 15.

A student can easily use this process by following a series of self-directed questions. To find 7 + 9, he or she must answer these questions:

What number goes inside? [9]
How many do I move? [1]
What's left outside? [6]
What's the answer? [16]

The make-10 strategy is a general strategy in that it works for all the hard basic addition facts. As a result, the children can always use it without having to decide what to do with each fact. It uses a process very much like the regrouping process used in the addition algorithm, so learning the make-10 strategy makes it easier to learn and remember the addition algorithm.

Mastery of the Hard Basic Addition Facts.   After the students have learned to use an efficient strategy, like the make-10 strategy, to find answers to the hard basic addition facts, rapid progress can be made toward mastery of those facts. As when working on the easy facts, the students need to figure out the answers to the hard facts. They should recognize and use relationships among the hard facts and commit them to memory.

If students do not know a hard fact, saying "I don't know" is not acceptable. They need to figure out the answer. Because we want them to do that efficiently and quickly, we encourage (almost require) them to use the thinking strategy that they learned. The students have, at this point, been using counting for over a year to find addition-fact answers. They are comfortable with counting—even when it takes a long time. Consequently, they will automatically fall back on counting because they are so comfortable with it. So, the teacher must continually lead the children to use the thinking strategy instead of counting.

If students do not know the answer to a fact, they need to think about what they already know that will help them find the answer. If they continually think about the relationships among the facts, they end up with fewer things to learn, and their retention of what they have learned is better.

Understanding the Addition Algorithm

Students are ready to develop a proficient use of the addition algorithm as the basis for complex mathematics. The use of the addition algorithm is also a basic skill. Most of the rest of the mathematics curriculum depends on the students' ability to add. Without addition, children will not be successful in multiplication. Without addition, the children will not be successful in measurement. And without addition, the children will not be successful in other complex mathematics skills such as decimals, percents, data analysis, and statistics.

Often, middle grade students who are having difficulty in middle grade mathematics are having that difficulty because they have not mastered basic skills of addition.

Remember that the addition algorithm is the step-by-step process by which the basic facts are used to find answers to any other whole number addition example. To say it another way, the addition algorithm is what is used to do multidigit addition, addition of numbers with more than one digit. Remember that when remediating the algorithm, you want to do several things:

- **Let the students see what it looks like.** Carefully model the operation with an appropriate physical or pictorial model. Use a model that lets them see what happens to the basic units—ones, tens, hundreds, and so on—when they add.
- **Deemphasize rote rules.** You might end up with rules, but they should be meaningful. They should arise out of the modeling process.
- **Emphasize big ideas.** These are the important generalizations that describe the process. They also arise out of the modeling process.
- **Let the written algorithm simply be a recording of what happens when the algorithm is modeled.** Everything you write should match something you do.
- **Watch your language.** The language you use should describe what the children see when the operation is modeled, not language that describes what you write down.

The next three activities introduce the first of the big ideas.

Activity 4.01   Sticks and Stones

Bring nine small sticks and nine small stones to class.

Have a child come forward and place three of the sticks and five of the stones into a box. Record on the board what was placed in the box.	3 sticks 5 stones
Have another child come forward and place two more sticks and three more stones into the box. Record on the board what was placed in the box.	3 sticks 5 stones 2 sticks 3 stones
Ask what is in the box. Ask how the students know. Repeat the activity with different numbers of sticks and stones.	

Activity 4.02   Gloves and Socks

Bring nine gloves and nine socks to class.

Have a child come forward and place six gloves and one sock into a box. Record on the board what was placed in the box.	6 gloves 1 sock
Have another child come forward and place three more gloves and two more socks into the box. Record on the board what was placed in the box.	6 gloves 1 sock 3 gloves 2 socks
Ask what is in the box. Ask how the students know. Repeat the activity with different numbers of gloves and socks.	

The First Big Idea

The first big idea in addition is to **always add like units.** Out of experiences like those illustrated in the preceding activities, it becomes apparent to the students that to decide what is in the box, they need to think about only what was put into the box. If sticks and stones are in the box, then they need to think about how many sticks and how many stones are in the box. If gloves and socks are put into the box and later some more gloves and socks are put into the box, then they need to think about only how many gloves are in the box and how many socks are in the box. And how can they figure this out? Add the number of gloves that were put into the box at first to the number of gloves put into the box later. To decide how many socks are in the box, add the number of socks that were put into the box at first to the number of socks that were put into the box later. This is so obvious to the children that it rarely needs to be pointed out. Why do they not add the number of gloves to the number of socks? Because in this setting that would make no sense.

When adding 26 and 53 by representing these numbers with a model that allows the students to see the basic units and then combining the numbers together, the students know the answer because they can see what it looks like. They can see that they need to tell only how many tens there are and how many ones there are. There is no tendency to add the number of tens to the number of ones. That makes no sense.

If they use the model to add 142 + 35, they will not be inclined to add the 1 and the 3. That does not make sense. However, if the typical rote rules are taught, children frequently combine "always go left to right" and "you must line up the columns" to get:

$$\begin{array}{r} 142 \\ +\ 35 \\ \hline \end{array}$$

This is obviously not correct. It makes no sense. When an appropriate model is used to help the students see what multidigit addition looks like, they will not make this common error. They can see what needs to be added to what (Tucker, 1989):

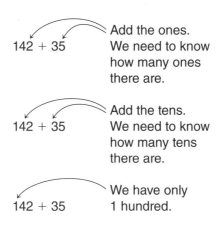

142 + 35   Add the ones. We need to know how many ones there are.

142 + 35   Add the tens. We need to know how many tens there are.

142 + 35   We have only 1 hundred.

We add ones to ones. We add tens to tens. We add hundreds to hundreds. *We always add like units.* This is the first of two big ideas that are used in the addition algorithm. Let's consider this big idea.

First, addition of like units is a constantly recurring idea. How do we add decimals? We add like units.

$2.481 + 47.2 = 49.681$ To find out how many tenths there are, tenths are added to tenths. *We must add like units.* It is interesting to note, though, that the decimal points do not need to be lined up. That's another rote rule that isn't even true.

Why is it easier to add $\frac{2}{5} + \frac{1}{5}$ than to add $\frac{2}{5} + \frac{1}{3}$? Because in $\frac{2}{5} + \frac{1}{5}$, the fractional units are the same in both fractions. In $\frac{2}{5} + \frac{1}{3}$, the fractional units are not the same. *We add like units.* In this case, we call them *like denominators,* but it is the same big idea.

When adding polynomials in algebra, we would add as follows:

$$(2x + 5y + 4xy) + (7x + 3xy) = 9x + 5y + 7xy$$

Why do we add the *x*s together? Why do we add the *xy*s together? Why did we not add the 5*y* to anything? Because *we add like units.* In this case, we call them *like terms,* but it is the same big idea.

As students will discover when studying foundations of algebra, this big idea (always add like units) is really an application of the *distributive property:*

$$23 + 42 = (20 + 3) + (40 + 2)$$
$$= 2 \times 10 + 3 \times 1 + 4 \times 10 + 2 \times 1$$
$$= 2 \times 10 + 4 \times 10 + 3 \times 1 + 2 \times 1$$
$$= |2 + 4| \times 10 + |3 + 2| \times 1$$
$$= 6 \times 10 + 5 \times 1$$
$$= 65$$

The Second Big Idea

The second of the two big ideas that are the basis of the addition algorithm also arises out of the modeling process. We first provide experiences to establish that a number can be named in many ways. We then create an addition dilemma and use the students' understanding of renaming numbers to resolve it. The following activity illustrates how this can be done.

Activity 4.04 Too Many to Write

Write the addition problem 54 + 28 on the board in vertical form. Have a student come forward and represent the two numbers by using bundled Popsicle sticks or base-10 blocks. Have the student place the numbers into a box. Ask the class to tell you what is in the box. How many tens are there? [7] Record this under the tens.

$$\begin{array}{r} 54 \\ +28 \\ \hline \end{array}$$

Ask how many ones are in the box. [12] Record this under the ones. Restate that we have 7 tens and 12 ones. Point to the answer on the board. Ask if this looks like 7 tens and 12 ones. [No, it looks like 7 hundreds, 1 ten, and 2 ones.]

$$\begin{array}{r} 54 \\ +28 \\ \hline 7 \end{array}$$

Ask if anyone knows what is wrong. [When you write 12 ones, it does not look like 12 ones.] Point out that we have room, in each position, for only a one-digit number. In this case, *we have too many to write.* Ask what we can do to get rid of this problem. [Trade 10 ones for a ten.]

$$\begin{array}{r} 54 \\ +28 \\ \hline 712 \end{array}$$

Have the students help you make a trade. Ask what we have after the trade. Point out that this is another name for the same number.

Repeat the activity with other numbers.

The second big idea in addition is **when there are too many to write, make a trade.** The second of the two big ideas that are the basis for the addition algorithm is: *When there are too many to write, make a trade,* meaning too many to write in standard notation. If the example given in Activity 4.04 had been done by using a base-10 chart, there would have been no confusion caused by the way the answer was written. But, neither would there have been a need to make the trade.

tens	ones
5	4
+2	8
7	12

Use of the Addition Algorithm. So, building on the students' experiences with the model, we can show that there are only two things in the addition algorithm to do: *Add like units* and *when there are too many to write, make a trade.* That is all there is to the addition algorithm. When the children learn there two things, they can add any two whole numbers. It does not make any difference whether we are adding three-digit numbers without regrouping, adding two-digit numbers with regrouping from ones to tens, adding five-digit numbers with regrouping from tens to hundreds and also regrouping from hundreds to thousands, or adding any combination of whole numbers. And, looking ahead to addition of decimals, there will not be anything new, because we just add like units and make a trade when there are too many to write.

Use of the Developmental Sequence to Remediate Addition

Establish the meaning of the operation	1. Associate addition with combining quantities.
	2. Learn to use counting to find answers.
Develop the easy basic facts	1. Find the answers by using the meaning of addition.
	2. Discover relationships among the facts.
	3. Memorize the facts.
Develop thinking strategies for hard addition facts	1. Use mental strategies.
	2. Use memorized easy facts to find answers for the hard facts.

Develop the hard basic facts	1. Find the answers by using the thinking strategies.
	2. Review helpful relationships among the facts.
	3. Memorize the facts.
Develop the algorithm	1. Always add like units.
	2. If there are too many to write, make a trade.

Remediation of Student Difficulties with Whole Number Addition

The preceding summary of the developmental sequence to remediate addition is not only a sequence for teaching whole number addition; it also provides a sequence for diagnosis and then remediation of student difficulties with whole number addition.

First, *check to see if the student associates combining of quantities with addition*. For example, show the student two paper bags. Tell her or him that one bag contains three pencils, and the other bag contains five pencils. Ask the student how to figure out how many pencils there are, all together. If the student says to add, go on to the next step in the sequence. If she or he does not say to add, ask for another way to find out how many pencils there are. Continue with similar examples until the meaning of addition is established as the combining of quantities.

Second, *check to see if the student has mastered the easy basic addition facts*. For purposes of the diagnosis, as you are checking for mastery of the easy facts, consider answers that are found by counting or guessing to be wrong answers.

If the child is having difficulties with only a few, isolated facts, a successful remediation can usually be accomplished by identifying one fact at a time and telling him or her that you want that fact to be remembered. Then, continually focus the student's attention on that fact.

For example, suppose that fact is $4 + 3 = 7$. Say, "Four plus three equals seven." Then immediately turn back to the student and ask, "What is four plus three?" Once again, tell the child, "I want you to remember that." You repeat this over and over throughout the day. You ask during reading. You ask on the way to lunch. If he or she begins to count, interrupt and say, "I don't want you to count. I want you to remember. What is four plus three?" At the end of the day, stop the student and ask again.

On the second day, mix in two facts that the child already knows (for example, $3 + 3 = 6$ and $1 + 4 = 5$). Part of the time, ask, "What is three plus three?" Part of the time, ask, "What is four plus three?" Part of the time, ask, "What is one plus four?"

If the student is having difficulties with many facts, a successful remediation can usually be accomplished by emphasizing the relationships that exist among the facts. As it was demonstrated earlier, emphasizing these relationships reduces the number of things that need to be learned. And, of course, *it is always easier to remember things that are related to other things that we know*.

Third, check to see if the student has mastered the hard basic addition facts. As with the easy basic addition facts, a child may be having difficulty with many of the hard basic facts or with one or two isolated hard basic facts. The same remediation technique that was suggested for isolated easy basic facts is recommended for isolated hard basic addition facts. Another method that provides an effective memory aid for isolated easy or hard addition or subtraction basic facts is described in Activity 4.05.

If the student is having difficulty with many of the hard basic facts, the best way to remediate that difficulty is normally to emphasize the make-ten thinking strategy for hard basic addition facts. Do not emphasize speed because that will encourage wild guessing. Rather, emphasize the steps in the thinking strategy.

Fourth, check to see if the student is using the addition algorithm correctly. If he or she is having difficulty with the addition algorithm, identify the big idea that is causing the difficulty. Use a model that lets the student see the basic units (ones, tens, hundreds) and that demonstrates the big idea.

Review and Remediation of Whole Number Subtraction

The developmental sequence for teaching whole number subtraction is similar to that for addition. The first step is to establish the meaning of the operation by associating subtraction with a physical operation. Two physical settings are related to subtraction. One setting calls for comparison subtraction, and the other calls for take-away subtraction.

Developing the Meaning of Subtraction

Comparison Subtraction.   We first consider *comparison subtraction*. Beginning with two quantities, we compare them to find the difference. The process used to find the difference is one-to-one matching. Students can easily learn to use this matching process to find answers to specific subtraction examples.

Take-Away Subtraction.   Now let's consider the second of the physical settings that students should associate with subtraction. In this setting, we start with one number, take some of it away, and find the remainder (Page, 1994).

There are two distinct types of subtraction. Students should understand both comparison and take-away situations and relate both to subtraction. They will encounter both kinds of situations in solving problems, so it's important that they recognize that *we can use subtraction here*. However, once the meaning of subtraction has been established, take-away subtraction is used almost exclusively in whole number subtraction.

Remediation of the Easy Basic Subtraction Facts

The students should figure out the correct answers for any facts that they do not know. As they figure out those facts, they should be compiled in some organized form. As this is being done, the teacher should help the students recognize the following relationships:

1. When you subtract zero from a number, the answer is always that number.
2. When you subtract a number from itself, the answer is always zero.
3. When you subtract one from a number you always get the number that comes before it in the counting sequence.
4. The part-part-whole relationship yields pairs of related facts.

   $5 - 3 = 2$ and $5 - 2 = 3$ $8 - 2 = 6$ and $8 - 6 = 2$ $7 - 3 = 4$ and $7 - 4 = 3$
   $4 - 1 = 3$ and $4 - 3 = 1$ $9 - 5 = 4$ and $9 - 4 = 5$ $9 - 2 = 7$ and $9 - 7 = 2$

5. There is a strong relationship between subtraction facts and addition facts.

   $5 - 3 = 2$ and $2 + 3 = 5$ $8 - 2 = 6$ and $6 + 2 = 8$ $7 - 3 = 4$ and $4 + 3 = 7$
   $4 - 1 = 3$ and $3 + 1 = 4$ $9 - 5 = 4$ and $4 + 5 = 9$ $9 - 2 = 7$ and $7 + 2 = 9$

The most effective plan for remediation of easy basic subtraction facts is to emphasize these relationships. Relationships such as these reduce the number of things that need to be learned and remembered. Since *it is always easier to remember things that are related to other things that you know*, these relationships also improve recall.

Often, students who have mastered most of the easy subtraction facts still have difficulty remembering easy facts. Activity 4.05 describes a particularly good procedure for remediating this problem.

Activity 4.05 Peek If You Need To

When an individual child is having difficulty remembering a particular fact—for example, 9 – 4—fold a small piece of paper, write the problem on the outside, write the answer on the inside, and tape it to the child's desk.

Each time the student is asked this fact, he or she tries to remember the answer. If the student cannot remember, he or she is allowed to look inside at the answer. Tell the child each time to remember the answer and then ask, "What is 9 – 4?"

Remediation of the Hard Basic Subtraction Facts

The objective is for students to commit the hard basic facts to memory so that they can be recalled whenever they are needed. When they encounter hard basic facts that they have not memorized, we do not want students to make wild guesses, nor do we want them to count on their fingers. We want students to think about what they already know that can help them figure out what they do not know.

The *subtract-from-10* strategy is an effective strategy that has proven successful for finding answers to the hard basic subtraction facts. It requires students to already know the facts having a minuend of ten (10 − 5, 10 − 7, 10 − 4, and so forth). It uses the idea that the teen numbers can be thought of as "ten and some more."

This strategy is the reverse of the make-10 strategy that was suggested for finding answers to the hard addition facts. Since subtraction from 10 is easy, we will have the students subtract from 10 to find answers to all the hard basic subtraction facts. The 10-frame is an effective tool for developing understanding of and mental imagery for the subtract-from-10 thinking strategy. For example, suppose we want to find the answer to 13 − 7. We begin by using the 10-frame to represent 13, the number that we start with:

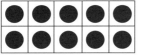

When we take away 7, we will take seven counters from the 10-frame:

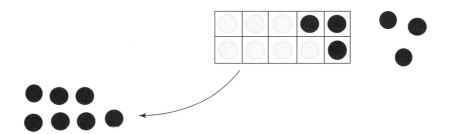

Three counters are left in the 10-frame. Altogether, 3 + 3, or six, counters are left. So, 13 − 7 = 6. Or, suppose we want to find 14 − 8:

Start with 14.

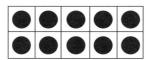

Take 8 from the 10.

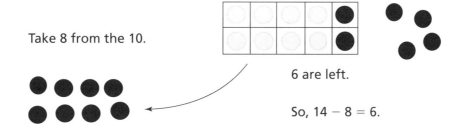

6 are left.

So, $14 - 8 = 6$.

This is a nice way to record the steps:

$$\begin{array}{c} 13 \\ \underline{-7} \end{array} \longrightarrow \begin{array}{c} 10 + 3 \\ \underline{-7} \end{array} \longrightarrow \begin{array}{c} 10 + 3 \\ \underline{-7} \\ 3 \end{array} \longrightarrow \begin{array}{c} 10 + 3 \\ \underline{-7} \\ 3 + 3 = 6 \end{array}$$

Remediation of the Subtraction Algorithm

When remediating the subtraction algorithm, remember that the subtraction algorithm is the step-by-step process by which we can use the basic facts to find answers to any other whole number subtraction example. Remember, also, that when remediating the algorithm, you want to do several things:

- **Let the students see what it looks like.** Carefully model the operation with an appropriate physical or pictorial model. Use a model that lets them see what happens to the basic units—ones, tens, hundreds, and so on—when they subtract.
- **Deemphasize rote rules.** You might end up with rules, but they should be meaningful. They should arise out of the modeling process.
- **Emphasize big ideas.** These are the important generalizations that describe the process. They also arise out of the modeling process.
- **Let the written algorithm simply be a recording of what happens when the algorithm is modeled.** Everything you write should match something you do.
- **Watch your language.** The language you use should describe what the children see when the operation is modeled, not language that describes what you write down.

The Big Ideas for the Subtraction Algorithm

The two big ideas for the subtraction algorithm are **always subtract like units** and **when there are not enough, make a trade.**

Students will never try to take the ones from the tens or take the tens from the hundreds. That makes no sense when they see what it looks like. It is not necessary to tell the students how to subtract two- and three-digit numbers. Their common sense will tell them. We take the hundreds from the hundreds. We take the ones from the ones. We take the tens from the tens. *We always subtract like units.* This is the first of two big ideas that are used in the subtraction algorithm.

The second big idea, *when there are not enough, make a trade,* comes just as naturally as did the first one. Activity 4.06 illustrates how this second big idea can be introduced.

Use of the Subtraction Algorithm.   Out of the students' experiences with the model, we can show that there are only two things to do in the subtraction algorithm: *Subtract like units* and *when there are not enough, make a trade.* That is all there is to the subtraction algorithm. When the children learn to do these two things, they can complete any whole-number subtraction example. It does not make any difference whether we are subtracting three-digit numbers without regrouping, subtracting two-digit numbers with regrouping from tens to ones, subtracting five-digit numbers with regrouping from hundreds to tens and also regrouping from thousands to hundreds, or any combination of whole numbers. *Always subtract like units. When there are not enough, make a trade.* And, looking ahead to subtraction of decimals, there will not be anything new, because we just subtract like units and make a trade when there are not enough.

Use of the Developmental Sequence for Remediation of Subtraction

Establish the meaning of the operation	1. Associate subtraction with comparison and with take away.
	2. Learn to use counting to find answers.
Develop the easy basic facts	1. Find the answers by using the meaning of subtraction.
	2. Discover relationships among the facts.
	3. Memorize the facts.
Develop thinking strategies for hard subtraction facts	1. Use mental strategies.
	2. Use memorized easy facts to find answers for the hard facts.
Develop the hard basic facts	1. Find the answers by using the thinking strategies.
	2. Review relationships among the facts.
	3. Memorize the facts.
Develop the algorithm	1. Always subtract like units.
	2. If there are not enough, make a trade.

Remediation of Student Difficulties with Whole Number Subtraction

The developmental sequence for subtraction, like the one for addition, provides the following sequence for diagnosis and remediation of student difficulties with whole number subtraction.

Diagnoses	Remediation
Problems with easy basic facts	Work on relationships among the facts.
Problems with hard basic facts	Work on an efficient thinking strategy (subtract from 10).
Problems with the subtraction algorithm	Use a model that allows the students to see the basic units and that lets them see what the two subtraction big ideas look like.

Teaching Problem Solving Using Addition and Subtraction

Problem solving is a high-priority topic in the elementary school mathematics curriculum. The ability to use addition and subtraction to solve problems is found in the way that the meanings of the operations are developed. When the arithmetic operations are related to physical operations, students are better able to look at problem situations and determine if addition or subtraction can be used to find the solution.

If the essence of the problem is that some of a quantity is being taken away, students can look at the situation and tell that subtraction should be used to find the answer. If the essence of the problem is that quantities are being combined and we want to find how many altogether, students can look at the situation and tell that addition should be used to find the answer. And, if the essence of the problem is that two quantities are being compared and you want to find which is more and how much more, students can look at the situation and tell that subtraction should be used.

Translate Word Problems into Situations

When problems are posed as word problems, the students should not be taught to look for key words like *and* or *of,* but rather they should think about the situation being described and think about what is happening to the quantities. They should think about what operation they see happening in the problem. The reason many students are unable to solve word problems is that they have not learned to convert the word problem (a bunch of words) into a situation. It is not that they lack the needed mathematical understanding and ability. Most often, once they are able to "see" the situation, the solution is simple for them.

Sometimes special help must be provided so the students can make the conversion from a bunch of words to a situation. Remediation techniques that have proven to be successful are *dramatization of the problem, modeling the problem, partnering,* and *group explanations.* These techniques are illustrated in the following activities.

Activity 4.07   Act It Out

Form groups of students. Give each group a word problem and have each group plan how to act out its problem before the rest of the class. When the groups are ready, have each group act out its problem and then ask the question that needs to be answered. The other class members must figure out the answer. The teacher should use some students to show the first one.

Activity 4.08   Show It with Stuff

Form groups of students. Give each group a word problem and have each group plan how to use materials like counters and boxes to show its problem to the rest of the class. When the groups are ready, have each group show its problem and then ask the question that needs to be answered. The other class members must figure out the answer. The teacher should do the first one.

Activity 4.09   Partners Can

Have the children work with partners. Give the partners a word problem and have them discuss the problem and agree on how to explain what is happening in the problem. When the partners are ready, the teacher should go to them and have them explain the problem. What is happening? What do we want to find out?

Activity 4.10   Teacher's a Dummy

Have the students look at a word problem. Tell them that you don't understand the problem and you don't know what to do. Ask them to explain the problem to you. Try to get even the weakest students involved. Play dumb. Ask really stupid questions. Loosen up and have fun with it.

Exercises and Activities

1. Compare the two earlier subtraction lesson plans.
   a. Identify where the adapted plan provides more kinesthetic activity.
   b. Identify where the adapted plan provides more opportunity for communication from the children.
   c. Identify where the adapted plan provides more opportunity for communication among the children.
2. Choose a lesson on either addition or subtraction of whole numbers from a published elementary school mathematics textbook series.
   a. Identify the parts of the lesson that develop the concept(s) or skill(s).
   b. Identify the parts of the lesson that provide visual information about the concept(s) or skill(s) being taught.
   c. Expand the lesson by adding activities that provide more visual information about the concept(s) or skill(s) being taught.
   d. Identify kinesthetic activity that is included in the lesson.
   e. Add more kinesthetic activity to the lesson.
   f. Identify parts of the lesson that include student communication about the concept(s) or skill(s) taught in the lesson.
   g. Add more opportunities for communication from or among students to the lesson.
   h. Identify the parts of the lesson designed to assess the learning of the students.
   i. Add more continual assessment (monitoring of learning) to the lesson plan.
3. An interesting process can be used to change a hard subtraction fact into an easier one. If we think of the answer as the difference between the two numbers, that difference can be illustrated on the number line:

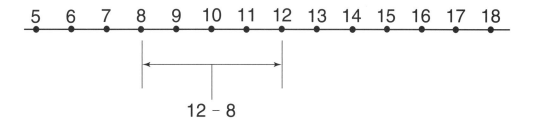

Notice that if 2 is added to both numbers, they shift two spaces to the right on the number line, but they are the same distance apart:

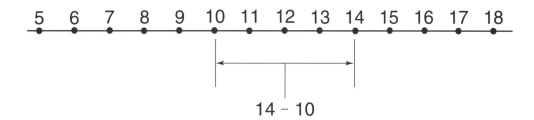

Adding the same number to both numbers does not change the difference. Notice that although the difference (the answer) is the same, this new fact is a lot easier.

a. Use this equal-additions process to change 15 − 8 into an easier fact.

b. Develop an activity to teach children to use this strategy to find answers to the hard basic subtraction facts.

4. The following addition results illustrate an error pattern like those that were related by Robert Ashlock in his book, *Error Patterns in Computation: Using Error Patterns to Improve Instruction*:

$$
\begin{array}{r} 8\ 4 \\ +\ 5\ 6 \\ \hline 1310 \end{array}
\qquad
\begin{array}{r} 3\ 5 \\ +\ 7\ 2 \\ \hline 107 \end{array}
\qquad
\begin{array}{r} 6\ 9 \\ +\ 2\ 8 \\ \hline 817 \end{array}
\qquad
\begin{array}{r} 1\ 8 \\ +\ 9\ 7 \\ \hline 1015 \end{array}
$$

a. What is this student's error pattern? What is the student doing to produce the incorrect answers?

b. Plan a mini-lesson to correct this student's error pattern.

5. The following subtraction results illustrate an error pattern like those that were related by Robert Ashlock in his book, *Error Patterns in Computation: Using Error Patterns to Improve Instruction*:

$$
\begin{array}{r} 76 \\ -58 \\ \hline 18 \end{array}
\qquad
\begin{array}{r} 64 \\ -28 \\ \hline 36 \end{array}
\qquad
\begin{array}{r} 457 \\ -168 \\ \hline 299 \end{array}
\qquad
\begin{array}{r} 317 \\ -158 \\ \hline 169 \end{array}
$$

a. What is this student's error pattern? What is the student doing to produce the incorrect answers?

b. Plan a mini-lesson to correct this student's error pattern. Build on what the student does do correctly when solving these problems.

References and Related Readings

Ashlock, R. B. (2002). *Error patterns in computation: Using error patterns to improve instruction* (8th ed.). Upper Saddle River, NJ: Prentice Hall.

Bishop, J. W., Otto, A. D., & Lubinski, C. A. (2001). Promoting algebraic reasoning using students' thinking. *Mathematics Teaching in the Middle School, 6,* 508–514.

Fernandez, M. L., & Anhalt, C. O. (2001). Transition toward algebra. *Mathematics Teaching in the Middle School, 7,* 236–241.

Huinker, D., Freckman, J. L., & Steinmeyer, M. B. (2003). Subtraction strategies from children's thinking: Moving toward fluency with greater numbers. *Teaching Children Mathematics, 9,* 347–353.

Isaacs, A. C., & Carroll, W. M. (1999). Strategies for basic-facts instruction. *Teaching Children Mathematics, 5,* 508–515.

Kamii, C., & Lewis, B. (2003). Single-digit subtraction with fluency. *Teaching Children Mathematics, 10,* 230–236.

Martinez, J. G. R. (2002). Building conceptual bridges from arithmetic to algebra. *Mathematics Teaching in the Middle School, 7,* 326–331.

National Council of Teachers of Mathematics. (1989). *Curriculum and evaluation standards for school mathematics.* Reston, VA: Author.

National Council of Teachers of Mathematics. (2000). *Principles and standards for school mathematics.* Reston, VA: Author.

Page, A. (1994). Helping children understand subtraction. *Teaching Children Mathematics, 1,* 140–143.

Postlewait, K. B., Adams, M. R., & Shih, J. C. (2003). Promoting meaningful mastery of addition and subtraction. *Teaching Children Mathematics, 9,* 354–357.

Thornton, C. A., Tucker, B. F., Dossey, J. A., & Bazik, E. F. (1983). *Teaching mathematics to children with special needs.* Menlo Park, CA: Addison-Wesley.

Tucker, B. F. (1981). Give and take: Getting ready to regroup. *The Arithmetic Teacher, 28*(8), 24–26.

Tucker, B. F. (1989). Seeing addition: A diagnosis/remediation case study. *The Arithmetic Teacher, 36*(5), 10–11.

Websites

www.corestandards.org/the-standards/mathematics
The Common Core State Standards for Mathematics can be found at this site.

www.proteacher.com/100009.shtml
Lesson plans on addition and subtraction, by teachers.

http://mathforum.org/
Math forum links to math discussions and ideas.

www.sasked.gov.sk.ca/docs/elemath/numop.html
A scope and sequence chart for numbers and operations.

five

COMPUTATION WITH WHOLE NUMBERS

Development of Multiplication and Division

CHAPTER OUTLINE

Teaching Multiplication of Whole Numbers

Now we examine the developmental sequence as it is applied to teaching whole number multiplication. As when teaching or remediating addition and subtraction, the teacher must first establish the meaning of multiplication.

Developing the Meaning of Multiplication

Students need to *associate multiplication with the combining of equal-sized quantities.* The association must be so strong that when students see the symbols 3×4, they visualize three groups of four things being combined. When they see a situation where equal quantities are being combined, they will think, "That's multiplication!" After multiplication has been mastered, the students will see problem settings where equal quantities are being combined and think, "I can use multiplication to solve this problem."

Counting.   The students must also realize that, after equal quantities have been combined, they can *count to find how many there are altogether.*

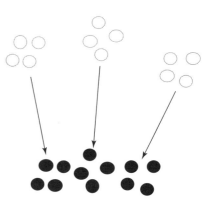

If I combine three groups of 4,

I can count them to see that there are 12 altogether. So, 3 × 4 = 12.

Addition.   Because counting so many objects becomes tedious and is time consuming, we want to lead the students to understand that we can also use addition to find the answer:

Start with three groups of 4.

Combine two of the groups. That's 4 + 4.

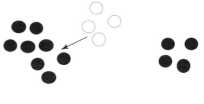

Then, I can add the other group of 4. That's 4 + 4 + 4.

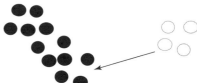

Teaching Both Counting and Addition.   We want to teach students that they can figure out the answer to multiplication examples in two ways: Count to get the answer, or add to get the answer. If the students have already developed a level of proficiency with simple addition, it is easier and quicker to get multiplication answers by adding. These are two ways that work, but the students should be encouraged to use the most efficient method.

The teacher should review the operation of multiplication by using physical materials and using concepts and language that are already available to the students. In this natural setting, the teacher should then utilize the new mathematical terms and notation that is used to write them.

In the next activities, multiplication is developed as a physical operation on equal-sized groups. Then, the language of multiplication is used along with the multiplication (or "times") sign. Finally, we use the written notation for multiplication. The sequence of activities is particularly helpful when remediating the meaning of multiplication.

Activity 5.01 Putting Bunches Together

Bring about 25 small sticks that are about the same size to class.

Using rubber bands, tell the students to make three bunches of five sticks. Have them put the three bunches into a box. Write on the board what is in the box. [three bunches of 5] Ask how we can figure out how many sticks are in the box. [We count them.]

Point out that the bunches are being combined. Ask what we call it when we put numbers of things together. [Addition] Show how addition can be used to find how many sticks. [First, put two bunches together into the box. That's 5 + 5. Then add the other bunch. That's 5 + 5 + 5.] Tell the students to find how many sticks are in the box by using both methods. Write the answer. [Three bunches of 5 is 15.]

Repeat the activity with other numbers.

Activity 5.02 Money in My Pocket

Bring to class about 30 pennies. Have four children come forward. Give each of them 6 pennies. Have them put the pennies in their pockets. Ask the class to figure out how to find how many pennies there are in all four pockets. [By taking them out, combining them, and counting. By adding.] Have the children find the answer both ways.

Repeat the activity with different numbers.

Activity 5.03 The Way to Say It

Have six students come to the front of the room and get four blocks each. Then have the other students watch carefully as your six helpers, one at a time, place their blocks in a paper bag.

Ask the class to describe what was done. [Four was placed in the bag 6 times.] Have the students figure out how many blocks are in the bag. Write, "Four, 6 times = 24" on the board.

Do another example (perhaps seven, 3 times) and write it on the board. Then explain to the class that instead of four, 6 times, we usually say 6 times 4. Point to the other example and ask how we usually say it. [3 times 7]

Finally, use the multiplication sign [×] and show how to use it to write the examples. [6 × 4 = 24, 3 × 7 = 21] Tell the students how to read each example. [6 times 4 equals 24, 3 times 7 equals 21]

Do other examples with the blocks and paper bag. Tell the students to use multiplication language and notation to say, write, and read the examples.

Activity 5.04 Fact Finders

Prepare two spinners—one with the numbers 2 to 9, used to determine the size of the groups, and the other with the numbers 2 to 4, used to determine the number of groups:

Group Size

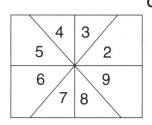

Number of Groups

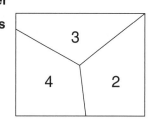

Have a child spin the group-size spinner and have another child spin the number-of-groups spinner. The children form and combine the groups and then figure out the total number. Remind them to use appropriate multiplication language to describe what they are doing and to use appropriate multiplication notation to write their results. Have them read what is written.

As they figure out answers, encourage the students to use the most efficient method.

Developing the Easy Basic Multiplication Facts

To reinforce the meaning of multiplication, the teacher should expose the students to a wide variety of multiplication examples using objects that are familiar to them. The students should use appropriate terminology to describe the multiplication verbally and use the times sign and equal sign to write it. In every example, students should figure out the answer for themselves, and the teacher should continually emphasize how much easier it is. The students can find the answers by themselves. Three examples of instructional activities follow that illustrate how this can be accomplished.

Activity 5.05   How Much Paper Do I Need?

Tell the students that you are thinking about doing an art activity where each person needs five sheets of paper. Ask the class to figure out how many sheets of paper are needed for a group of four students.

Get out some paper, and use it to check the answer.

Activity 5.06   What Do We Need to Play the Game?

Show this game to the children: Have cards, each with one letter on it. Shuffle the cards, and give seven cards to each of three children. They are to use their cards to spell the longest word that they can. But, before spelling their words, they may trade three cards if someone else is willing to trade with them. After the trades, whoever spells the word with the most letters wins.

Have the students figure out how many cards were used in the game. How many cards would be needed if there were four players? Five players?

Activity 5.07   Is That Enough Milk?

Have the students count to find out how many children are in the class. Then explain that we would like to get enough cartons of milk so that everyone can have one drink. How many cartons are needed?

Tell them that one person can carry four cartons without dropping them. Have four students come to the front. Ask the class whether there would be enough milk if each of these children brought back four cartons. Would there be enough if five students went for milk? Six students?

Note that this process requires a lot of adding. We want to speed it up as much as possible. One way to accomplish this is to have the students think about what multiplication they have already done that might help. Often, several related multiplications are done together or in succession. For example, if you have just found the answer to 3×6 by adding $6 + 6 + 6$, then 4×6 is easy:

$$4 \times 6 = 6 + 6 + 6 + 6$$

I already know that this is 18, so the answer to 4×6 is

$$4 \times 6 = 18 + 6$$
$$= 24$$

The teacher should continually emphasize that with every problem that the children face, they should first think about what they already know that will help.

Discovering Relationships among the Easy Basic Multiplication Facts.
After the meaning of multiplication has been established and the students can confidently find answers on their own, we focus on the easy basic multiplication facts, with our goal being for the students to commit those facts to memory. Which multiplication facts are included in the easy ones will vary from program to program, but whichever are included, there is a sense that they are easier than the others. For purposes of our discussion here, we will consider multiplication facts with multipliers of 0 to 3 to be the easy ones. There are 64 of these easy basic multiplication facts.

While focusing on the easy facts, in addition to figuring out the answers for themselves, the students need to review helpful relationships that exist among the multiplication facts. In particular, the teacher needs to ensure that the students understand four relationships.

First, the students should recognize that the facts where one of the numbers being multiplied is 0 all have something in common. The answer for these facts is always 0:

X	0	1	2	3	4	5	6	7	8	9
0	0	0	0	0	0	0	0	0	0	0
1	0	1	2	3	4	5	6	7	8	9
2	0	2	4	6	8	10	12	14	16	18
3	0	3	6	9	12	15	18	21	24	27
4	0	4	8	12						
5	0	5	10	15						
6	0	6	12	18						
7	0	7	14	21						
8	0	8	16	24						
9	0	9	18	27						

$$0 \times 4 = 0 \qquad 0 \times 7 = 0 \qquad 6 \times 0 = 0$$
$$9 \times 0 = 0 \qquad 0 \times 3 = 0 \qquad 4 \times 0 = 0$$
$$0 \times 8 = 0 \qquad 1 \times 0 = 0$$

There are 19 facts with the multiplier or the multiplicand equal to 0. That's 19 of the 64 easy basic multiplication facts, but because of this relationship, it is only 1 fact for the students to learn.

A second important relationship is evident in the next group of facts:

$$1 \times 4 = 4 \qquad 1 \times 7 = 7 \qquad 6 \times 1 = 6$$
$$9 \times 1 = 9 \qquad 1 \times 3 = 3 \qquad 4 \times 1 = 4$$
$$1 \times 8 = 8 \qquad 1 \times 1 = 1$$

There are 19 basic multiplication facts in which one of the numbers being multiplied is 1. In each of these cases, the answer will be the other number. Two of those are $0 \times 1 = 0$ and $1 \times 0 = 0$, and they have been dealt with earlier. So, we have 17 new facts in this group. But, because of this relationship, it is only 1 new fact to memorize.

The third relationship that we want the students to recognize is that certain pairs of facts are related:

$$3 \times 4 = 12 \quad \text{and} \quad 4 \times 3 = 12$$
$$9 \times 2 = 18 \quad \text{and} \quad 2 \times 9 = 18$$
$$4 \times 5 = 20 \quad \text{and} \quad 5 \times 4 = 20$$
$$4 \times 8 = 32 \quad \text{and} \quad 8 \times 4 = 32$$

Students should recognize from these pairs of facts that changing the order of the numbers being multiplied does not change the answer. This rearrangement principle tells us that the answer to 5×6 is also the answer to 6×5. The answer to 3×9 is also the answer to 9×3. And, 8×74 has the same answer as 74×8 (this is the *commutative property of multiplication*).

A fourth important relationship between other pairs of facts should also be recognized by the students. This time, the relationship is between certain multiplication facts and certain addition facts:

$$2 \times 4 = 8 \quad \text{and} \quad 4 + 4 = 8$$
$$2 \times 9 = 18 \quad \text{and} \quad 9 + 9 = 18$$
$$2 \times 5 = 10 \quad \text{and} \quad 5 + 5 = 10$$
$$2 \times 8 = 16 \quad \text{and} \quad 8 + 8 = 16$$

Multiplying 2 times a number is exactly the same as adding that number to itself. This is a direct result of the meaning of multiplication. Children who recognize this relationship realize that these are just the doubles that were already memorized as addition facts, so there is nothing new to learn here. Also, the numbers being multiplied may be rearranged without affecting the answer, $4 \times 2 = 2 \times 4$. Therefore, 4×2 is also a double. There are 15 of these doubles that have not been previously dealt with as multiplication by 0 or by 1. If the students are aware of how multiplication is related to addition, they will already know these 15 facts. That's 15 facts, but nothing new to learn.

There are just six remaining rearranged pairs that were not included in multiplication by 0, by 1, or by 2. That's 12 multiplication facts, but if the students have learned that rearranging the numbers does not change the product, it is only six things to learn. So, of the 64 easy basic multiplication facts, the only one not yet discussed is $3 \times 3 = 9$. That's 1 fact to learn. Let's summarize the impact of such an emphasis on relationships:

Group of Facts	Number of Facts	Things to Learn
× 0	19	1
× 1	17	1
× 2	15	0
Commutative pairs	12	6
3 × 3	1	1
All easy facts	**64**	**9**

The emphasis on relationships provides a tremendous advantage to the students. The 64 easy basic multiplication facts can be mastered by learning only nine new things. This certainly increases the number of students who actually have the facts committed to memory and increases the speed with which memorization takes place. But, even more importantly, it significantly increases retention of those facts once they have been memorized. Remember: *It is always easier to remember things that are related to other things that are already known.*

Memorization of the Easy Basic Multiplication Facts.
After the students understand the relationships among the facts, they should commit the easy basic multiplication facts to memory. The instructional activities that are selected to lead the students to memorizing the easy basic multiplication facts should have certain characteristics. These are the same eight characteristics presented in Chapter 4 for addition facts:

1. Students should be aware that the objective is to memorize the facts. They should be told to remember.
2. The activities should use an interesting and fun format.
3. The activities should have a high level of involvement. Minimize time spent waiting. Maximize time spent thinking about the facts.
4. The activities should focus on a small number of unmemorized facts at any given time.

5. Some already memorized facts should be mixed in with the target unmemorized facts. This will improve retention.

6. If a child does not know an answer, then he or she should figure it out. This implies that the child will have time to figure it out. Discourage guessing by asking, "How did you figure that out?"

7. To figure out an answer, the student should think about what he or she already knows that will help find the answer: What other already known facts will help? What already known relationship will help? Counting or adding should be used only as a last resort.

8. Emphasize accuracy, not speed. Accuracy is of great importance. Speed is of little importance. Speed will come after accuracy and confidence.

The following examples of memorization activities demonstrate these characteristics.

Activity 5.08   Doubles and One More

Have a student come to the front and demonstrate 3 × 6 by using counters. After he or she has shown three groups of 6, suggest that the student start by combining two of the groups. Point to the two groups of 6 that have been combined. Point out that it is 6 + 6. Point out that it is also 2 × 6. Then point out that there is still one more 6. Three 6s are the same as two 6s and one more 6. Write it on the board:

$$3 \times 6 = 2 \times 6 + 6$$

Emphasize to the students that they already know the double, so they just need to add one more 6.

Repeat this process with other multiplications by 3: 3 × 7, 3 × 5, 3 × 9, 3 × 4, 3 × 8, 3 × 3.

Activity 5.09   Facts of the Day

Identify two facts that a student needs to work on. Have her or him figure out the answers and write each fact on a piece of paper. Tell the student to remember both of the facts. Immediately ask the child for both answers. Tell her or him again to remember the answers. Frequently during the day, ask the child to give you one or the other of these answers. Each time, tell the child to remember. At the end of the day, send the two pieces of paper with the facts written on them home with the student, along with a note explaining what you are doing. Ask the parents to ask their student to give them the answers to both facts.

Activity 5.10   'Round We Go

Prepare cards showing multiplication facts without answers:

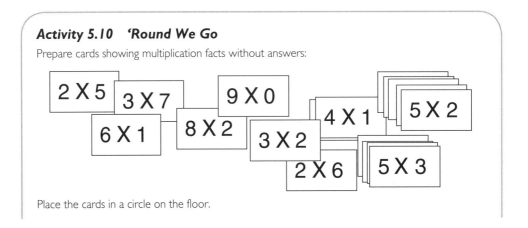

Place the cards in a circle on the floor.

Have the students march around the circle, chanting this rhyme:

Marching, marching, 'round we go,

Not too fast and not too slow.

We won't run and we won't hop.

We're almost there. It's time to stop.

When the rhyme is finished, hold up a card with an answer. Students who are standing by facts with that answer hold up their hands. Repeat the procedure several times.

Developing the Hard Basic Multiplication Facts

Thinking Strategies for the Hard Basic Multiplication Facts. During development of the hard basic multiplication facts (for example, those with multipliers greater than 3), answers can still be found by counting or by adding. However, with the larger numbers, both counting and adding are inefficient and consequently very slow. At this point in the development, more efficient strategies are needed that allow the students to find answers quickly and accurately.

Our objective is for these facts to be committed to memory. Remember from our discussion of strategies for the hard basic addition facts that some strategies seem to lead to memorization while others do not. Recall, also, that the strategies that are successful have two common characteristics.

Successful strategies are mental strategies. They consist of a series of quick, easy mental procedures. They are not pencil-and-paper strategies, nor are they performed by manipulating fingers or other objects. Also, *successful strategies require the child to use facts that are already memorized to figure out the facts that are not yet memorized.* The student is constantly thinking about what he or she already knows that can help figure out what he or she does not know. The student has a sense of building on what is already known. New knowledge is closely related to existing knowledge, and it is always easier to remember things that are related to other things that we know.

One More Strategy The simplest thinking strategy for hard basic multiplication facts is the *one more strategy*. The thinking is very simple, so it is easy for students to use. Every hard basic multiplication fact can be found by using this strategy. If we want to find 6 × 8, we think of six 8s as being five 8s and one more 8. We visualize 6 × 8 as six rows of 8 objects:

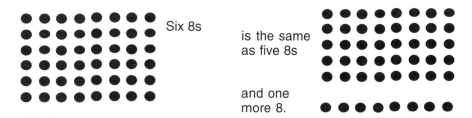

If we know what five 8s is equal to, then we simply need to add one more 8. That will give the answer to six 8s:

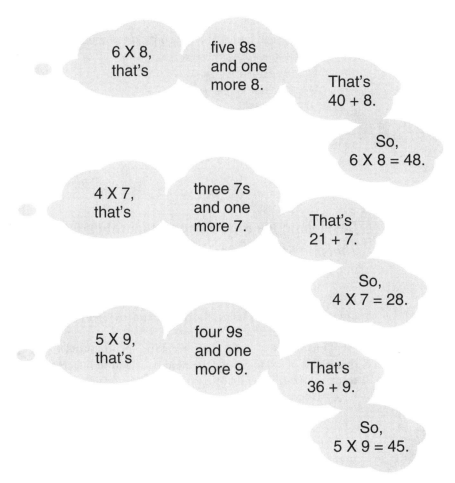

To use the one-more strategy to find answers to a hard basic multiplication fact, we must, in each case, know another fact first. For example, to find 6 × 8, we must already know 5 × 8. To find 7 × 9, we must already know 6 × 9. To find 5 × 7, we must already know 4 × 7. To find 6 × 6, we must already know 5 × 6.

Textbooks frequently use the one-more strategy to develop the hard facts in carefully controlled sequence. The authors know which facts have previously been developed, and all new facts build on them. However, in practice, the students do not memorize the facts in the same sequence in which they are developed in the textbook. They typically remember some and not others. As a result, at any given time, the students in any class will have mastered varied combinations of facts, and, of course, they will not have mastered other combinations.

When it is time for the students to figure out the answer to 6 × 8, we cannot be sure that they already know 5 × 8. When we are ready for them to figure out the answer to 7 × 9, we cannot depend on their already knowing 6 × 9. Some students already know the necessary facts. Some do not. Although the one-more strategy works well in the textbook, and although it may work well when you are working with a single student (when you can keep track of which facts are already memorized), it is difficult to use in a large group setting (when it is hard to keep track of which facts each student has already memorized). But, there is another thinking strategy that seems to work more effectively in a whole-class setting.

Partial-Products Strategy The other thinking strategy for hard basic multiplication facts that has proven to be more successful in a whole-class environment is the *partial-products strategy*. In fact, the one-more strategy is really a special case of the partial-products strategy, which is an application of the distributive property. The simplest description of this strategy is that we take the "big" fact that we do not know *and break it into easier facts that we do know.* For example, suppose we do not know the answer to 6×7. We visualize this as 6 rows of 7 objects. We break it into two easy parts and then combine those two parts:

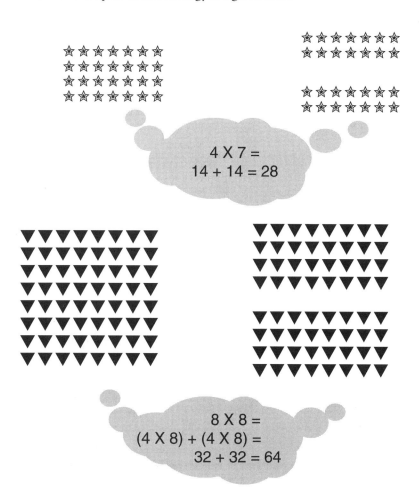

Other examples of this strategy are given next:

Success with this strategy depends on getting the students to think about *what easier facts they already know* that can help them find the answer. This kind of thinking is good problem-solving behavior, and we would want them to think like this even if it did not help them with their multiplication facts.

Teachers who use the partial-products strategy find that a fair amount of time and effort is required to get the students to use this thinking pattern. But, after they become comfortable with it, they are able to find answers much more quickly, and they make rapid progress toward mastery of the multiplication facts. In addition to providing quicker mastery of the hard basic multiplication facts, this strategy introduces the concept of *partial products*, which will be used later in multidigit multiplication. In other words, the instructional goal is achieved more quickly if time is spent on learning the thinking strategies.

Use of the Thinking Strategies   After the students have learned to use the partial-products strategy to find answers to the hard basic multiplication facts, rapid progress can be made toward mastery of these facts. As when working on the easy facts, the students should be able to figure out the answers to the hard facts. They need to recognize and use relationships among the hard facts. And, we want them to commit the hard facts to memory.

If students do not know a hard multiplication fact, they cannot just say, "I don't know." They must figure out the answer. And since we want them to figure out the answer efficiently and quickly, we encourage (almost require) them to use the thinking strategy that has been learned. The students have, at this point, been using repeated addition for over a year to find multiplication-fact answers. They are comfortable using repeated addition—even when it takes a long time. Consequently, they will automatically fall back on repeated addition because they are comfortable with this process. So, the teacher must continually lead the children to use the thinking strategy instead.

If the students do not know the answer to a hard basic multiplication fact, *they need to think about what they already know that will help them with the fact that they do not know.* If the students continually think about the relationships among the facts, they end up with fewer things to learn, and their retention of what they have learned is better.

Memorization of the Hard Basic Multiplication Facts.   The following group of activities demonstrates how a teacher can *help students think about what they already know that will help them with what they are trying to figure out.*

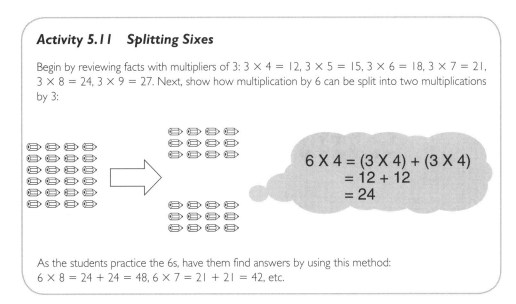

Activity 5.11   Splitting Sixes

Begin by reviewing facts with multipliers of 3: $3 \times 4 = 12$, $3 \times 5 = 15$, $3 \times 6 = 18$, $3 \times 7 = 21$, $3 \times 8 = 24$, $3 \times 9 = 27$. Next, show how multiplication by 6 can be split into two multiplications by 3:

$$6 \times 4 = (3 \times 4) + (3 \times 4)$$
$$= 12 + 12$$
$$= 24$$

As the students practice the 6s, have them find answers by using this method:
$6 \times 8 = 24 + 24 = 48$, $6 \times 7 = 21 + 21 = 42$, etc.

Activity 5.12   Thirty-Six vs. Twenty-Four

Prepare a set of 50 cards with one-digit numbers on them. Each of the numbers 0 through 9 should appear on 5 cards. This is a game for two players.

Shuffle the deck and place it facedown on the table between the players. Turn 1 card faceup. The players take turns. One player tries to find pairs of numbers with a product of 36. The other player tries to find pairs of numbers with a product of 24. On each turn, the player turns over an additional card and looks at all the numbers that are showing. If the player sees two numbers with his or her product, he or she takes those 2 cards.

After all the cards in the deck have been turned over, the game ends, and the player who has taken the most cards is the winner. Most of the cards will not be used and will remain on the table.

Activity 5.13   Finding My Answers

Prepare a set of 50 cards like those described for Activity 5.12. This is a game for three players.

Shuffle the deck and place it facedown on the table. Turn 1 card faceup. The players take turns. One player tries to find pairs of numbers with a product of 63, 48, or 49. The second player tries to find pairs of numbers with a product of 72, 64, or 42. The third player tries to find pairs of numbers with a product of 81, 56, or 32. On each turn, the player turns over an additional card and looks at all the numbers that are showing. If the player sees two numbers with one of his or her products, he or she takes those 2 cards.

After all the cards in the deck have been turned over, the game ends, and the player who has taken the most cards is the winner. Most of the cards will not be used and will remain on the table.

Activity 5.14   Some Easy and Some Hard

Prepare a set of 50 cards like those described for Activity 5.12.

Follow the procedures of Activity 5.12, except have the three players find the following sets of products: 12, 16, or 56; 8, 36, or 48; and 6, 25, or 42.

Activity 5.15   Line Up

Prepare large flash cards showing multiplication facts without answers. Include the facts that are currently being emphasized. Include enough so that every student will have one. Shuffle them and give one card to each student.

Separate the class into two groups. Have one group go to one side of the room, and have the other group go to the opposite side of the room. Tell the two groups to line up so that the answers to their multiplication facts are in order. Allow them to talk and help each other. When they are lined up, have them hold their cards so the other group can see them. Each group should then check the other group.

Collect the cards, reshuffle them, and repeat the activity.

Activity 5.16 Scavenger Hunt

Prepare five lists of answers to multiplication facts. Each list should have seven answers. Also prepare cards showing the multiplication facts that have the answers on the lists, but do not include the answers on these cards. Be sure that there is a fact card for each answer on each list, but include some extra fact cards that do not go with any of the answers.

Tape the fact cards on the walls all around the classroom. Form five teams and give each team one of the lists of answers. Tell the teams that they must find facts to go with all the answers on their lists.

The first team to collect facts for all their answers wins.

Teaching the Multiplication Algorithm

When the basic multiplication facts have been mastered, the student is ready to begin work on the multiplication algorithm. The multiplication algorithm is the step-by-step process by which we use the basic facts to find answers to any other whole number multiplication example. We use the multiplication algorithm to do multidigit multiplication. Several principles related to teaching algorithms have been mentioned earlier. Let's review those principles:

- **Let the students see what it looks like.** Carefully model the operation with an appropriate physical or pictorial model. We should use a model that lets them see what happens to the basic units—ones, tens, hundreds, and so on—when they multiply.
- **Deemphasize rote rules.** You may end up with rules, but they should be meaningful. They should arise out of the modeling process.
- **Emphasize big ideas.** These are the important generalizations that describe the process. They also arise out of the modeling process.
- **Let the written algorithm simply be a recording of what happens when the algorithm is modeled.** Everything you write should match something you do.
- **Watch your language.** The language you use should describe what the children see when the operation is modeled, not language that describes what you write down.

The First Big Idea

Multiplication by Ten The first of the big ideas that form the basis of the multiplication algorithm is *multiplication by 10*. It is important that the students discover that multiplication by 10 is really easy. It is not unusual to see a child multiply by 10 something like this:

$$
\begin{array}{r}
236 \\
\times\ \ 10 \\
\hline
000 \\
\underline{236\ \ \ } \\
2,360
\end{array}
$$

When we see this, we know that the algorithm has been taught rotely, and the child has not been taught the first big idea for the multiplication algorithm. Most adults know (and who knows how they learned it) that when multiplying by 10, we simply "add a zero." Multiplication by 10 is easy. But we do not want to just give the students this "rule" without teaching it meaningfully. To do this, we need a model for numbers that lets the students see ones, tens, and hundreds. For our discussion here, we begin by using bundled sticks:

We begin by using the bundled sticks to represent 21.

Then, we use the bundled sticks to represent 21 ten times, and we write 10×21 on the board.

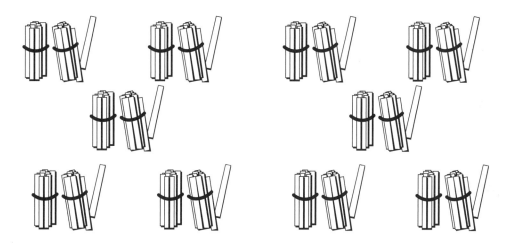

Next, we put all the tens together and put all the ones together.

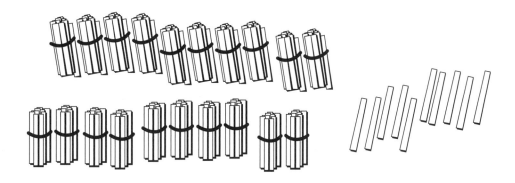

And, finally, we group the tens together to make hundreds and group the ones together to make a ten.

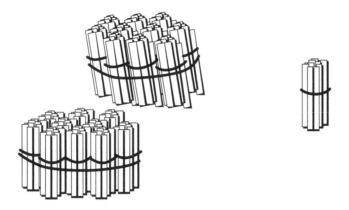

We record the result on the board: $10 \times 21 = 210$.

We repeat this process with a variety of examples and record all the results together on the board. For example, we might use:

$$10 \times 21 = 210$$
$$12 \times 10 = 120 \ (10, \text{twelve times})$$
$$10 \times 36 = 360$$
$$42 \times 10 = 420$$
$$10 \times 8 = 80$$

When these examples have been completed using the model to get the answers, we ask the students if they see a pattern. Do they see how they might get the answer without using the model? When it has been suggested that they can just "add" a zero to get the answer, write another example (for example, 10×18) on the board, and ask what the answer is. Record the answer that the students give, but then do this example with the model to verify that their answer is correct.

Out of experiences like those just illustrated, it becomes apparent to the students that multiplication by 10 is easy, that you "just add a zero." The next step is to extend the notion of multiplication by 10 as follows:

$$30 \times 7 = \overset{\text{This is 30.}}{10 \times 3} \times 7$$

We have a basic fact (3×7) and a multiplication by 10.

The answer is $10 \times 21 = 210$.

Similarly, $50 \times 9 = 10 \times 5 \times 9 = 10 \times 45 = 450$. Again, we have a basic fact and a multiplication by 10. Another example is $4 \times 60 = 4 \times 6 \times 10 = 240$, which is also a basic fact and a multiplication by 10. Answers to all of the examples— 70×8, 30×6, 7×20, 40×3, 5×80, and so on—are easily found by multiplying the answer to a basic fact by 10.

The answer to an example like 30 × 70 can be found by extending the notion of multiplication by 10 still further:

$$30 \times 70 = \underset{\underset{30}{\rule{1.2cm}{0.4pt}}}{10 \times 3} \times \underset{\underset{70}{\rule{1.2cm}{0.4pt}}}{10 \times 7} = 10 \times 10 \times 3 \times 7 = 2{,}100$$

In this case, we end up with a basic fact and two multiplications by 10. Each multiplication by 10 "adds a zero." Similar examples also result in a basic fact and two multiplications by 10:

$$40 \times 30 = 4 \times 3 \times 10 \times 10 = 1{,}200$$
$$20 \times 90 = 2 \times 9 \times 10 \times 10 = 1{,}800$$
$$50 \times 70 = 5 \times 7 \times 10 \times 10 = 3{,}500$$
$$80 \times 50 = 8 \times 5 \times 10 \times 10 = 4{,}000$$

This one has 3 zeros. Why?

One final extension of multiplication by 10 is needed. Since $100 = 10 \times 10$ and $1{,}000 = 10 \times 10 \times 10$, and $600 = 6 \times 10 \times 10$ and $4{,}000 = 4 \times 10 \times 10 \times 10$, it follows then, that

$7 \times 600 = 7 \times 6 \times 10 \times 10 = 4{,}200$
(A basic fact and two multiplications by 10)

This one has 4 zeros. Why?

$70 \times 600 = 7 \times 6 \times 10 \times 10 \times 10 = 42{,}000$
(A basic fact and three multiplications by 10)

$4000 \times 30 = 4 \times 3 \times 10 \times 10 \times 10 \times 10 = 120{,}000$
(A basic fact and four multiplications by 10)

$60 \times 500 = 6 \times 5 \times 10 \times 10 \times 10 = 30{,}000$
(A basic fact and three multiplications by 10)

After each step in the development of the concept of multiplication by 10 and the extensions of that concept, the students need to have a variety of experiences where they practice and apply their current level of understanding. The following activities illustrate ways to practice this concept.

Activity 5.17   Easy Tens

Prepare a set of 50 cards like those described for Activity 5.12. Also prepare a spinner with three options: 1, 10, and 100.

Have three or four students take turns playing the game. All players start with 0 points. On each turn, the player turns up the next card and spins the spinner. The product of the two numbers is then added to that player's score.

Each player is responsible for checking the other players' arithmetic. After each player has had 10 turns, the game is over, and the player with the most points wins.

Activity 5.18 Tossing for Points

Draw a series of shapes on the bottom of the inside of a box and write a number like 5, 30, 4, 200, 70, or 8 in each shape. Also prepare a cube with 4, 5, 6, 7, 8, and 9 written on the six faces. Place the box against one wall, and use masking tape to place a line on the floor about 6 feet from the wall.

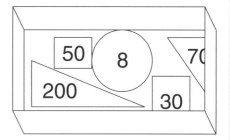

Have a small group of students play. Players take turns standing behind the line and tossing the cube into the box. If the cube lands on one of the shapes, the player's score for that toss is the product of the number in the shape and the number on the cube. If the cube is not touching a shape, the player's score for that toss is the number on the cube. If the cube is touching two shapes, the player's score is the product of the number on the cube times the greater of the numbers in the two shapes. After each player has had five tosses, the one with the greatest total score wins.

Activity 5.19 That One!!!

Prepare a set of about 30 cards with multiplication examples such as 6 × 80, 200 × 4, 30 × 60, 800 × 70, 300 × 200, 90 × 80, and 600 × 6.

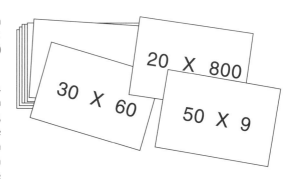

Have two students play the game. Shuffle the deck and place it facedown between the players. On each play, both players take 1 card. At the same time, they place the 2 cards faceup on the table. The players decide which card has the greatest product. The first player to touch that card and say "That one!" takes both cards. After all the cards have been played, the player who has taken the most cards is the winner of the game.

The students should settle any disputes by discussing the basic fact and how many multiplications by 10 there are.

The Second Big Idea

Partial Products   The second of the two big ideas that are the basis of the multiplication algorithm also develops from the modeling process. This big idea was used earlier when we worked on the hard basic multiplication facts. It is the notion of *partial products*. Recall that when the students were faced with a hard multiplication fact that they did not know the answer to, they could use partial products to break it into easier facts. For example, 8 × 7 can be broken into 4 × 7 + 4 × 7:

$$8 \times 7 \qquad\qquad 4 \times 7 + 4 \times 7$$

Similarly, if the students want to multiply a one-digit number by a two-digit number, they can break this hard-to-find product into two easy parts, called *partial products*. To multiply 12×7, the students do this:

$$12 \times 7 \qquad\qquad 10 \times 7 + 2 \times 7$$

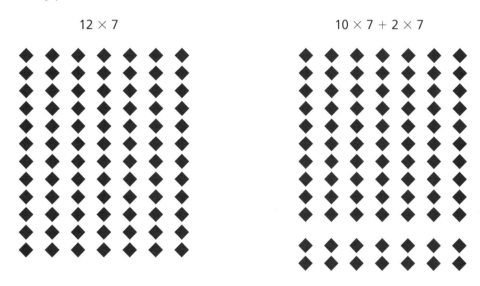

And, since $10 \times 7 = 70$, and $2 \times 7 = 14$, $12 \times 7 = 70 + 14 = 84$. In the same way, $36 \times 4 = 30 \times 4 + 6 \times 4$:

$$30 \times 4 \qquad\qquad\qquad\qquad\qquad\qquad 6 \times 4$$

Note that 30×4 is a basic fact and a multiplication by 10, and 6×4 is a basic fact. So, we have broken 36×4 into two easy partial products:

$$36 \times 4 = 30 \times 4 + 6 \times 4 = 120 + 24 = 144$$

When the notion of *area of rectangles* has been developed, the array model for multiplication evolves into the area model. If the sides of a rectangle are 8 and 3, the area of that rectangle is 8 × 3 = 24:

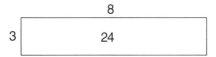

In the same way, 36 × 4 can be represented by a rectangle with sides of 36 and 4. The area of this rectangle is equal to 36 × 4:

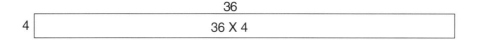

If we cut the rectangle into two parts, we see a representation of the two partial products:

In this example, we also end up with nothing but basic facts and multiplication by 10. If we follow the same procedure with 53 × 8, we have 53 × 8 = 50 × 8 + 3 × 8. Once again, there is nothing but basic facts and multiplication by 10:

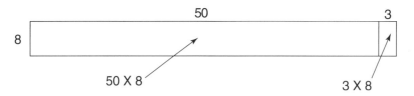

Partial products can also be used to break an example like 29 × 70 into easy partial products:

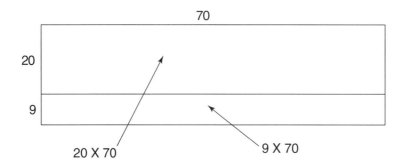

Notice that 20 × 70 is a basic fact and two multiplications by 10, while 9 × 70 is a basic fact and one multiplication by 10.

When the students are multiplying two multidigit numbers, partial products still allow them to find the answer by using only basic multiplication facts and multiplication by 10. For example, consider 35 × 46 and 179 × 38:

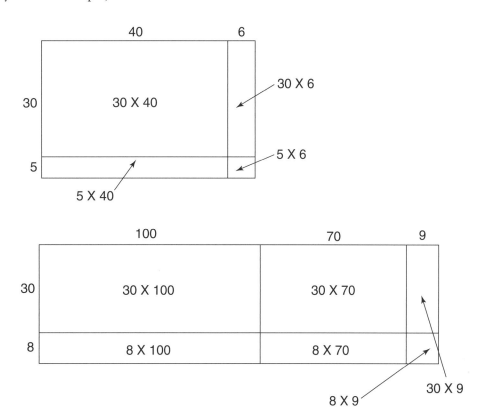

In every whole number multiplication example, regardless of how large or small the numbers, *partial products allow students to find the answer by using only basic facts and multiplication by 10*. Once the partial products have been found, they are added to get the total product. We find then that the algorithm for multidigit multiplication consists of a series of easy steps.

When multiplying a three-digit number by another three-digit number, we have 9 partial products. When multiplying two four-digit numbers, we have 16 partial products. Keeping track of such a large number of partial products is a problem. So, to condense the recording of the algorithm, we must regroup as in addition. First, consider 54 × 7:

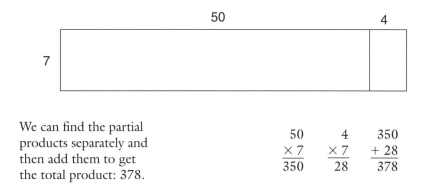

We can find the partial products separately and then add them to get the total product: 378.

$$\begin{array}{r} 50 \\ \times 7 \\ \hline 350 \end{array} \qquad \begin{array}{r} 4 \\ \times 7 \\ \hline 28 \end{array} \qquad \begin{array}{r} 350 \\ + 28 \\ \hline 378 \end{array}$$

Or, we can do the two multiplications and use regrouping to find the answer. First, multiply 7 times 4. That's 28—or 2 tens and 8 ones. Record the 8 ones in the ones place and keep track of the 2 tens.

$$\begin{array}{r} {}^{2} \\ 54 \\ \times\ 7 \\ \hline 8 \end{array}$$

Next, we multiply 7 times 50. That's 7 times 5 tens, or 35 tens. But we already had 2 tens, so, altogether, we have 37 tens. That's the same as 3 hundreds and 7 tens.

$$\begin{array}{r} {}^{2} \\ 54 \\ \times\ 7 \\ \hline 378 \end{array}$$

We use regrouping in a similar fashion to multiply 3×486:

First, multiply 3 times 6. That's 18, or 1 ten and 8 ones. Record the 8 ones in the ones place and keep track of the ten.

$$\begin{array}{r} {}^{1} \\ 486 \\ \times\ 3 \\ \hline 8 \end{array}$$

Next, multiply 3 times the 8 tens. That's 24 tens. With the ten that we already had, we have 25 tens or 2 hundreds and 5 tens. Record the 5 tens in the tens place and keep track of the 2 hundreds.

$$\begin{array}{r} {}^{21} \\ 486 \\ \times\ 3 \\ \hline 58 \end{array}$$

Finally, multiply 3 times the 4 hundreds. That's 12 hundreds. But we already had 2 hundreds, so that's 14 hundreds, or 1 thousand and 4 hundreds. Record this.

$$\begin{array}{r} {}^{21} \\ 486 \\ \times\ 3 \\ \hline 1{,}458 \end{array}$$

If the student can use regrouping to find $54 \times 7 = 378$, then 54×70 is the same, except there is also a multiplication by 10. If the student can use regrouping find to $483 \times 6 = 2898$, then 483×600 is the same, except there are also two multiplications by 10. To multiply 342×90, the student would think and do this:

I know I will multiply by 9 and also by 10. Since I can multiply in either order, I'll multiply by 10 first. I know to "add a zero" to the answer, so I'll go ahead and write the zero.

$$\begin{array}{r} 342 \\ \times\ 90 \\ \hline 0 \end{array}$$

Now, I'll multiply 9 times 2. That's 1 ten and 8 ones. I'll record the 8 ones and keep track of the ten.

$$\begin{array}{r} {}^{1} \\ 342 \\ \times\ 90 \\ \hline 80 \end{array}$$

Now, I'll multiply 9 times 4 tens. That's 36 tens. But I already had 1 ten, so that makes 37 tens. That's the same as 3 hundreds and 7 tens.

$$\begin{array}{r} {}^{31} \\ 342 \\ \times\ 90 \\ \hline 780 \end{array}$$

Now, I'll multiply 9 times 3 hundreds. That's 27 hundreds. But I already had 3, so that makes 30 hundreds. That's the same as 3 thousands and no hundreds.

$$\begin{array}{r} {}^{31} \\ 342 \\ \times\ 90 \\ \hline 30{,}780 \end{array}$$

Similarly, the student can multiply 264×400:

There are two multiplications by 10. I'll do that first. I'll need to add two zeros.

$$\begin{array}{r} 264 \\ \times\ 400 \\ \hline 00 \end{array}$$

Then, I'll multiply 264 by 4.

$$
\begin{array}{r}
{\scriptstyle 21} \\
264 \\
\times\ \ 400 \\
\hline
105,600
\end{array}
$$

We can now do any whole-number multiplication example by using an efficient, written algorithm. For example, consider 316×274:

First, multiply by 4.

$$
\begin{array}{r}
316 \\
\times\ 274 \\
\hline
1,264
\end{array}
$$

Next, multiply by 70.

$$
\begin{array}{r}
316 \\
\times\ 274 \\
\hline
1264 \\
22120
\end{array}
$$

Then, multiply by 200.

$$
\begin{array}{r}
316 \\
\times\ 274 \\
\hline
1264 \\
22120 \\
63200
\end{array}
$$

Finally, add the partial products.

$$
\begin{array}{r}
316 \\
\times\ 274 \\
\hline
1264 \\
22120 \\
\underline{63200} \\
86,584
\end{array}
$$

The following activities illustrate how a teacher might introduce and have the students use partial products.

Activity 5.20   *Pieces of the Problem*

Show a graph-paper representation of a multiplication on a transparency. For example, you might use 8 × 23. Lay a piece of yarn across the transparency to separate the multiplication into two parts:

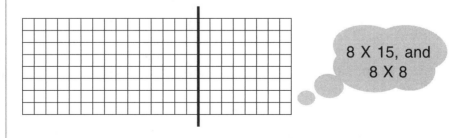

8 X 15, and
8 X 8

Repeat by placing the yarn in different places.

Activity 5.21 Use the Easy Tens

This is a continuation of Activity 5.20. Show a graph-paper representation of another multiplication example on a transparency. For example, you might use 7 X 27. Lay a piece of yarn across the transparency to separate the multiplication into two parts. Have the children name the two parts:

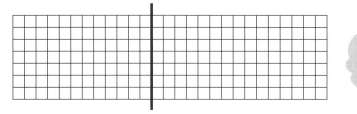

7 X 12, and
7 X 15

Then, move the yarn so that all the tens are in one piece. Have the children name the two parts:

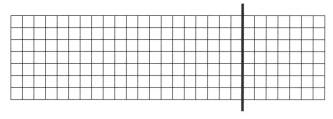

7 X 20, and
7 X 7

Ask, "Which would be easier to do: 7 X 12 and 7 X 15, or 7 X 20 and 7 X 7?"

Repeat the process with other multiplication examples.

Activity 5.22 Putting the Pieces Together

Prepare sets of three cards. In each set, one card will show a multiplication example where a two-digit number is being multiplied by a one-digit number. The other two cards in the set will show the two partial products:

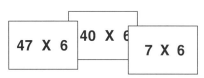
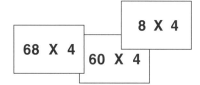

Pass out the cards and have the students find their two partners. When the three partners are together, they then find answers to the two partial products and add them to get the total product.

Use of the Multiplication Algorithm. So, we find that the two big ideas on which the multiplication algorithm is based are *multiplication by* 10 and *partial products*. Multiplication by 10 is easy, and using partial products reduces the algorithm into a series of steps that involve nothing but basic multiplication facts, multiplications by 10, and addition with regrouping.

Complex paper-and-pencil computations is an area that should have decreased emphasis. The availability and use of calculators support the students' ability to compute answers to complex problems. However, using calculators does not replace the need to learn basic facts or how to do mental computation.

The authors of this text believe that when teaching the two big ideas—*multiplication by 10* and *partial products*—as the basis of the multiplication algorithm, our goal is not to develop a high level of skill with the algorithm. Rather, the goal is to develop a high level of understanding of the algorithm and of how it simplifies multiplication with large numbers. In practice, for example, we would want the student to know how to use the algorithm to find 2794 × 2836, but we would not make a homework assignment that includes more than one exercise like this. Rather, we would have the student think about the partial products to mentally estimate such products and then have her or him use a calculator to check the accuracy of the estimates.

The following activities describe two estimation games where the students think about the partial products. To encourage this kind of thinking, the teacher should have the student who wins explain to the other players how to make good estimates in a hurry.

Activity 5.23 Shuffle

Prepare a set of 30 cards showing multiplication examples. The examples should include some with one-digit multipliers and some with two-digit, three-digit, and four-digit multipliers:

```
  4 0 9 1        829         490       5 1 6        1609
X       2      X   62      X   906     X     8     X    2138
```

Form a group of two to four students. Shuffle the deck. Players take turns being the dealer. On each play, the dealer gives each player 5 cards, facedown. When the dealer says "go," the players race to arrange their cards in order from least answer to greatest answer. The first player to finish says "Done," and play stops. If everyone agrees that the answers are in order, that player gets a point.

If there is a disagreement about the order of the answers, the students should each explain their reasons. If they cannot agree, then they should use a calculator to resolve the disagreement.

The game continues until a player has 5 points. That player wins.

Activity 5.24 Guesstimation

Prepare a set of cards like those described in Activity 5.23. Form a group of two to four students. Shuffle the deck and place it facedown on the table.

One card is turned over and all the players write their best estimate of the answer. They are not to do any written computation. The estimate must be done mentally. When everyone is finished, they use a calculator to find the exact answer. The player with the best estimate gets 1 point.

If there is a disagreement about which estimate is closest to the answer, the students should each explain their reasons. If they cannot agree, then they should use the calculator to resolve the disagreement by finding the difference between the estimates and the answer.

The game continues until a player has 10 points. That player wins.

Use of the Developmental Sequence for Remediation of Multiplication

Establish the meaning of the operation	1. Associate multiplication with combining groups of the same size. 2. Learn to use addition to find answers.
Develop the easy basic facts	1. Find the answers by using the meaning of multiplication. 2. Discover relationships among the facts. 3. Memorize the facts.
Develop thinking strategies for hard multiplication facts	1. Use mental strategies. 2. Use memorized facts to find answers for the hard facts.
Develop the hard basic facts	1. Find the answers by using the thinking strategies. 2. Review helpful relationships among the facts. 3. Memorize the facts.
Develop the algorithm	1. Multiply by 10. 2. Use partial products.

Remediation of Multiplication

As was true with the addition and subtraction developmental sequences, the developmental sequence for multiplication can serve as a framework for diagnosis and remediation of student difficulties in multiplication. Once you determine where in the development sequence the student difficulty is occurring, you know where in the sequence to begin remediation.

Has the meaning of multiplication been established?	If the student cannot use physical or pictorial materials to explain what 3×12 means, start remediation at this point If the student is able to do this, go on to the easy basic multiplication facts.
Has the student mastered the easy basic multiplication facts?	If the student cannot give answers to the easy basic multiplication facts without counting, focus the remediation on the relationships that exist among the easy basic multiplication facts. As students practice on the easy facts, they should be continually reminded of the relationships. If the student can demonstrate mastery of the easy basic multiplication facts, go on to the hard basic multiplication facts.
Has the student mastered the hard basic multiplication facts?	If the student cannot give answers to the hard basic multiplication facts without counting, teach the student how to use the partial-products thinking strategy. When the student does not know the answer to a hard basic fact, insist that she or he use that thinking strategy. If the student can demonstrate mastery of the hard basic multiplication facts, go on to the multiplication algorithm.
Is the student able to use the multiplication algorithm to find answers to multidigit multiplication examples?	If the student cannot complete examples using the multiplication algorithm, analyze the errors to see which of the big ideas needs to be retaught. Emphasize how partial products allow the student to get multiplication answers using only basic facts and multiplications by ten.

Adapting a Multiplication Lesson   Now we adapt a fifth-grade lesson on multiplication. As we have done before, we begin with a traditional plan, taken directly from suggestions like those that might appear in a teacher's guide of a published textbook program. You should note that this plan is a good one. However, its focus is to teach the textbook page. Notice also that the developmental part of the lesson consists of a detailed explanation of a single example, and that the lesson consists mainly of practice. (It was pointed out earlier that the most important thing a teacher can do to make a lesson appropriate for all students is to thoroughly develop the concepts and skills.)

LESSON OBJECTIVE

The learner will multiply a two-digit number and a one-digit number.

Lesson Opener

Have students find each of the following products:

$$10 \times 5 \qquad 31 \times 3 \qquad 7 \times 34$$

$$2 \times 18 \qquad 42 \times 3 \qquad 26 \times 2$$

Ask students if they have estimated how many people are in a room by using multiplication. For example, they may have estimated by multiplying a row of 10 by 5 (the number of rows). Explain that this will help them to understand the multiplication of a two-digit number and a one-digit number.

Development

Direct the attention of the class to the example on the first page of the lesson: 4×34. Point out that 34 is between 30 and 40, so 4×34 will be between 4×30 and 4×40. Ask what 4×30 equals. [120] What does 4×40 equal? [160] So, the answer to 4×34 must be between 120 and 160.

Point out the picture of the base-10 blocks used to illustrate the example. Multiply the ones. Record it as 1 ten and 6 ones. Point out the second picture that shows the renaming. Multiply the tens. Add the extra ten. Write the tens.

Ask if this answer is reasonable. Is it between 120 and 160?

Monitoring Learning

Have the students do the *Check Understanding* examples. Watch for students who add the extra ten to the tens digit before multiplying.

Practice

Have students complete the practice exercises on the second page of the lesson. Students who had difficulty with the *Check Understanding* examples may be assigned the reteaching worksheet instead of the practice exercises.

This lesson will be adapted to make it more effective in meeting the needs in a diverse classroom. The adapted lesson plan that follows includes an increased amount of developmental instruction. Notice the shift in instructional emphasis from teaching the pages of the student book toward an emphasis on teaching the concept. We have also increased visual input, kinesthetic activity, student communication, and monitoring of learning.

LESSON OBJECTIVE

The learner will multiply a two-digit number and a one-digit number.

Lesson Opener

Prepare pairs of cards. One card of each pair will show a multiplication example like 30 × 7; the other card of the pair will show the answer to the multiplication:

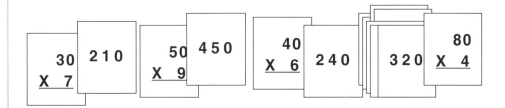

Shuffle the cards and give a card to each student. If there is an odd number of students, the teacher should keep a card and participate. Have the students find their partners. After everyone has found a partner, call on several students to tell how they were able to figure out the correct answers. **Monitor understanding.** Observe the students carefully throughout this activity. Direct leading questions to students who are unable to find their partners. (For example, ask, "How many tens are you starting with? How many times do you have those tens?")

Write 4 × 90 on the board. Point out that this is an easy multiplication to do. Then, write 4 × 93 on the board and tell the class that today they will learn that multiplying these numbers is also easy.

Development

Show 6 × 8 as an array of squares. Draw a line through the array to show that 6 × 8 can be broken into two easy parts:

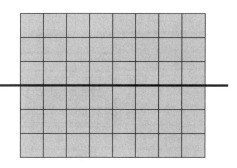

6 × 8 is the same as 3 × 8 + 3 × 8

Monitor understanding. Observe the students carefully throughout this activity. If a student seems not to understand, explain the two partial products by showing them in the pictorial model.

Next, use the same model to show that 6 × 14 is the same as 6 × 10 plus 6 × 4:

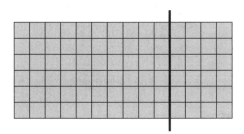

Next, show that 4 × 28 is the same as 4 × 20 + 4 × 8:

Monitor understanding. Continue to observe the students to see if they understand. Provide extra explanations as needed.

Next, use base-10 blocks to model similar examples. Show 4 × 36. Show the students that the 6 ones are there four times, and that the 3 tens are there four times:

3 tens, four times

6 ones, four times

Help the students to see that these two parts show the two multiplications that must be completed to get the answer to the original problem: 4 × 30 and 4 × 6. Have the students find these two partial products and add them to get the final product. **Monitor understanding.** Watch the students to be sure that they understand.

Also use the base-10 blocks to show the multiplication of 6 × 43:

6 × 40

6 × 3

Once again, have the students find the two partial products and add them to get the final product.

Point out to the students that although it is necessary to do both multiplications, it is not really necessary to write the two partial products separately. Redo the two previous examples using base-10 blocks to illustrate how to use regrouping. Be sure to record each step so that the students can see the relationship between the written steps and the steps using the model. Show 4 × 36 and write it on the board in vertical form.

3 tens, four times

6 ones, four times

Point out that we have some tens and we have some ones. We think first about how many ones there are. We have 6 ones, four times. That's 24 ones. But, as we learned in relationship to addition, that is too many to write, so we must make a trade. We trade 20 of the ones for 2 extra tens. **Monitor understanding.** If students do not understand, a short review of regrouping in addition may be needed.

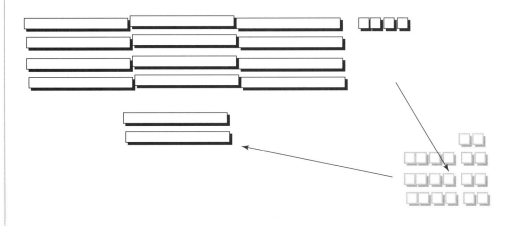

There are 4 ones left after the trade. We record the 4 ones in the ones place and keep track of the 2 extra tens.

$$\begin{array}{r} 2 \\ 36 \\ \times\ 4 \\ \hline 4 \end{array}$$

Next, we think about how many tens we have. There are 3 tens, four times. That's 12 tens. But we must also count the 2 extra tens that we traded for, so altogether we have 14 tens. But that's too many to write, so we trade 10 tens for a hundred:

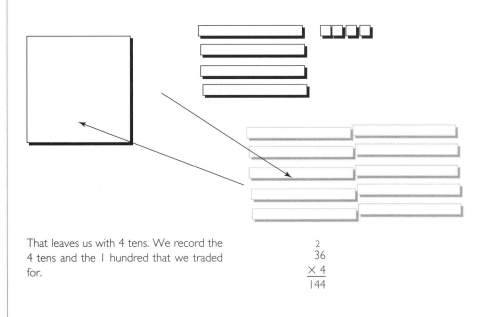

That leaves us with 4 tens. We record the 4 tens and the 1 hundred that we traded for.

$$\begin{array}{r} 2 \\ 36 \\ \times\ 4 \\ \hline 144 \end{array}$$

Use the base-10 blocks to show the multiplication of 6 × 43:

6 × 40 6 × 3

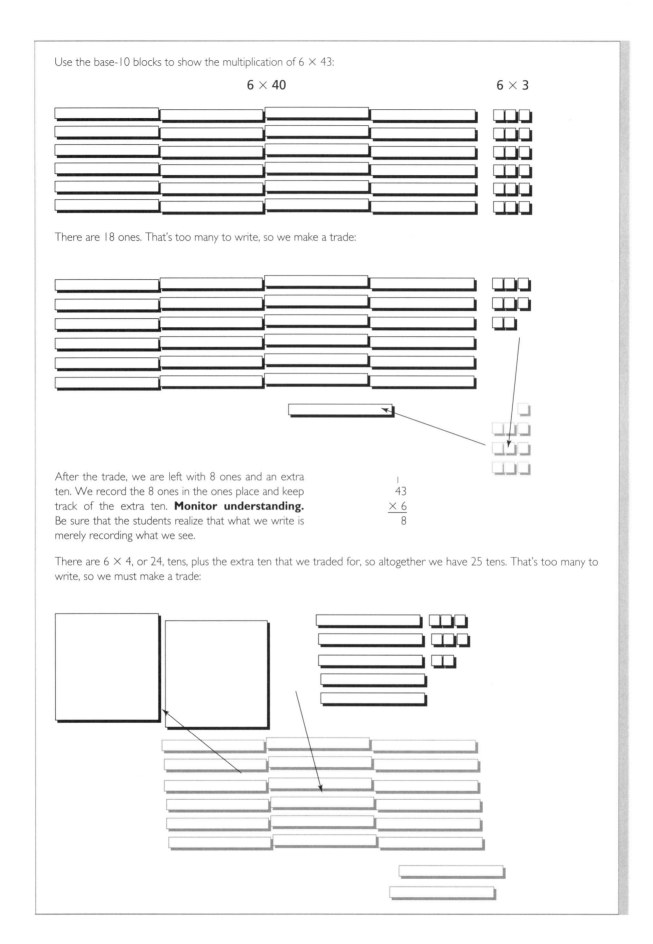

There are 18 ones. That's too many to write, so we make a trade:

After the trade, we are left with 8 ones and an extra ten. We record the 8 ones in the ones place and keep track of the extra ten. **Monitor understanding.** Be sure that the students realize that what we write is merely recording what we see.

$$\begin{array}{r} 1 \\ 43 \\ \times\ 6 \\ \hline 8 \end{array}$$

There are 6 × 4, or 24, tens, plus the extra ten that we traded for, so altogether we have 25 tens. That's too many to write, so we must make a trade:

After the trade, we have 2 hundreds and 5 tens, in addition to the 8 ones that we already recorded. We record the tens and hundreds.

$$\begin{array}{r} 1 \\ 43 \\ \times\ 6 \\ \hline 258 \end{array}$$

Practice

Have students work with partners to complete practice examples 10, 13, and 17.

Closure

Ask the students what they learned today. Hand out papers with one multiplication example. Have the students take this example home and show a parent how to do it.

Teaching Division of Whole Numbers

The same developmental sequence used for addition, subtraction, and multiplication is used to teach whole-number division. As with the other operations, the first major instructional task is to establish the meaning of division.

The Meaning of Division

There are several different ways that division can be approached. However, when division is introduced at the elementary school level, it is nearly always considered to be the separation of a quantity into equal-sized parts. Therefore, we want students to *associate division with separating a quantity into equal-sized parts*. The association should be so strong that when students see the symbols 12 ÷ 4, they visualize a group of 12 things being separated into equal groups. When the child sees a situation where a quantity is being separated into equal parts, he or she will think, "That's division!" After division has been mastered, the student will see problem settings where quantities are being separated into equal parts and will think, "I can use division to solve this problem."

There are two distinct kinds of division when a quantity is being separated into equal parts: *measurement division* and *partition division*. The easiest way to understand the difference between them is to consider an example of each.

Measurement Division. Suppose in a game where players use chips, there are 20 chips and all 20 must be used. If we know that each player must use 4 chips, how many players must there be in the game? To answer this question, we set aside 4 chips (that's enough for one player), then set aside 4 more chips (that's enough for another player), and continue this process until all the chips have been set aside. We then count the groups of 4 chips to see how many players there would be. Since there are five groups of 4 chips, there would be five players:

In this example, we know how many chips we are starting with and we know the size of the groups. We want to find out how many groups there are. The division we described is 20 ÷ 4 = 5:

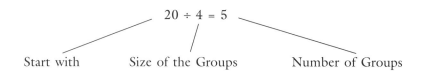

Start with   Size of the Groups   Number of Groups

This is called *measurement division. In measurement division, we know the beginning number, we know the size of the groups, and we want to find the number of groups.*

Partition Division.   Now, let's consider the other type of division. Suppose this time there is another game where the players use chips. In this game, there are also 20 chips and every chip must be used. However, there are four players and every player must have the same number of chips. This time, we know that there are four groups of chips (one group of chips for each player), but we don't know how many chips are in each group. To find out how many chips each player gets, we designate four players and give each of them a chip. Then we give each of them another chip, and we continue this process until all the chips have been passed out. Finally, we count to see how many chips each of the four players has after all the chips have been passed out:

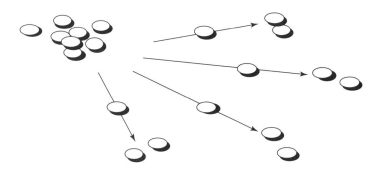

In this example, we know how many chips we are starting with and we know the number of groups. We want to find out how many chips are in each group. The division that we described is 20 ÷ 4 = 5:

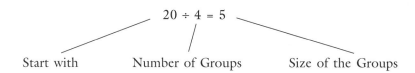

Start with   Number of Groups   Size of the Groups

This kind of division is called *partition division. In partition division, we know how many we are starting with, we know the number of groups, and we want to find out how many are in each group* (Moyer, 2000; Tucker, 1973).

Teaching Both Measurement Division and Partition Division.   The two kinds of division seem to be the same, but actually they are different in three ways. First, we know different information: In measurement division, we know the size of the groups, whereas in partition division, we know the number of groups. Second, we want to find different things: In measurement division, we want to find the number of groups; in partition division, the size of the groups. Third, we use different procedures to get the answer: In measurement division, we repeatedly remove (subtract) the same amount, but in partition division, we distribute (pass out) the objects equally.

Because the students encounter both kinds of division situations, it is important that they be exposed to both as they are learning the meaning of the operation. The following activities illustrate how a teacher might lead students to understand the meaning of division. The activities provided here illustrate only partition division. Development of similar activities for measurement division is left as an exercise for the reader.

Activity 5.25   Equal Sharing

Place a transparency on the overhead projector. Put 24 raisins in one corner. Use a marker to draw four 3-inch circles on the transparency.

Explain that you have four students to whom you want to give the raisins and that you want them all to have the same number. Tell the students' that you want to put each child's raisins in one of the four circles.

Ask the students how to do it. Follow their directions exactly until there are the same number of raisins in each circle. If the students' directions do not lead to equal groups, let them figure out what to do. When the groups are all the same size, write the word **divide** on the board. Explain that when you separate a number of things into equal-sized groups, it is called **division**.

Repeat the activity, but this time, start with 36 raisins.

Activity 5.26   Equal Sharing–Write It

Follow the procedures of Activity 5.25, but for the first two examples, write the division sentence.

Write $24 \div 4 = 6$, and explain that 24 is the number that you start with (24 raisins), 4 is the number of equal groups (there are four students), and 6 is the number in each group (each student gets 6 raisins). Also explain the division sign and demonstrate how to read the division sentence.

On the third example, have a student read the division sentence. For the rest of the examples, ask a student to tell you what the division sentence is, and have another student write the division sentence.

Activity 5.27   Acting Out Division

Write $12 \div 3 = 4$ on the board. Ask the students to help you recall what the division sentence means. Point to the 12. Ask what that number tells us. [It's the number of objects that we start with.] Point to the division sign. Ask what it tells us. [It tells us to separate the 12 into equal groups.] Point to the 3. Ask what it tells us. [We have three equal groups.] Point to the = 4, and ask what it tells us. [It tells us the number in each group.] Identify 12 objects and do what the number sentence says.

Next, write $27 \div 3 =$. Explain that this time we don't have the entire division sentence. Ask what we know. [We know that we are to start with 27 objects and separate them into three equal groups.] Identify 27 objects and carry out the division to find how many are in each group. When finished, write the answer part of the division sentence.

Repeat this procedure with other examples: $15 \div 5$, $24 \div 6$, $35 \div 7$.

> ### Activity 5.28 Fact Finders–Division
>
> Prepare lists of four division facts without the answers. The lists should be different, but be sure that each fact that you include appears on two lists. Form groups of two or three students. Give each group a list and a set of objects. It is best if you are able to provide each group with objects that are different from the ones used by other groups. For example, one group may be given small stones, another group blocks, and another group pencils.
>
> Have each group use their objects to figure out the answers to all their facts. When everyone is finished, talk about the answers. When each answer is given, ask if anyone else had that same problem. Did they get the same answer?

Developing the Easy Basic Division Facts

To reinforce the meaning of division, the teacher should expose the students to a wide variety of division examples by using familiar objects. The students should use appropriate terminology to describe the division verbally and use the division sign and equal sign to write the division sentence. In each example, they should figure out the answer for themselves, and the teacher should continually say how easy it is. The teacher should emphasize that they can find the answers by themselves.

Relationships among the Easy Basic Division Facts.   After the meaning of division has been established and children can confidently find answers on their own, we focus on the easy basic division facts. For purposes of our discussion here, we consider division facts with divisors of 1 to 5 to be the easy ones. There are 50 of these easy basic division facts.

As these facts are discovered, organized, and reorganized, the students are led to discover as many relationships among them as possible. Many of these relationships, in effect, reduce the amount of memorization that is necessary. All of them contribute to improved retention of the facts that are memorized. It is always easier to remember things that are related to other things that are already known. Among the relationships that the teacher should be sure to emphasize are the following five:

1. When 0 is divided by any number, the answer will always be 0. (There are 5 of these facts among the 50 facts that we are considering easy basic division facts. That's *5 facts* but *only one thing to remember.*)
2. When any number is divided by 1, the answer will be the starting number. (In addition to 0 ÷ 1, there are 9 of these facts among the 50 easy basic division facts. That's *9 facts* but *only one thing to learn.*)
3. When any number is divided by itself, the answer will always be 1. (In addition to 1 ÷ 1, there are 4 of these facts among the 50 easy basic division facts. That's *4 facts* but *only one thing to learn.*)
4. There are several pairs of facts that are related:

$6 \div 2 = 3$ and	$6 \div 3 = 2$	$8 \div 2 = 4$ and	$8 \div 4 = 2$
$10 \div 2 = 5$ and	$10 \div 5 = 2$	$12 \div 4 = 3$ and	$12 \div 3 = 4$
$15 \div 3 = 5$ and	$15 \div 5 = 3$	$20 \div 4 = 5$ and	$20 \div 5 = 4$

Each of these pairs has the same dividend, and the numbers that are the divisor and quotient in 1 fact of the pair are the quotient and divisor in the other fact of the pair. The 2 facts in a pair should be learned together. Then, each pair of facts becomes one thing to learn. (That's *12 facts* but *only six things to learn.*)

5. Every division fact is related to a multiplication fact. For example, consider these pairs of facts:

$12 \div 2 = 6$	and	$6 \times 2 = 12$	$18 \div 3 = 6$	and	$6 \times 3 = 18$
$21 \div 3 = 7$	and	$7 \times 3 = 21$	$24 \div 4 = 6$	and	$6 \times 4 = 24$
$30 \div 5 = 6$	and	$6 \times 5 = 30$	$36 \div 4 = 9$	and	$9 \times 4 = 36$

Once this relationship is discovered, students can use it to find answers to division facts without counting objects. However, they are able to do this only if they already know the related multiplication facts.

Memorization of the Easy Basic Division Facts. When the students have become familiar with the helpful relationships among the easy basic division facts, we can expect them to make fairly rapid progress toward memorizing these facts. The instructional activities that are selected to lead the students to memorizing the easy basic division facts should have certain characteristics. These are the same eight characteristics presented earlier in this chapter for multiplication facts:

1. Students should be aware that they are to memorize the facts.
2. The activities should use an interesting and fun format.
3. Activities should have a high level of involvement.
4. Activities should focus on a small number of unmemorized facts at any given time.
5. Some already memorized facts should be mixed in with the target unmemorized facts. This will improve retention.
6. Students should be allowed enough time to figure out facts that they do not know.
7. To figure out answers, students should think about what they already know that will help them find this answer. What other facts or relationships do they already know that will help?
8. Accuracy, not speed, should be emphasized.

The following examples of memorization activities have these eight characteristics.

Activity 5.29   One Is Important!

Write the following problems on the chalkboard:

$4 \div 1 =$ $8 \div 1 =$ $3 \div 1 =$

Have the children figure out the answers. Ask them what the pattern is. Once they are sure of the pattern, have them use it to find the answers to these examples:

$7 \div 1 =$ $5 \div 1 =$ $6 \div 1 =$

Erase the board and write these examples:

$3 \div 3 =$ $9 \div 9 =$ $7 \div 7 =$

Have the children figure out the answers. Ask them what the pattern is. Once they are sure of the pattern, have them use it to find the answers to these examples:

$2 \div 2 =$ $8 \div 8 =$ $5 \div 5 =$

Finally, use flash cards showing a mixture of the two types of division just illustrated. Show a flash card. Call on a child to answer. Ask the other students if the answer is correct. Ask how they know. What pattern are they using?

Activity 5.30   Related Pairs

Write the following pairs of problems on the board:

$15 \div 3 =$ $20 \div 5 =$ $6 \div 3 =$

$15 \div 5 =$ $20 \div 4 =$ $6 \div 2 =$

Have the students figure out the answers. Ask them what the pattern is. Once they are sure of the pattern, write these facts on the board:

$$8 \div 2 = 4 \qquad 10 \div 5 = 2 \qquad 12 \div 3 = 4$$

$$15 \div 5 = 3 \qquad 6 \div 2 = 3 \qquad 20 \div 4 = 5$$

Use flash cards showing the facts $6 \div 3 =$, $8 \div 4 =$, $10 \div 2 =$, $12 \div 4 =$, $15 \div 3 =$, and $20 \div 5 =$. Show a card. Call on a student. Ask which of the facts on the board can help us with this one.

Activity 5.31   Line Up

Prepare large cards showing easy basic division facts without the answers. Distribute one card to each student. Separate the class into two groups. Have one group move to one side of the room, and have the other group move to the opposite side of the room.

Tell the students to line up with the others in their group so that the answers to their problems are in order from least to greatest. Allow them to talk to help one another. If they have difficulty, have them think about the helpful relationships.

When they are lined up, have them hold their cards so that the other group can check to see if they are in the correct order. If the students think someone in the other group is not lined up correctly, they should tell that student what other fact(s) to think about to get the correct answer.

Activity 5.32   Problems and Answers

Prepare about 25 pairs of cards. In each pair, one card should show an easy basic division fact without the answer. The other card in the pair should show the answer to the fact.

Form a group of two or three students. Shuffle the cards and place the deck face down on the table. To start play, each player draws three cards. Players take turns playing. On each play, the player draws one card from the deck and then lays down any matching problem cards and answer cards that he or she has. Other players check each fact to be sure it is correct. It a fact is incorrect, the player must pick up the incorrectly matched cards.

Play continues until all the cards have been drawn from the deck. The player who has completed the most facts is the winner.

Developing the Hard Basic Division Facts

Thinking Strategies for the Hard Basic Division Facts.   Before beginning remediation work on the hard basic division facts, the students must have learned to use an efficient thinking strategy to figure out answers. The most effective fact strategies have two characteristics: They are mental strategies, and they require the student to use facts that are already memorized to figure out the ones that are not memorized. We consider two of those strategies.

Use Partial Quotients.   The *partial-quotients strategy* (Tucker, Singleton, & Weaver, 2002) for hard basic division facts is similar to the partial-products strategy that was used for hard basic multiplication facts. In this strategy, the student thinks about what easier division facts with the same divisor can help. For example, suppose the student needs to find 48 ÷ 6:

48 ÷ 6 = ?

> I can't divide 48 by 6, but I can divide 30 by 6. So, I'll separate 48 into 30 and 18 and divide each part by 6.

30 ÷ 6 = 5

18 ÷ 6 = 3

> Then I'll add the two partial quotients to get the total quotient, 8.

48 ÷ 6 = 8

If the student does not know the answer to 56 ÷ 8, he or she can break 56 into two easy parts and use partial quotients to find the answer:

56 ÷ 8 = ?

> I can't divide 56 by 8, but I can divide 40 by 8. So, I'll separate 56 into 40 and 16 and divide each part by 8.

40 ÷ 8 = 5

16 ÷ 8 = 2

> Then I'll add the two partial quotients to get the total quotient, 7.

56 ÷ 8 = 7

In the same way, we can find the answer to 28 ÷ 7. Separate 28 into 14 + 14. Divide each part by 7 and add the partial quotients to get the total quotient, 4. Using this strategy lays the groundwork for the algorithm. However, partial quotients are seldom used in textbooks for basic division facts.

Think of a Related Multiplication Fact. The strategy that is most commonly taught in elementary school mathematics textbooks comes from one of the relationships that exists among the basic facts. Most commonly, the thinking strategy taught for hard basic division facts is: *Think of a related multiplication fact.* For example, if a student needs to find the answer to 36 ÷ 9, he or she should think, "What number times 9 will equal 36?"

36 ÷ 9 = ?

> If I don't know the answer to 36 ÷ 9, I think about the related multiplication fact.

? X 9 = 36

> Since 4 X 9 = 36, I know that 36 ÷ 9 must equal 4.

Similarly, if a student does not know the answer to 72 ÷ 8, she or he can think about the related multiplication fact: "What number times 8 equals 72?" Since 9 × 8 = 72, we know that 72 ÷ 8 = 9. This strategy works well if the students are thoroughly familiar with the relationship between division facts and multiplication facts and if they have mastered the required multiplication facts before they try to use them to find answers to division facts.

A Remediation Note.   Students who have difficulty using related multiplication facts to find answers to the hard basic division facts often have that difficulty because they have not yet mastered the hard basic multiplication facts. *We cannot use facts that we do not know.*

Teaching the Hard Basic Division Facts.   When students have developed an efficient thinking strategy to quickly and accurately find answers to the hard basic division facts, it is relatively easy for them to achieve mastery of those facts. The teacher should *revisit the relationships* that were discovered during development of the easy division facts to ensure that the students realize that they also apply to the hard division facts. And, the students should *work toward memorization* of those facts.

Remediating the Division Algorithm

After the basic division facts have been mastered, it is possible to develop the division algorithm very quickly. Rapid success depends, however, on the application of the same principles that were presented for each of the other operations:

- **Let the students see what it looks like.** Carefully model the operation with an appropriate physical or pictorial model. We should use a model that lets them see what happens to the basic units—ones, tens, hundreds, and so on—when they divide.
- **Deemphasize rote rules.** You may end up with rules, but they should be meaningful. They should arise out of the modeling process.
- **Emphasize big ideas.** These are the important generalizations that describe the procedures. They also come from the modeling process.
- **Let the written algorithm simply be a recording of what happens when the algorithm is modeled.** Everything you write should match something you do.
- **Watch your language.** The language you use should describe what the children see when the operation is modeled, not language that describes what you write down.

Although the division algorithm can be developed by using measurement division, there are many points at which difficulties arise (Tucker, 1973). Consequently, since the early 1980s, textbook writers have used, almost without exception, partition division to develop the algorithm. We also use partition division in our development. We proceed by describing how a physical model can be used to clarify and give meaning to the algorithm. We see, too, how the entire algorithm is based on the application of two big ideas.

The First Big Idea
Divide One Unit at a Time   This big idea is developed in the next two examples. Consider, first, the example 48 ÷ 4. We want to divide 48 into four equal parts. To do this, we begin by using bundled sticks to represent 48:

Next, we write the division problem on the chalkboard:

$$4\overline{)48}$$

We want to separate 48 into four equal parts, so we designate four places to put those four equal parts. We begin by distributing the tens:

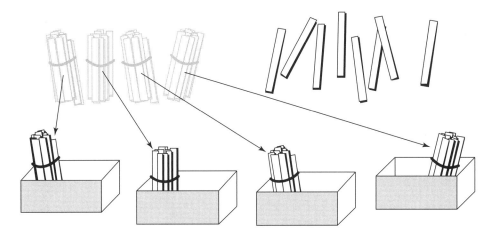

We record that 1 ten is placed in each of the equal parts:

$$\overset{1}{4\overline{)48}}$$

And, we record that 4 tens are taken away from the original number. After the subtraction, we see that we still have 8 ones to distribute:

$$\begin{array}{r} 1 \\ 4\overline{)48} \\ -4 \\ \hline 8 \end{array}$$

Next, we distribute the ones. We are able to place 2 ones in each of the equal parts:

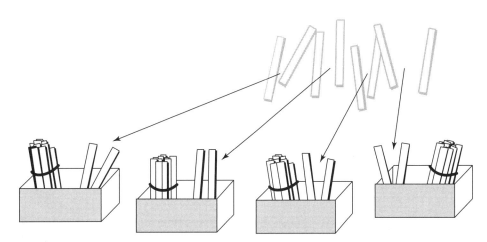

Finally, we record the 2 ones that we placed in each of the equal groups, record that we took 8 ones away from what was left of the beginning number, and record that nothing is left of the original number to be distributed. We were able to place 1 ten and 2 ones (12) in each of the four equal parts.

$$\begin{array}{r} 12 \\ 4\overline{)48} \\ -4 \\ \hline 8 \\ -8 \\ \hline 0 \end{array}$$

One key to successfully teaching the division algorithm or any of the algorithms is to help the students to understand that the written algorithm is nothing more than an orderly recording of what is being done with the model. To accomplish this, the teacher must model the process one step at a time, and each step should be recorded immediately after it is completed. We look at one more example: 639 ÷ 3. This time we use base-10 blocks to model the process. We begin by writing the problem and representing the beginning number with the model:

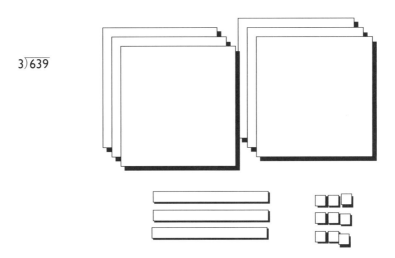

Then, we designate three locations where we place the three equal parts:

We distribute the hundreds first. We have 6 hundreds, so we can place 2 hundreds in each of the three equal parts:

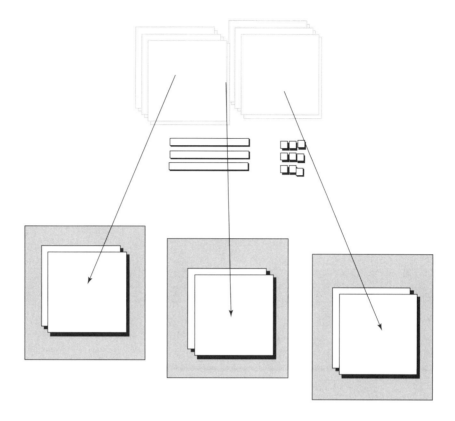

We took 6 hundreds away from our beginning number. We record that and see that after the subtraction, we still have 3 tens and 9 ones to distribute:

$$
\begin{array}{r}
2 \\
3{\overline{\smash{)}}}639 \\
-600 \\
\hline
39
\end{array}
$$

Next, we distribute the tens. We have 3 tens to distribute, so we are able to place 1 ten in each of the three equal parts:

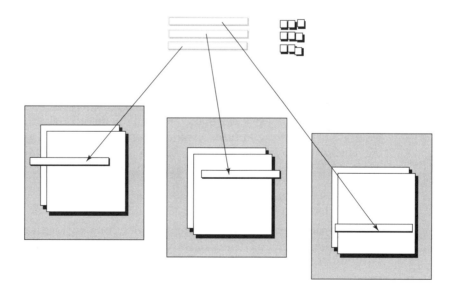

We took 3 tens away from what was left of the beginning number. We record that and find that there are still 9 ones to be distributed:

$$
\begin{array}{r}
21 \\
3\overline{)639} \\
-6 \\
\hline
39 \\
-3 \\
\hline
9
\end{array}
$$

Finally, we distribute the 9 ones. We are able to place 3 ones in each of the three equal parts:

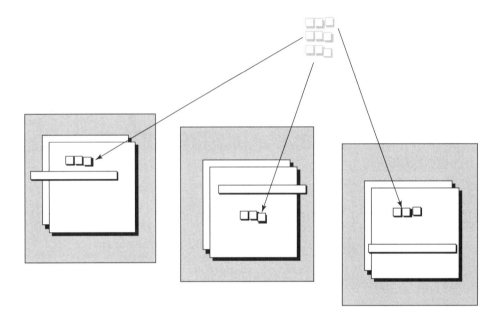

We record the 3 ones that we placed in each of the equal parts. In this step, we distributed 9 ones. These were taken away from what was left of the beginning number, so we record this subtraction. We have nothing left to distribute.

$$
\begin{array}{r}
213 \\
3\overline{)639} \\
-6 \\
\hline
39 \\
-3 \\
\hline
9 \\
-9 \\
\hline
0
\end{array}
$$

We were able to place 2 hundreds, 1 ten, and 3 ones in each of the three equal parts. The answer to the division problem is 213.

In the preceding two examples, we have the first of the two big ideas that are the basis of the division algorithm: *Divide one unit at a time.* What we are really doing is using *partial quotients* in the same way that they were suggested for simplifying hard basic division facts.

The Second Big Idea

Trade Remainders for Smaller Units The second big idea for the division algorithm also arises out of the modeling of division examples. This time, we begin with $92 \div 4$. First, we write the division problem and represent 92 (the number that we start with) using base-10 blocks:

We designate four locations where we place the four equal parts:

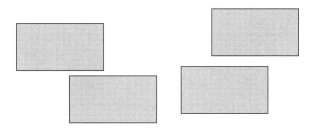

We begin the division process by distributing the tens. Since there are 9 tens, we have enough to place 2 tens in each of the four equal parts. Notice that there is 1 ten leftover:

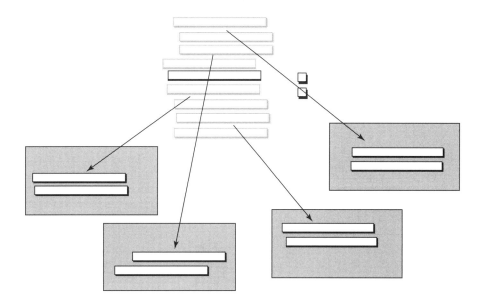

We place 2 tens in each of the four equal parts. We took 8 tens away from the starting number. We are left with 1 ten and 2 ones:

$$
\begin{array}{r}
2 \\
4\overline{)92} \\
-8 \\
\hline
12
\end{array}
$$

Now we are faced with a problem that we have not seen before. What do we do with the ten that we were unable to distribute? Whenever we have "leftovers," we trade them for smaller units. So, in this case, we trade the leftover ten for 10 ones:

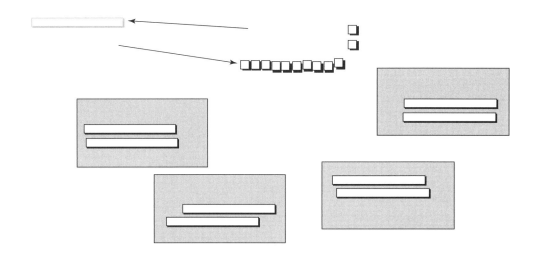

Before the trade, we had 1 ten and 2 ones. After the trade, we have 12 ones:

$$\begin{array}{r} 2 \\ 4{\overline{\smash{)}92}} \\ -8 \\ \underline{12} \end{array}$$

The bracket shows that a trade has been made.

These 12 ones need to be distributed to the four equal parts. We can place 3 ones in each of the four equal parts:

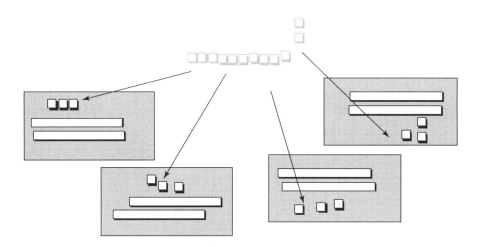

We record the 3 ones that were placed in each equal part. In this step, we took 12 ones from what was left of the beginning number. We record this subtraction and see that there is nothing left to be distributed.

$$\begin{array}{r} 23 \\ 4{\overline{\smash{)}92}} \\ -8 \\ \underline{12} \\ -12 \\ \underline{0} \end{array}$$

The answer to the division problem is 23.

The preceding example illustrated the second big idea on which the division algorithm is based: *Trade remainders for smaller units.* We next examine another example in which this big idea is used. To find the answer to 625 ÷ 5, we write the problem and represent the beginning number, 625, with base-10 blocks. We begin by distributing 1 hundred to each of five equal parts:

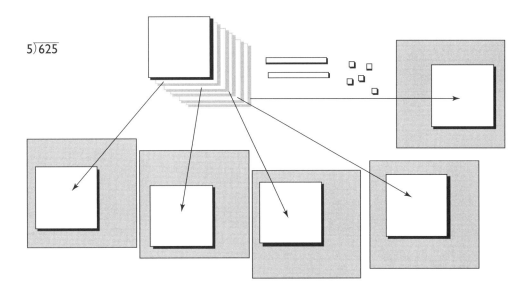

In this step, we took 5 hundreds away from our beginning number. After we record this subtraction, we have 1 hundred, 2 tens, and 5 ones that still need to be distributed:

$$\begin{array}{r} 1 \\ 5\overline{)625} \\ -5 \\ \hline 125 \end{array}$$

The remaining hundred can be traded for 10 tens. We now have 12 tens:

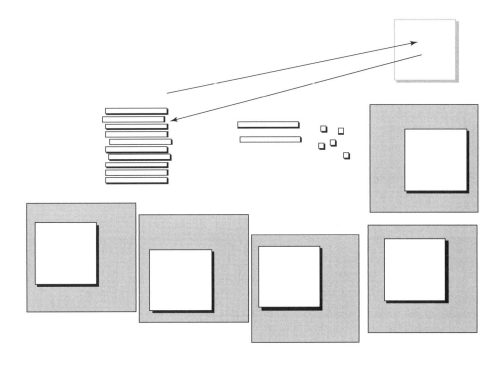

Now, we can place 2 tens in each of the five equal parts:

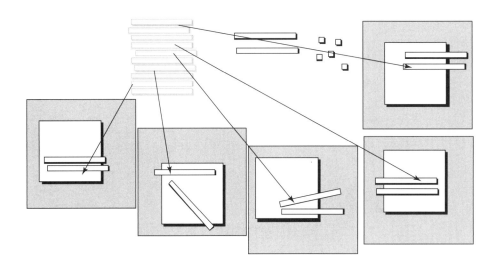

We record the 2 tens that we placed in each of the equal parts. To do this, we take 10 tens away from what is left of our starting number. We record this subtraction and we have 2 tens and 5 ones left to distribute.

$$
\begin{array}{r}
12 \\
5\overline{)625} \\
-5 \\
\hline
125 \\
-10 \\
\hline
\underline{25}
\end{array}
$$

We then trade the remaining 2 tens for 20 ones. Now we have ones to distribute:

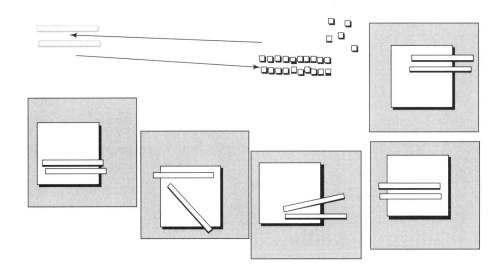

We place 5 ones in each of the five equal parts:

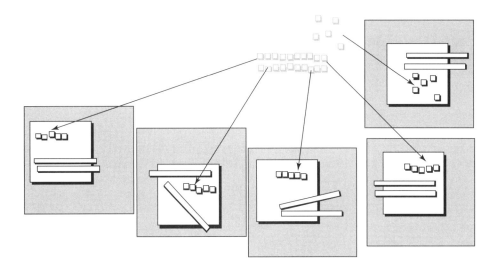

Finally, we complete the recording of the process. We record 5 in the ones place, and since we took 25 ones away from what was left of the beginning number, we record this subtraction. We see that there is nothing left to distribute: $625 \div 5 = 125$.

$$
\begin{array}{r}
125 \\
5{\overline{\smash{)}625}} \\
-5 \\
\hline
125 \\
-10 \\
\hline
25 \\
-25 \\
\hline
0
\end{array}
$$

Use of the Division Algorithm. Both big ideas for the division algorithm arise out of experiences as we model division examples: *Divide one unit at a time* and *trade remainders for smaller units.* Regardless of what the numbers are, that's all there is to the division algorithm.

Notice that all the examples we examined had one-digit divisors. If we want students to be able to use pencil-and-paper computation to divide by large divisors, a great deal of time must be spent teaching them to estimate partial quotients. However, we should seriously question the practice of using pencil-and-paper computation for these examples. With the availability of calculators, we do not need to teach today's students, to do complex, pencil-and-paper division computation. The time can be better spent on literally hundreds of other things—things that will be far more useful to the students.

In the spirit of the NCTM Standards, it is more important for students to understand how the algorithm works than for them to become proficient with long division involving multidigit divisors. It is more important that they can use the principles that are the basis of the algorithm to make quick and accurate estimates. It is also more important that they become able to intelligently decide whether it is appropriate to estimate the answer, use a calculator to get the exact answer, or use pencil-and-paper computation.

The following activities illustrate how a teacher might teach the first big idea: *Divide one unit at a time.* Notice that the early examples involve common objects.

Activity 5.33 Rocks and Blocks

Bring about 20 small rocks to class. Place 18 rocks into a box with 12 wooden blocks. Write "18 rocks and 12 blocks" on the board. Have six students come to the front of the room. Tell the class that you want to share the rocks and blocks equally among these six people, but that you want the class to tell how to do the sharing so it will be equal.

Call on other students to give directions. Do exactly as you are told, but keep asking, "Is that right?" "Now what do I need to do?" "Are we done yet?"

When the sharing is complete, repeat the process by sharing 20 rocks and 15 blocks among five students.

Activity 5.34 Buttons and Bows

Follow the procedures of Activity 5.33, except use buttons and bows instead of rocks and blocks.

Activity 5.35 Nuts, Bolts, and Screws

Follow the procedures of Activity 5.33, except use groups of three different kinds of objects: nuts, bolts, and screws.

Activity 5.36 Pennies and Dimes

Share nine dimes and six pennies among three people.

Record the results as a division example. Point out how you can share the tens (the dimes) first and then share the ones (the pennies).

The following activities illustrate how a teacher might remediate the second big idea: *Trade remainders for smaller units*. Once again, the early examples involve common objects.

Activity 5.37 Eggs and More Eggs

Bring seven egg cartons to class. Fill the egg cartons by placing a block in each space. Place the seven full cartons and six blocks on a table. Explain that the blocks represent eggs. Write "7 cartons and 6 eggs" on the board. Tell the students that you want to divide the eggs into three equal groups.

Start with the cartons. Ask how many eggs are in each carton. [12] Ask how many cartons should be placed in each of the three groups. [2] Do that. Then, ask what to do with the extra carton of eggs. [Take them out of the carton.] Ask how many eggs still need to be divided. [12 + 6 = 18] Ask how many eggs go into each of the three groups. [6 eggs]

Write the final result on the board. Each group has two cartons and 6 eggs.

Activity 5.38   Sharing Beads

Prepare about 12 strings of beads. Place 7 beads on each string.

Place the 12 strings of beads on the table with 1 extra bead. Point out to the students that each string has 7 beads on it. Explain that you want to divide the beads into five groups with the same number of beads in each group.

Divide the strings of beads first. Cut the 2 strings that were leftover and take the beads off the strings. Divide the resulting 15 beads.

Activity 5.39   More Pennies and Dimes

Share nine dimes and 6 pennies among four people.

Record the results as a division example. Point out how you can share the dimes first, trade the leftover dime for 10 pennies, and then share the 16 pennies.

The following activities illustrate how a teacher can encourage students to use the principles of the division algorithm to estimate division answers.

Activity 5.40   Best Guess

Write $12\overline{)384}$ on the board. Tell the class that you want everyone to guess what the answer is and to write it on a sheet of paper.

When everyone has written a guess, start to work through the example.

Ask how many hundreds are in each part. [There are 12 parts but only 3 hundreds. We cannot put any hundreds in each part.] Ask what to do with the 3 hundreds. [Trade them for 30 tens. We now have 38 tens.]

Ask how many tens can be placed in each part. [3 tens] Ask if anyone's guess had 3 tens.

Continue until the example is finished. Decide whose guess was closest to the answer. Repeat the process with other examples.

Activity 5.41   Guesstimation

Prepare cards with division examples on them. Some should have one-digit divisors and some should have two-digit divisors. Form a group of two or three students. Shuffle the cards and place the deck facedown on the table.

On each play, one card is turned over and the students estimate the answer and write down the estimate. Then they should use a calculator to find the answer. The student with the best estimate gets a point. If there is a tie, all who tied get a point. After each play, the one(s) with the best estimate must explain how the estimate was figured out.

When all the cards have been played, the player with the most points wins.

Use of the Developmental Sequence for Remediation of Division

Establish the meaning of the operation	1. Associate division with separating a quantity into equal-sized parts. 2. Learn to use subtraction to find answers.
Develop basic division facts	1. Find basic division facts using the meaning of division. 2. Discover relationships among the facts. 3. Learn to use a thinking strategy for finding hard division facts. 4. Memorize the facts.
Develop the division algorithm	1. Divide one unit at a time. 2. Trade remainders for smaller units.

Remediation of Division

The developmental sequence for division can be a tool for diagnosis and remediation of student difficulties with division. After determining where in the sequence the student's difficulty is occurring, you know where in the sequence to begin remediation.

If the student is having trouble with easy basic facts, the remediation emphasis should be on relationships among the easy basic facts.

If the student is having trouble with the hard basic facts, the remediation emphasis should be on using an effective thinking strategy.

If the student is having trouble with the division algorithm, the remediation emphasis should be on the two big ideas.

Adapting a Division Lesson

Now we adapt a fifth-grade lesson on division. As we have done before, we begin with a traditional plan that follows the kind of suggestions that would be found in a teacher's guide of a published textbook program. Note that this plan is a good one. As with previous textbook lessons that we examined, the focus is to teach the textbook page. The developmental part of the lesson consists of a detailed explanation of a single example, and the lesson consists mainly of practice.

LESSON OBJECTIVE

The learner will record the steps in division computation.

Lesson Opener

Have students find each of the following quotients:

30 ÷ 3   60 ÷ 3   80 ÷ 4   40 ÷ 2

Have students separate 26 pennies into three equal parts. How much is in each part? How much is leftover?

Development

Direct the attention of the class to the example on the first page of the lesson. Forty-two cents (4 dimes and 2 pennies) is being separated into three equal parts. Refer to the pictures on the page. The dimes are separated first. One dime is placed in each part, and one dime remains. Point out the written steps that are shown on the page.

The next picture shows 10 pennies in place of the dime. Altogether, there are 12 pennies to be divided. Four pennies are placed in each part. Point out the written steps that are shown on the page.

Ask if the students understand that the written division is just the recording of the steps.

Monitor Learning

Have the students do the *Check Understanding* examples.

Practice

Have the students complete the practice exercises on the second page of the lesson. Students who had difficulty with the *Check Understanding* examples can be assigned the reteaching worksheet instead of the practice exercises.

Closure

Ask the students what they learned about recording division.

Next, we adapt this lesson to make it more effective in meeting the learning needs in a diverse classroom. We increase the amount of developmental instruction, visual input, kinesthetic activity, and student communication, and we make monitoring of learning a more integral part of the lesson. These adaptations make the lesson appropriate for almost all students. But, remember that some students with severe needs might require further instructional adaptations.

LESSON OBJECTIVE

The learner will record the steps in division computation.

Lesson Opener

Make enough copies of each of the following division examples so that there will be enough for all the students:

30 ÷ 3	40 ÷ 2	40 ÷ 4	50 ÷ 5
60 ÷ 2	60 ÷ 3	60 ÷ 6	80 ÷ 2
80 ÷ 4	80 ÷ 8	90 ÷ 3	90 ÷ 9

Write the numbers 10, 20, 30, and 40 on pieces of paper and put the pieces of paper at different locations on the wall. Tell the students that the numbers on the wall are the answers. Have the students go stand by the answers to their problems. **Monitor understanding.** Watch the students during this activity to be sure that they understand. Provide help as it is needed. Explain that today the class will divide two-digit numbers and will learn how to record the steps.

Development

Show the students seven strings of beads with 6 beads on each string and 9 beads not on strings. Ask the students to tell you how to separate the beads into three equal groups. Record the steps using a chart like this one. Begin by placing two strings of beads in each part. Record the two strings that were placed in each part and subtract the six strings that were distributed.

STRINGS	BEADS	
2		In each group
7	9	Starting amount
−6		
1	9	

Ask what to do with the leftover string of beads. [Take them off the string.] Record this result. **Monitor understanding.** At each step, watch for students who do not understand. Provide extra explanation as needed.

STRINGS	BEADS	
2		In each group
7	9	Starting amount
−6		
̶1̶	̶9̶	
	15	

Distribute the 15 beads. Record the number placed in each group, and subtract the number that was used.

STRINGS	BEADS	
2	5	In each group
7	9	Starting amount
−6		
̶1̶	̶9̶	
	15	
	−15	
	0	

Using blocks to represent eggs, show the students five cartons of eggs and 8 eggs not in cartons. Tell them that you want to separate the eggs into four equal groups. Follow the steps outlined for the previous example and record the steps on a chart like this one:

CARTONS	EGGS	
		In each group
5	8	Starting amount

Monitor understanding. At each step, watch for students who do not understand. Provide extra explanation as needed. For example, you might need to remind some students that there are 12 eggs in each carton.

Show the students 75 cents (seven dimes and five pennies). Tell them that you want to separate the money into five equal parts. Follow the same procedures that were used in the previous two examples.

DIMES	PENNIES	
		In each group
7	5	Starting amount

Record the steps on a chart like this one.

Monitor understanding. Continue watching for students who do not understand. Provide help as needed.

Tell the students that you are now going to do this example again, but that you will record the steps a little bit differently. Point out that since each dime is equal to 10 pennies, we can think of the dimes and pennies as tens and ones. Write the division and record the steps using standard division notation:

```
        Tens ─────────────┐ ┌─ Ones
                        15 ── Amount in each group
Number of groups ───── 5)75 ── Starting number
                       −5 ── Amount distributed in first step
Amount left to distribute  25 ── (After the trade, 25 ones)
                       −25 ── Amount distributed in second step
Nothing left to distribute ──  0
```

Monitor understanding. Be sure that students understand that everything we write is a recording of something that we do.

Direct the attention of the class to the example on the first page of the lesson. Forty-two cents (four dimes and 2 pennies) is being separated into three equal parts. Refer to the pictures on the page. The dimes are separated first. One dime is placed in each part and one dime remains. Point out the written steps that are shown on the page.

The next picture shows 10 pennies in place of the dime. Now, there are 12 pennies to be divided. Four pennies are placed in each part. Point out the written steps that are shown. **Monitor understanding.** Ask if the students understand that the written division is just the recording of the steps.

Form groups of four students. Give each group eight dimes and 16 pennies. Write the example $7\overline{)84}$ on the board and have each group use the dimes and pennies to find the answer to the division example. Have the groups record each step the way you have been doing it. **Monitor understanding.** Move around to observe the work in the groups. If a group is having difficulty, ask leading questions to help them. Emphasize the recording of the steps.

Practice

When all the groups have finished, have the students do the *Check Understanding* examples for practice. **Monitor understanding.** Move around the room, checking the students' work. Catch the errors and misconceptions and get them corrected. If some students need reteaching, form a group and reteach the concepts and skills.

Closure

Pick one more example and ask for volunteers to come to the front to find the answer. Have a student separate the dimes and pennies. Have the other student record the steps.

Follow-Up

Assign one example for homework. Tell the students that they are to explain to a parent how to do the division and record the steps.

Teaching Problem Solving Using Multiplication and Division

The beginning of the ability to solve problems involving multiplication and division is found in the way that the meanings of those operations are developed. If the essence of the problem is that several equal-sized quantities are being combined, the student can look at the situation and tell that multiplication can be used to find the answer. If the essence of the problem situation is that a quantity is being separated into equal parts, the student can look at the situation and tell that division can be used to find the answer. Students should be led to analyze the problem situation, decide what "physical action" is taking place, and relate that physical action to the appropriate arithmetic problem.

All of the remarks in Chapter 4 about teaching students to solve problems using addition and subtraction also apply when teachers are teaching students how to use multiplication and division to solve problems. The student should experience *problems that they care about* and that involve *familiar objects*. They should experience *mixed examples and nonexamples* where they must decide when they can and cannot use each of the operations. And, finally, when solving word problems, the students should be led to focus not on key words, but on what is happening in the problem situation.

Exercises and Activities

1. Compare the two multiplication lesson plans in this chapter.
   a. Identify where the adapted plan provides more developmental work.
   b. Identify where the adapted plan provides more kinesthetic activity.
   c. Identify where the adapted plan provides more opportunity for communication from the students.
   d. Identify where the adapted plan provides more opportunity for communication among the students.

2. Adapt Activities 5.25 to 5.28 so that measurement division is being developed and used.

3. Develop an instructional activity that uses a physical model to help students understand relationship 4 in the section Discovering Relationships among the Easy Basic Division Facts (page 80).

4. Develop an instructional activity that uses a physical model to help students understand relationship 5 in the section Discovering Relationships among the Easy Basic Division Facts (page 81).

5. Following the steps described in the Divide One Unit at a Time section (page 84), develop an instructional activity that has students use one-, ten-, and hundred-dollar bills to divide 852 by 3.

6. Revise Activity 5.25 to make it more kinesthetic.

7. Develop a kinesthetic practice activity for multiplication of two-digit numbers by one-digit numbers.

8. Develop a kinesthetic practice activity for division of two-digit numbers by one-digit numbers.

9. All of the generalizations that are referred to in this text as "big ideas" are direct results of the properties of operations in the set of real numbers. What properties give us the big idea of partial products?

10. Describe activities similar to Activities 5.25 to 5.27 that will develop the concept of *measurement division*.

11. Develop an activity similar to Activity 5.30 that will encourage students to think about related multiplication facts to find answers to division facts.

12. All of the generalizations that are referred to in this text as "big ideas" are direct results of the properties of operations in the set of real numbers. Division distributes over addition from the right. Explain how the big idea *divide one unit at a time* results from this property.

13. Choose a lesson on either multiplication or division of whole numbers from a published elementary school mathematics textbook series.

    a. Write a lesson plan that follows the teaching suggestions in the teacher's guide.

    b. Identify the parts of the lesson that provide visual information about the concept(s) or skill(s) being taught and expand the lesson by adding activities that provide more visual information about the concepts or skills being taught.

    c. Identify all kinesthetic activity that is included in the lesson and add more kinesthetic activity to the lesson.

    d. Identify parts of the lesson that include student communication about the concept(s) or skill(s) taught in the lesson and add more opportunities for communication from or among students to the lesson.

    e. Identify the parts of the lesson designed to assess students' learning and add more continual assessment (monitoring of learning) to the lesson plan.

14. Read the article "Using Modeling, Manipulatives, and Mnemonics with Eighth-Grade Students," by David H. Allsopp, which is in the November/December 1999 issue of *Teaching Exceptional Children*.

    a. How do the teaching suggestions made in the article disagree with those included in this text?

    b. When the teaching suggestions made in the article disagree with those included in this text, which approach do you prefer? Explain why.

15. Read the discussion related to "Standard 7: Concepts of Whole Number Operations," which is found on pages 41–43 of *Curriculum and Evaluation Standards for School Mathematics*, published in 1989 by the NCTM. Relate the teaching suggestions in this chapter to Standard 7.

16. The following multiplication results illustrate an error pattern like the error patterns that were related by Robert Ashlock in his 2002 book, *Error Patterns in Computation: Using Error Patterns to Improve Instruction:*

$$
\begin{array}{cccc}
\overset{1}{1}4 & \overset{3}{3}4 & \overset{5}{4}7 & \overset{4}{6}8 \\
\underline{\times\,4} & \underline{\times\,9} & \underline{\times\,8} & \underline{\times\,5} \\
86 & 546 & 726 & 500
\end{array}
$$

a. What is this student's error pattern? What is the student doing to produce the incorrect answers?

b. Plan a mini-lesson to correct this student's error pattern.

17. The following division results illustrate an error pattern like the error patterns that were related by Robert Ashlock in his 2002 book, *Error Patterns in Computation: Using Error Patterns to Improve Instruction:*

$$
\begin{array}{cccc}
33 & 24 & 69 & 37 \\
2\overline{)66} & 4\overline{)168} & 3\overline{)288} & 5\overline{)365} \\
\underline{60} & \underline{160} & \underline{270} & \underline{350} \\
6 & 8 & 18 & 15 \\
\underline{6} & \underline{8} & \underline{18} & \underline{15}
\end{array}
$$

a. What is this student's error pattern? What is the student doing to produce the incorrect answers?

b. Plan a mini-lesson to correct this student's error pattern.

References and Related Readings

Allsopp, D. H. (1999). Using modeling, manipulatives, and mnemonics with eighth-grade children. *Teaching Exceptional Children, 32,* 74–81.

Ashlock, R. B. (2002). *Error patterns in computation: Using error patterns to improve instruction* (8th ed.). Upper Saddle River, NJ: Prentice Hall.

Fuson, K. C. (2003). Toward computational fluency in multidigit multiplication and division. *Teaching Children Mathematics, 9,* 300–305.

Graeber, A. O., & Campbell, P. F. (1993). Misconceptions about multiplication and division. *Arithmetic Teacher, 40,* 408–411.

Moyer, P. (2000). A remainder of one: Exploring partitive division. *Teaching Children Mathematics, 6,* 517–521.

National Council of Teachers of Mathematics. (1989). *Curriculum and evaluation standards for school mathematics.* Reston, VA: Author.

National Council of Teachers of Mathematics. (2000). *Principles and standards for school mathematics.* Reston, VA: Author.

Roberts, S. K. (2003). Snack math: Young children explore division. *Teaching Children Mathematics, 9,* 258–261.

Tucker, B. F. (1973). The division algorithm. *The Arithmetic Teacher, 20*(8), 639–646.

Tucker, B. F., Singleton, A. H., & Weaver, T. L. (2002). Partial quotients: An optional thinking strategy for hard division facts. *The Illinois Mathematics Teacher, 53*(1), 23–30.

Wickett, M. S. (2003). Discussion as a vehicle for demonstrating computational fluency in multiplication. *Teaching Children Mathematics, 9,* 318–321.

Websites

www.corestandards.org/the-standards/mathematics
The Common Core State Standards for Mathematics can be found at this site.

www.proteacher.com/I00009.shtml
Lesson plans on multiplication and division, by teachers.

http://mathforum.org/
Math forum links to math discussions and ideas.

SIX

FRACTIONS

Working with Units Smaller Than One

Defining Fractions

Understanding and using whole numbers is a basis for the study of fractions. Similarly, understanding and using fractions are basic for the study as other kinds of numbers such as mixed numbers, decimals, and percents. There are three ways that a fraction can be interpreted. In other words, there are three distinct meanings for each fraction. For example, $\frac{2}{3}$ can be interpreted as 2 divided by 3:

Suppose we start with 2.

Now, we divide 2 by 3. That is, we divide 2 into three equal parts.

One of these three equal parts (the shaded part) is $\frac{2}{3}$. It is 2 divided by 3.

102

The fraction $\frac{2}{3}$ can also be interpreted as a ratio, which is a kind of comparison. Suppose we want to compare 2 and 3. The ratio is 2 to 3, which can be written as $\frac{2}{3}$. We can say that 2 is $\frac{2}{3}$ as big as 3:

Finally, the fraction $\frac{2}{3}$ can be interpreted as two of three equal parts. If we have a region (quantity) that is equal to 1 and divide that region into three equal parts, then two of those three equal parts would be written as $\frac{2}{3}$:

The shaded part is equal to $\frac{2}{3}$.

This last interpretation is typically used when children are first learning about fractions.

Three Sides of Fractions

Children should be able to achieve three goals with numbers (Thornton, Tucker, Dossey, & Bazik, 1983). First, they should be able to identify the quantity that is named by the number. They should be able to show how much it is. Second, they should be able to name the number and be able to say it. Third, they should be able to write the number clearly using standard notation that communicates the number unambiguously. Indeed, these goals imply that there are six tasks that the students should be able to complete. This is just as true when the numbers are fractions as when they are whole numbers:

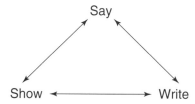

1. If the student is shown some fractional quantity, he or she should be able to say the number (the fraction) that names that quantity.
2. If the student is shown some fractional quantity, he or she should be able to write the number (the fraction) that names that quantity.
3. If the student is shown a numeral (a fraction), he or she should be able to show that fractional quantity.
4. If the student is shown a numeral (a fraction), he or she should be able to say that number (the fraction).
5. If the student hears a number (a fraction) spoken, he or she should be able to show that fractional quantity.
6. If the student hears a number (a fraction) spoken, he or she should be able to write that number (the fraction).

Because we want students to be able to perform these tasks with fractions, our instruction must be designed so that these abilities are explicitly taught.

Fractional Units

Fractions are introduced to students very early (kindergarten or first grade). Although this early encounter with fractions is normally limited, it lays important groundwork for a later, more formal treatment of the topic. However, remediation of this important concept may be needed in later grades. Usually, at the beginning level, students are introduced to only $\frac{1}{2}$ and $\frac{1}{3}$. The three big emphases at this level are that one of something is separated into *equal parts*, the number on the bottom (the *denominator*) *tells how many parts*, and the number on top (the *numerator*) indicates that we are considering *one of those equal parts*.

The equal parts are the *fractional units*. If the fraction is $\frac{1}{3}$, then the fractional unit is thirds. Since the numerator is 1, we are considering one of those fractional units (one third). Fractions with a numerator of 1 are called *unit fractions* because they name one fractional unit. One half is also a unit fraction, but the fractional unit is halves. When learning $\frac{1}{2}$, the students need to see many examples where objects are separated into two equal parts. The objects must be cut exactly in half. The students should see many nonexamples where objects are cut into more than two equal parts and other nonexamples where objects are cut into unequal parts. When learning $\frac{1}{3}$, the children need to see many examples where objects are cut into three equal parts. The objects must be cut into exact thirds. The students should see many nonexamples where objects are cut into more than or less than three equal parts and other nonexamples where objects are cut into unequal parts.

The children should learn to identify the fractions, to say the fraction names, and to write the fractions. The following activities illustrate the way that the fraction $\frac{1}{2}$ can be redeveloped. It is left as an exercise for the reader to develop similar activities for redeveloping other fractions.

Activity 6.01 Fair Sharing

Bring two apples and a knife to class. You also need three sheets of paper, three 1-foot lengths of yarn, and a pair of scissors.

Hold up one of the apples and tell the class that you want to cut the apple into two parts. Cut the apple into two parts that are unequal. Have two children come to the front of the class. Give each child one of the two parts of the apple. Have them hold their pieces so the class can see. Ask if they both got a fair share. [No.] Ask why not. [One got more. One didn't get as much. The two parts were not equal. They weren't the same size.] Hold up the second apple. Ask what to do so that both children will get a fair share. [Cut it into two equal parts.]

Cut the second apple into two equal parts and give each child one part. Ask if they both got a fair share. [Yes.] Write the fraction $\frac{1}{2}$ on the board. Tell the class that this is a *fraction*. It is one half. Point out the top number and the bottom number. Tell the class that the 2 tells us that there are two equal parts. Show the two equal apple parts. Hold up one of these parts and tell the class that this is one half of the apple. Hold up the other part and tell the class that this is also one half of the apple.

Show the class the two unequal apple parts. Ask if they are the same size. [No.] Hold up one of the unequal parts and tell the class that since the parts are not equal, this is not one half of the apple.

Repeat the activity using the three lengths of yarn. Cut one length of yarn into two equal parts to illustrate one half. Cut the second length of yarn into two unequal parts to illustrate a nonexample of one half. Cut the third length of yarn into three equal parts to illustrate another nonexample of one half. For each nonexample, ask why it is not one half.

Repeat the activity again using the three sheets of paper.

Activity 6.02   Putting Halves Together

Prepare a number of shapes. Cut each shape into two equal parts. Be sure that you make enough shapes so that there will be enough for all the students.

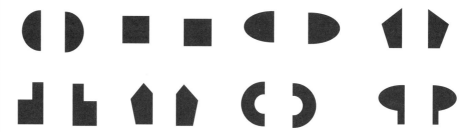

Give each child one of the pieces. If there is an odd number of children, keep one piece and participate in the activity so every child will have a partner. Tell the children that they each have one half of a shape. Have them find the person who has the other half of the shape. When they have all found their partners, have them put the two pieces together to see what the whole shape looks like.

Write $\frac{1}{2}$ on the board. Remind the class that this is the way to write one half. Point to the denominator. Ask what this number tells us. [The number of equal parts.]

Activity 6.03   Halves and Not Halves

Prepare a number of shapes like those used for Activity 6.02. Cut some of them into two equal parts. Cut some into two unequal parts. Cut the rest into three parts. Use a piece of yarn to divide the bulletin board into two sections. Place a card showing the fraction $\frac{1}{2}$ in the middle of one section of the bulletin board.

Show the students the parts of each shape. Let them decide whether the shape was cut into halves. If it was cut into halves, place the two halves on the section of the bulletin board with the fraction $\frac{1}{2}$. If the students decide that the shape was not cut into halves, place the parts of the shape in the other section of the bulletin board.

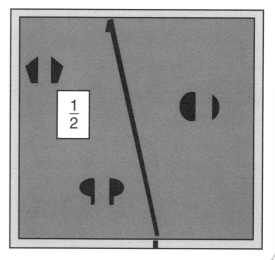

Activity 6.04   Writing Fractions

Prepare a number of shapes like those used for Activity 6.02. Cut some of them into two equal parts. Cut some of them into two unequal parts. Cut the rest into three parts. Tape the parts of each shape side by side on the board.

Show the students the parts of each shape. Let them decide which shapes are cut into halves. If the children decide that a shape is cut into halves, have a child come forward and write $\frac{1}{2}$ below the parts of that shape. Draw an arrow from the fraction to one of the two equal parts.

Beyond Unit Fractions

After the students understand unit fractions (usually $\frac{1}{2}$, $\frac{1}{3}$, and $\frac{1}{4}$), the fraction concepts are generalized to include fractions with numerators other than 1. This is usually accomplished by the end of second grade. The notion that the parts must be equal is revisited, and then the students learn to write a numerator to indicate how many equal parts are being considered and a denominator to indicate the total number of equal parts.

For example, when a shape is divided into four equal parts and three of the parts are shaded, then the fraction $\frac{3}{4}$ names the shaded part of the shape:

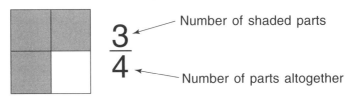

Once again, we want the students to be able to show the fractional quantity, name the fractional quantity using appropriate fraction terminology, and write the fraction name by using appropriate fraction notation. The following sequence of activities illustrates how a teacher might redevelop a student's appropriate fraction notation.

Activity 6.05   Naming Fractions

Prepare cards showing pictures of fractional quantities.

Show the pictures to the class. Call on individuals to give the fraction name for the shaded part in the pictures. Ask how they can tell what the fraction name is.

Activity 6.06   Find the Fraction

Show the children a set of fraction circles:

Write $\frac{2}{3}$ on the board. Point out the circle that is divided into thirds. Pick up two of those three parts and tell the class that this is two thirds of the circle.

Write other fractions on the board and call on students to come to the front and use the fraction circles to show the fractions.

Activity 6.07   Fraction Match

Prepare pairs of cards. One card of each pair should show a picture of a fraction. The second card should show the fraction.

Shuffle the cards and give each student a card. If there is an odd number of students, the teacher should keep a card and participate in the activity so everyone has a partner.

Have the children find their partners so that one partner has the fraction and the other partner has the picture of that fraction.

When all the students have a partner, they should hold their cards so that the other students can check to see if they are correct.

Fractions of a Set

Another way that fractions are used is to name a part of a set of objects. For example, consider this set of circles:

Since four out of six circles are black, we can name the part of the set consisting of black circles using the fraction $\frac{4}{6}$. We can find another fraction name by forming groups of two circles:

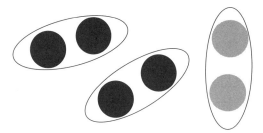

We can see that two out of three groups are black, so $\frac{2}{3}$ is another fraction name for the part of the set made up of black circles.

Now consider this set of shapes. Three of the five shapes are squares, so we can say that $\frac{3}{5}$ of the shapes are squares:

But, all the shapes are not the same size. This illustrates the primary difference between the way we use a fraction to name a part of a region and the way we use a fraction to name a part of a set. When we name a *fraction of a region,* all the *parts must be the same size.* But, when we name a *fraction of a set,* all the *parts must have the same number of objects.*

In the following set of people, even though the men are not the same size as the women, $\frac{1}{2}$ of the set is men. There are the *same number* of men as women:

Equivalent Fractions

When two different fractions name the same quantity, the fractions are equal. We say that they are *equivalent fractions.* Consider this square, which has been divided by a vertical line into two equal parts. The shaded part is $\frac{1}{2}$ of the square.

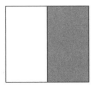

$\frac{1}{2}$

Suppose we cut the square, with horizontal lines, into three equal parts. Notice that each of the two original parts has been cut into three equal parts, which leaves us with six equal parts. Three of those six parts are shaded, so another

$\frac{3}{6}$

name for the shaded part of the square is $\frac{3}{6}$. The fractions $\frac{1}{2}$ and $\frac{3}{6}$ are equal. They are equivalent fractions. A similar procedure is illustrated next to show other pairs of equivalent fractions: $\frac{2}{3} = \frac{6}{9}$, $\frac{3}{4} = \frac{6}{8}$, and $\frac{2}{5} = \frac{4}{10}$:

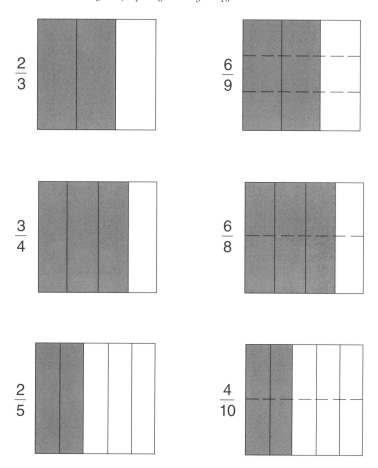

Fractions of sets can also be used to develop the idea of equivalent fractions. For example, in the following set of objects, 12 out of 18 are pentagons. One fraction name for the part of the set that is made up of pentagons is $\frac{12}{18}$:

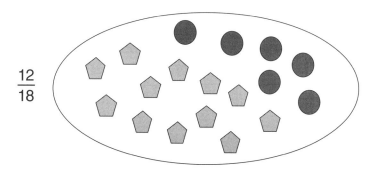

By grouping the objects, we can see other fraction names for the same part of the set:

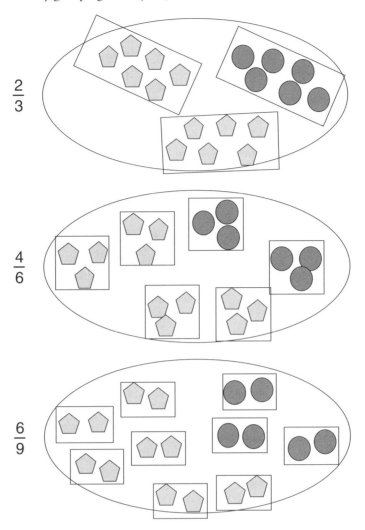

Using the Laboratory Approach

One effective way to teach equivalent fractions is to use the laboratory approach that was described in Chapter 3. Recall that in the laboratory approach, the students are led through a series of steps:

1. **Explore (or experiment).** In this step, a physical or pictorial model is used to find a variety of results (answers). Since the student can see where the answer came from, common sense tells the student whether the answer is correct.

2. **Keep an organized record of results.** The results are recorded in a way that facilitates recognition of the patterns that the teacher wants the student to notice.

3. **Identify patterns.** The children identify patterns that suggest ways to get the result (answer) without using the model.

4. **Hypothesize (or generalize) how to get results without the model.** In their own words, the children state the process that will produce the correct result.

5. **Test the hypothesis (the generalization).** Use the hypothesized procedure to get result(s). Then, do the same example(s) using the model to verify that the process does produce correct result(s).

Next, we examine how the laboratory process can be used to develop the concept of equivalent fractions:

1. **Explore.** Use fraction squares to find a new name for the same fractional quantity.
2. **Record each result.**

$$\frac{1}{2} = \frac{2}{4}$$

$$\frac{2}{3} = \frac{4}{6}$$

$$\frac{3}{4} = \frac{9}{12}$$

$$\frac{1}{2} = \frac{3}{6}$$

$$\frac{4}{5} = \frac{16}{20}$$

$$\frac{3}{5} = \frac{6}{10}$$

3. **Identify the pattern that is the relationship between the two equal fractions.** Students notice, "In the second fraction, both numbers are bigger." The teacher points to $\frac{3}{5} = \frac{6}{10}$ and asks, "How much bigger are they?" We want the students to see that both numbers are twice as big. The numerator was multiplied by 2 and the denominator was multiplied by 2.

In another example, we find that $\frac{3}{4} = \frac{9}{12}$. In this case, the numbers in the second fraction are three times as big. The numerator and denominator were both multiplied by 3 to produce an equivalent fraction.

In still another example, $\frac{4}{5} = \frac{16}{20}$, the numerator and denominator were both multiplied by 4. Point out that the horizontal lines separate every part into four smaller parts. So, we have four times as many parts altogether. The horizontal lines also separate every shaded part into four smaller parts, so we have four times as many shaded parts:

$$\frac{4}{5} \times_{4} = \frac{}{20}$$

$$\frac{4 \times 4}{5 \times 4} = \frac{16}{20}$$

4. **Generalize the pattern.** Help the students to see the same kind of pattern in all the other examples:

$$\frac{1 \times 2}{2 \times 2} = \frac{2}{4} \qquad \frac{2 \times 2}{3 \times 2} = \frac{4}{6}$$

$$\frac{3 \times 3}{4 \times 3} = \frac{9}{12} \qquad \frac{1 \times 3}{2 \times 3} = \frac{3}{6}$$

$$\frac{3 \times 2}{5 \times 2} = \frac{6}{10}$$

Ask the students if they think this always works. Can we always get an equivalent fraction if we multiply the numerator and denominator by the same number?

5. **Verify the generalization.** Write a fraction, such as $\frac{3}{4}$. Ask how to get an equivalent fraction. [Multiply the numerator and denominator by the same number.] Do this to get an equivalent fraction. Then, use the model to verify the result. For example, if the numerator and denominator were multiplied by 4 to find an equivalent fraction, the result would be:

$$\frac{3 \times 4}{4 \times 4} = \frac{12}{16}$$

To verify this result, start with a picture of $\frac{3}{4}$. To change from 4 equal parts to 16, cut each of the original parts into four pieces. When this is done, we can see that the shaded part of the square is 12 out of 16 equal parts:

So, we see that we obtain the correct result by multiplying the numerator and denominator by 4.

A natural extension of this idea is to find an equivalent fraction with a particular denominator. For example, we wish to find a fraction equivalent to $\frac{2}{3}$ that has a denominator of 15. It is left as an exercise for the reader to develop an instructional activity to teach this.

Comparison of Fractions

When fractions are being compared, extra attention must be given to the development of strong mental imagery for the fractional units. Along with this mental imagery must come an awareness that if the denominator is greater, there are more parts. And, if an object is divided into more parts, the parts are smaller. A natural sequence is to first compare unit fractions, such as $\frac{1}{2}, \frac{1}{3}, \frac{1}{4}, \frac{1}{5}, \frac{1}{7}$, and $\frac{1}{15}$. After the students are able to correctly compare unit fractions, the second step is to teach them to compare nonunit fractions that have the same numerators. For example, they might compare $\frac{2}{7}$ and $\frac{2}{4}$. The third step is to teach students to compare fractions with the same denominators—$\frac{5}{8}$ and $\frac{7}{8}$, for example. Finally, the fourth step is to teach the students to compare fractions that have unlike numerators and unlike denominators. In this final step, the students encounter, and must learn to use, the one big idea of comparison: *Compare like units.*

The following set of activities illustrates how a teacher can redevelop abilities to compare fractions.

Activity 6.09 Big and Little Pieces

Ask the students if they like candy. Ask if they would rather share a candy bar with two other people or with three other people. Ask why. What would be the difference? Show them two 2-inch by 6-inch rectangles of paper. Tell them to imagine that the two pieces of paper are two candy bars. Have the class tell you how to cut the first "candy bar" so it could be shared with two other people. [It needs to be cut into three equal pieces.] Have the class tell you how to cut the second candy bar so it could be shared with three other people. [It needs to be cut into four equal pieces.] Hold up a piece from each "candy bar" for the class to compare. Point out that the larger piece is $\frac{1}{3}$ and the smaller piece is $\frac{1}{4}$.

Point to the denominators and remind the students that when the denominator is bigger, the candy bar is cut into more pieces. So, the pieces are smaller.

Write $\frac{1}{3}$ and $\frac{1}{4}$ on the board, and ask which is is more.

Activity 6.10 More Big and Little Pieces

Show the class a set of fraction circles:

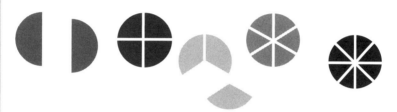

Write $\frac{1}{6}$ and $\frac{1}{4}$ on the board.

Ask which is greater. Have two children come forward and find the fraction piece that represents each of the fractions. Have them compare the two fraction pieces to verify which is greater. Repeat the activity with other pairs of unit fractions.

Emphasize repeatedly that a bigger denominator means smaller pieces.

Activity 6.11 When Three Pieces Is More Than Three Pieces

Tell the class to imagine that two people each have a candy bar. One cuts her candy bar into four equal parts. The other cuts hers into six equal parts. If both are willing to give you three pieces, who would be giving you more? Why?

Which is more, $\frac{3}{4}$ or $\frac{3}{6}$?

Show the class a set of fraction circles:

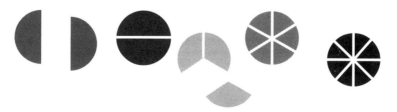

Write $\frac{3}{4}$ and $\frac{3}{6}$ on the board.

Ask which is greater. Have two students come forward and find the fraction pieces that represent each of the fractions. Have them compare the fraction pieces to verify which fraction is greater. Repeat the activity with other pairs of fractions. For example, you could use $\frac{2}{3}$ and $\frac{2}{6}$, $\frac{4}{6}$ and $\frac{4}{5}$, or $\frac{5}{8}$ and $\frac{5}{9}$.

Emphasize repeatedly that a bigger denominator means smaller pieces.

Activity 6.12   Fractions with Like Units

Show the class a set of fraction circles:

Write $\frac{5}{6}$ and $\frac{3}{6}$ on the board.

Ask which is greater. Have a student come forward and use the fraction circles to show the two fractions. Repeat the activity with other pairs of fractions with the same denominators. For example, you could use $\frac{3}{4}$ and $\frac{1}{4}$, $\frac{3}{8}$ and $\frac{5}{8}$, or $\frac{7}{9}$ and $\frac{8}{9}$.

Emphasize repeatedly that since the denominators are equal, the fractional units are the same. The numerator tells how many of those units you have. The fraction $\frac{8}{9}$ is greater than $\frac{7}{9}$ because eight of those units is more than seven of those units.

Activity 6.13   Getting Like Units

Write "7 feet" and "97 inches" on the board. Below them, write "23 yards" and "31 yards." Point to the top two lengths and ask which is longer. Then point to the bottom two lengths and ask which is longer.

Ask why the second pair of lengths is easier to compare. [The units are the same.]

Write "84 eggs" and "76 eggs" on the board. Below them, write "71 eggs" and "6 dozen eggs." Point to the top two amounts and ask which is more. Then point to the bottom two amounts and ask which is more.

Ask why the first pair of eggs is easier to compare. [The units are the same.] Explain that when we are comparing quantities, it is always easier when we compare *like units.*

Write $\frac{5}{8}$ and $\frac{3}{8}$ on the board. Below them, write $\frac{3}{4}$ and $\frac{7}{9}$. Point to the top two fractions and ask which is greater. Then point to the bottom two fractions and ask which is greater.

Ask why the first pair of fractions is easier to compare. [The units are the same.] It is always easier to compare quantities when the units are the same.

Write "13 inches" and "1 foot" on the board. Ask how many inches equal 1 foot. Mark out 1 foot and write 12 inches above it. Point out how easy it is to compare the two lengths when we rewrite them using the same units.

Write $\frac{2}{3}$ and $\frac{3}{4}$ on the board. Explain that you are going to show the class how to rewrite these fractions so that they have the same units. Show representations of these two fractions on an overhead transparency:

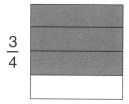   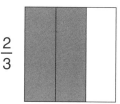

Tell the class that you want to cut the pieces so that you will have same-size pieces in both fractions. You can do that by cutting the first fraction vertically into three equal parts and cutting the second fraction horizontally into four equal parts. Do this on the transparency.

After doing this, write the new names for the fractions:

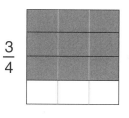   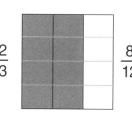

Ask the class to look at the new fraction names and decide which fraction is greater. [The fraction $\frac{3}{4}$ is greater than the fraction $\frac{2}{3}$.]

Show the class that you can get the new names for the two fractions by multiplying the numerator and denominator by the same number:

$$\frac{3 \times 3}{4 \times 3} = \frac{9}{12} \qquad \frac{2 \times 4}{3 \times 4} = \frac{8}{12}$$

Cross-multiplying is a process for comparing fractions that is often taught to elementary children. It is quick and easy to use. Unfortunately, though, it is most often taught as a rote process and consequently is generally not retained. Cross-multiplying works as follows:

Multiply each denominator times the numerator of the other fraction.

The greater product will be on the side of the greater fraction.

Multiply and compare products.

This is the greater fraction.

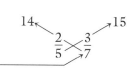

Let's consider how cross multiplication can be taught with meaning. We know that to compare $\frac{2}{5}$ and $\frac{3}{7}$, we need to rename the fractions using the same unit (the same denominator):

$$\frac{2 \times 7}{5 \times 7} = \frac{14}{35} \qquad \frac{3 \times 5}{7 \times 5} = \frac{15}{35}$$

The cross-multiplication process gives us the numerators of the renamed fractions that have the same fractional unit:

$$2 \times 7 \overset{\nwarrow}{} \quad \underset{\frac{2}{5}}{} \times \underset{\frac{3}{7}}{} \quad \overset{\nearrow}{} 3 \times 5$$

Since the units of these renamed fractions are the same, what we actually compare are the numerators (which tell us how many of those units we have). Although we need to know that the denominators are the same, we do not need to actually compute those denominators. When we use cross-multiplication, we are merely finding the numerators of the renamed fractions.

Adding Fractions

Recall that for whole numbers, two big ideas were identified for addition. The first of those big ideas was: *Always add like units*. The same big idea holds for addition of fractions. Addition of fractions with the same units (like denominators) is easy. The most effective way to show students how easy it is to add like fractions is to use a physical model such as fraction circles. For example, suppose we want to add $\frac{3}{8}$ and $\frac{2}{8}$. We represent both

fractions with the fraction pieces and then combine them. We have three of "these things" and two more of "these things." Altogether, there are five of "these things." "These things" are eighths, so $\frac{3}{8} + \frac{2}{8} = \frac{5}{8}$.

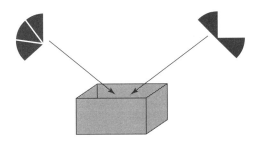

If we are adding like units (like fractions), we have to think about only how many of those units we have altogether. For $\frac{4}{7} + \frac{2}{7}$, we have 4 sevenths and 2 more sevenths. Altogether, we have 6 sevenths.

Addition of like fractions is easy if we use a physical model so the students can visualize combining the fractional units. If the fractions do not have the same fractional units (like denominators), then the students must be led to understand that the fractions can be renamed so that the fractional units are the same. That is, we change to equivalent fractions that have a **common denominator**. The students' previous work with equivalent fractions should have provided the needed understanding and skills, but rather than assuming that they remember, the teacher would be wise to redevelop the key ideas. It is not easy to add the fractions $\frac{3}{4}$ and $\frac{2}{3}$ because the fractional units are not the same. If we rename the two fractions so that both have the same denominator, 12, the addition becomes easy because we can *add like units*:

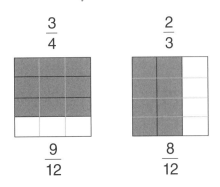

If we follow the same process for renaming fractions, it is easy to quickly rename the original fractions by using a common denominator. After seeing several examples completed by using the fraction-squares model, and after examining the results, the students notice that in every case, the product of the two given fractions can serve as a common denominator for the addition:

We can use 5×8 as the common denominator.

$$\frac{2}{5} + \frac{3}{8}$$

In the first fraction, we multiplied the denominator by 8, so we must also multiply the numerator by 8.

$$\frac{2 \times 8}{5 \times 8} + \frac{}{5 \times 8}$$

In the second fraction, we multiplied 5 times the denominator, so we must also multiply 5 times the numerator.

$$\frac{2 \times 8}{5 \times 8} + \frac{5 \times 3}{5 \times 8}$$

This process for obtaining common denominators is simple and easily justified by using the pictorial fraction-squares model. Using the model, students can quickly master addition of unlike fractions. Some teachers are not comfortable with this process, however, because although the product of the two denominators is always a common denominator, it is not always the *least* common denominator.

When most teachers learned to add unlike fractions as elementary students, they were taught that the least common denominator must first be found. They have been convinced by their own training that the least common denominator must be used in adding unlike fractions. This, of course, is not really true. Indeed, addition of fractions is typically defined in algebra as:

$$\frac{a}{b} + \frac{c}{d} = \frac{ad + bc}{bd}$$

So, then, does teaching students to find least common denominators not have any value? Of course least common denominators have value, and we should continue to teach students how to find them. However, it is actually much more difficult for students to find least common denominators than it is for them to add unlike fractions. It is recommended here to allow the students to first master addition of fractions and then to focus on least common denominators.

Subtracting Fractions

Developing understanding of subtraction of fractions exactly parallels the development of addition of fractions. Subtraction of fractions with like denominators is taught immediately after addition of like fractions. As with addition, subtraction of like fractions is most effectively taught by using a physical model. Select fraction pieces to represent the minuend, take away the pieces that represent the subtrahend, and recognize that the remaining fraction pieces represent the answer. It is helpful to point out how the process of subtracting fractions is like the process of subtracting whole numbers—we start with a number, take away a number, and see what number is left.

Immediately after addition of unlike fractions is taught, the students are taught subtraction of unlike fractions. The first of the big ideas for subtraction, *always subtract like units*, also applies to subtraction of fractions. So, subtraction of unlike fractions requires that we rename the two fractions by using the same fractional unit (a common denominator). Just as with addition, fraction squares are an excellent model for justifying the product of the two denominators as a common denominator. Once the two fractions have been renamed with a common denominator, the children can easily apply their ability to subtract like fractions:

$$\frac{a}{b} - \frac{c}{d} = \frac{ad}{bd} - \frac{bc}{bd} = \frac{ad - bc}{bd}$$

Least Common Denominators

Now we examine least common denominators. Mathematically, the *least common denominator* of two fractions is the *least common multiple* of the two denominators. The process for finding the least common multiple includes two distinct steps. First, we find the prime factorization of each denominator. Then, we form the least number that contains all the factors of the first denominator and also contains all the factors of the second denominator. This is a complex process to teach and students seldom retain it.

However, by being less mathematical, we can actually simplify the process. First, we help the students realize that although the product of the denominators is always a common denominator, sometimes there is another common denominator that is a smaller number:

$$\frac{1}{2} + \frac{1}{4} = \frac{4}{8} + \frac{2}{8} = \frac{6}{8} \text{ could be done like this: } \frac{1}{2} + \frac{1}{4} = \frac{2}{4} + \frac{1}{4} = \frac{3}{4}$$

$$\frac{5}{6} + \frac{3}{4} = \frac{20}{24} + \frac{18}{24} = \frac{38}{24} \text{ could be done like this: } \frac{5}{6} + \frac{3}{4} = \frac{10}{12} + \frac{9}{12} = \frac{19}{12}$$

Next, we need to help them to understand that since whole-number computation is generally easier with smaller numbers, fraction computation is also easier if we use smaller denominators. We can accomplish this by comparing several examples where the product of the denominators is a large number:

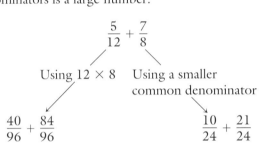

The next step is to discover a method for finding the least common denominator. For each of the two fractions, the students need to think about the denominators for all possible equivalent fractions. We get an equivalent fraction by multiplying numerator and denominator by the same number. We multiply by 2, 3, 4, 5, . . . to find the various possibilities. We do this for both fractions. Consider, for example, $\frac{2}{3}$ and $\frac{3}{5}$:

$$\frac{2}{3} = \frac{2 \times 2}{3 \times 2} = \frac{4}{6} \qquad \frac{2}{3} = \frac{2 \times 3}{3 \times 3} = \frac{6}{9} \qquad \frac{2}{3} = \frac{2 \times 4}{3 \times 4} = \frac{8}{12} \qquad \frac{2}{3} = \frac{2 \times 5}{3 \times 5} = \frac{10}{15}$$

$$\frac{3}{5} = \frac{3 \times 2}{5 \times 2} = \frac{6}{10} \qquad \frac{3}{5} = \frac{3 \times 3}{5 \times 3} = \frac{9}{15} \qquad \frac{3}{5} = \frac{3 \times 4}{5 \times 4} = \frac{12}{20} \qquad \frac{3}{5} = \frac{3 \times 5}{5 \times 5} = \frac{15}{25}$$

We can then create a list of denominators for fractions equivalent to each of the two fractions. We circle the possible denominators that appear in both lists. These are the possible common denominators:

$\frac{2}{3}$ 3   6   9   12   ⑮   18   21   24   27   ㉚   33   36   39   42   ㊺ . . .

$\frac{3}{5}$ 5   10   ⑮   20   25   ㉚   35   40   ㊺   50   55   60   65   70   75 . . .

The smallest of the numbers that appears in both lists is the least common denominator. The least common denominator of $\frac{2}{3}$ and $\frac{3}{5}$ is 15.

Suppose we want to find the least common denominator of $\frac{5}{6}$ and $\frac{3}{8}$:

$\frac{5}{6}$ 6   12   18   ㉔   30   36   42   ㊽   54   60   66   ㊼   78   84   90 . . .

$\frac{3}{8}$ 8   16   ㉔   32   40   ㊽   56   64   ㊼   80   88   96   104   112   120 . . .

The least common denominator of $\frac{5}{6}$ and $\frac{3}{8}$ is 24.

Addition and Subtraction Activities

The following sequence of activities illustrates how addition and subtraction of fractions can be taught or retaught.

Activity 6.14   Name the Rods

This activity uses colored number rods like Cuisenaire Rods (ETA/Cuisenaire, Vernon Hills, IL). Choose any of the rods in the set and let its length be equal to 1:

| 1 |

Then, find fraction names for all the other rods:

| 1 |

Each of these is $\frac{1}{6}$.

| 1 |

Each of these is $\frac{1}{3}$.

See if the students can find more than one name for some of the rods:

$\frac{1}{3}$

$\frac{2}{6}$

Activity 6.15   Give and Take

Prepare a large cube with $\frac{1}{8}$ on two faces, $\frac{2}{8}$ on two faces, and $\frac{3}{8}$ on two faces. Also prepare three circles divided into eighths.

Form a group of three students and seat them around a table. Give each child one of the circles cut into eighths, and show the group the cube with fractions on it.

The students take turns playing. On each play, the player tosses the cube and takes the fraction showing on top from the player on his or her left. Every player must write the fraction that he or she has after each play.

Players must check what everyone else has written. If any player has written an incorrect fraction, the other players must explain why it is not correct. If a player runs out of fraction pieces, he or she is out of the game but must continue to check the other players. After everyone has had three turns, the player with the largest fraction is the winner.

Activity 6.16   What Fraction Is in the Box?–Addition

This is a partner activity. The participants must have a set of fraction circles:

They should also be given a box and a set of cards showing examples of addition of like fractions:

After choosing a card, one student should place the fraction pieces for the first fraction into the box. The other student should place the pieces for the second number into the box. Then they both write what they think correct answer is. Finally, they look in the box to check their answers.

Activity 6.17 What Fraction Is in the Box?–Subtraction

This is a partner activity. The participants must have a set of fraction circles:

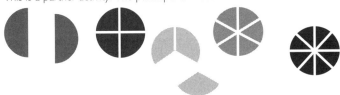

They should also be given a box and a set of cards showing examples of subtraction of like fractions:

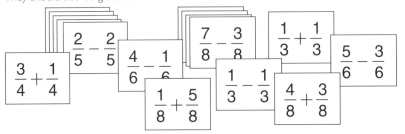

After choosing a card, one student should place the fraction pieces for the first fraction into the box. The other student should take the pieces for the second number out of the box. Then they both write what they think the correct answer is. Finally, they look in the box to check their answers.

Activity 6.18 Predictions

This is a partner activity. The participants must have a set of fraction circles:

They should also be given a box and a mixture of cards like those used in Activities 6.16 and 6.17:

After choosing a card, both students should write what they think the correct answer is. Then they use the fraction pieces to check their answers.

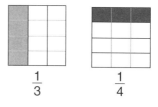
Improper Fractions and Mixed Numbers

Fractions with numerators greater than their denominators are called *improper fractions.* Improper fractions are greater than 1. There is not really anything improper about such fractions. In fact, mathematicians generally prefer using improper fractions to mixed numbers, because an improper fraction is considered to be a simpler form of the number than the equivalent mixed number. However, there are situations when a mixed number is preferable to an improper fraction. For example, if you went into a fabric store and told the clerk that you would like to buy $\frac{17}{4}$ yards of cloth, the clerk would probably look at you as if you were crazy. If a price tag indicated the price of some piece of merchandise as $\frac{874}{100}$ dollars, the customer would probably say, "Just forget it."

In their first encounter with improper fractions and mixed numbers, children learn that these are merely two ways to name the same amount. The work focuses on finding mixed numbers equal to given improper fractions and finding improper fractions equal to given mixed numbers. Either physical models or pictorial models can be used effectively to develop the concepts and skills. Using the fraction circles, we can show that $1 + \frac{2}{6} = \frac{8}{6}$:

  One and two sixths is the same amount as eight sixths.

And, using pictorial fraction squares, we can show that $1 + \frac{3}{4} = \frac{7}{4}$:

  One and three fourths is the same amount as seven fourths.

If we record the step where 1 is renamed as a fraction, we can see the steps that would be followed when a model is not being used:

$$1 + \frac{3}{4} = \frac{4}{4} + \frac{3}{4} + \frac{7}{4}$$

This is another name for 1.

We can then follow this same process for conversion of any mixed number to an improper fraction:

$$1\frac{5}{8} = \frac{8}{8} + \frac{5}{8} = \frac{13}{8} \qquad 3\frac{2}{3} = \frac{3}{3} + \frac{3}{3} + \frac{3}{3} + \frac{2}{3} = \frac{11}{3}$$

And we can follow a similar procedure to change an improper fraction to a mixed number:

$$\frac{14}{9} = \frac{9}{9} + \frac{5}{9} = 1\frac{5}{9} \qquad \frac{18}{7} = \frac{7}{7} + \frac{7}{7} + \frac{4}{7} = 2\frac{4}{7}$$

Addition and subtraction of mixed numbers is almost identical to addition and subtraction of whole numbers. For each operation, the procedures are based on the same two big ideas. First, when adding, *always add like units*:

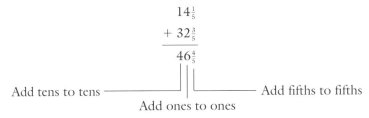

We also apply the second big idea of addition: *When there are too many to write* in standard form or as a proper fraction, *make a trade*:

$$\begin{array}{r} 1 \\ 14\frac{4}{5} \\ + 32\frac{3}{5} \\ \hline \frac{2}{5} \end{array}$$

Altogether, there are 7 fifths. That's the same as 5 fifths and 2 fifths. Trade the 5 fifths for 1 one. Record the extra one, and record the 2 fifths.

$$\begin{array}{r} 1 \\ 14\frac{4}{5} \\ + 32\frac{3}{5} \\ \hline 7\frac{2}{5} \end{array}$$

If we include the extra one that we traded for, we have 7 ones.

$$\begin{array}{r} \overset{1}{14\frac{4}{5}} \\ + \ 32\frac{3}{5} \\ \hline 47\frac{2}{5} \end{array}$$
And, we have 4 tens.

When subtracting, *we always subtract like units.*

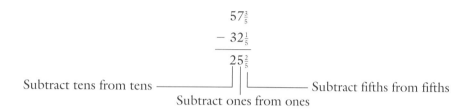

Subtract tens from tens ——————— | | ——————— Subtract fifths from fifths

Subtract ones from ones

We also apply the second big idea of subtraction—*when there are not enough, make a trade*:

$$\begin{array}{r} \overset{6}{4}\overset{7}{\cancel{7}}\frac{1}{5} \\ - \ 21\frac{4}{5} \end{array}$$
We need to subtract 4 fifths. There are not enough, so we trade 1 one for more fifths. In the trade, we get 5 extra fifths. Record the trade.

$$\begin{array}{r} \overset{6}{4}\overset{7}{\cancel{7}}\frac{1}{5} \\ - \ 21\frac{4}{5} \\ \hline \frac{3}{5} \end{array}$$
When we subtract 4 fifths, we are left with 3 fifths.

$$\begin{array}{r} \overset{6}{4}\overset{7}{\cancel{7}}\frac{1}{5} \\ - \ 21\frac{4}{5} \\ \hline 25\frac{3}{5} \end{array}$$
We then subtract the 1 one and the 2 tens.

A Remediation Note. The following incorrect computation illustrates what may be the most common error pattern among students who are subtracting mixed numbers:

$$\begin{array}{r} \overset{6}{4}\overset{12}{\cancel{7}}\frac{}{5} \\ - \ 21\frac{4}{5} \\ \hline 25\frac{8}{5} \end{array}$$
In this error pattern, the student is carrying over the rote borrowing procedure from whole-number subtraction. The student must be led to understand that the denominator tells how many pieces you get in the trade. Let the class see the example with a model.

Multiplying Fractions

Three different approaches to modeling multiplication of fractions have appeared in the professional literature. Two of these approaches have been demonstrated to be effective. They are reasonably easy to use and they are meaningful to the students. The third approach is easy to use, but it is not meaningful to the students. The rationale for the answer does not make sense. We examine all three approaches and discuss what the children must already understand before the approaches can be used effectively.

In the first approach, the students find a fraction of a fraction:

$$\frac{1}{2} \times \frac{2}{3}$$

This means $\frac{1}{2}$ of $\frac{2}{3}$

The teacher cannot assume that the students understand this. To help the students associate the word *of* with multiplication, begin with some whole-number examples. For example, show a group of three objects. Then show five *of* these groups. Write 5 × 3. Show a 7-inch strip of paper. Then show four *of* these strips end to end. Ask how long they are altogether. Write "4 *of* the strips." Write 4 × 7. Show three cartons of "eggs." Write 3 × 12. Then write "3 *of* the cartons."

Only after the students are comfortable with the relationship between multiplication and the word *of* should this method be attempted. To find $\frac{1}{2}$ of $\frac{2}{3}$, we must begin with $\frac{2}{3}$. We use a fraction square to represent the beginning fraction. The shaded part of the square represents $\frac{2}{3}$.

Now we want to find $\frac{1}{2}$ of that fraction. We can find half of the shaded part of the square by cutting it into two equal parts with a horizontal line. We then hatch $\frac{1}{2}$ of the beginning fraction.

The square is now divided into six equal parts. The hatched part is two out of six equal parts, or $\frac{2}{6}$:

$$\frac{1}{2} \text{ of } \frac{2}{3} \text{ is } \frac{2}{6}$$
$$\frac{1}{2} \times \frac{2}{3} = \frac{2}{6}$$

This is exactly what we would have expected if we had used a physical model. If we used the fraction circles to represent $\frac{2}{3}$, we would have two of those pieces. Of course, half of those two pieces is one of those pieces ($\frac{1}{3}$), and $\frac{1}{3} = \frac{2}{6}$.

For another example, we model $\frac{2}{5} \times \frac{3}{4}$. Before we can find $\frac{2}{5}$ of $\frac{3}{4}$, we must first have $\frac{3}{4}$. We use a fraction square to represent $\frac{3}{4}$. We divide the square into fourths with horizontal lines. Three fourths of the square is shaded.

Now we divide the square into fifths using vertical lines. We hatch $\frac{2}{5}$ of the fraction $\frac{3}{4}$:

$$\frac{2}{5} \text{ of } \frac{3}{4} \text{ is } \frac{6}{20}$$
$$\frac{2}{5} \times \frac{3}{4} = \frac{6}{20}$$

The second method for modeling fraction multiplication uses the area model that we have already seen with whole-number multiplication. Recall that the area of a rectangle is equal to the product of the length and the width.

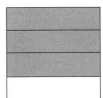

In this model, the length of one side times the length of the other side equals the area:

$3 \times 4 = 12$

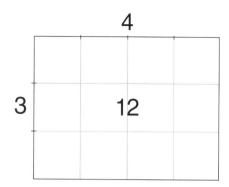

Now, suppose we want to find the answer to $\frac{1}{2} \times \frac{2}{3}$. If we have a rectangle with a length of $\frac{1}{2}$ and a width of $\frac{2}{3}$, then the area of that rectangle would be $\frac{1}{2} \times \frac{2}{3}$. We start with a unit square (a square that is 1 unit on each side). The area of the unit square is also 1. We divide one side into three equal parts and highlight $\frac{2}{3}$ of that side:

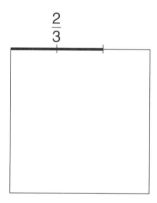

Next, we divide an adjacent side into two equal parts. We highlight $\frac{1}{2}$ of that side. We subdivide the square and shade the rectangle that has a length of $\frac{2}{3}$ and a width of $\frac{1}{2}$. The area of the shaded rectangle is $\frac{1}{2} \times \frac{2}{3}$. The area of the shaded rectangle is also two out of six equal parts of the unit square, so $\frac{1}{2} \times \frac{2}{3}$ and $\frac{2}{6}$ are two names for the same area, and they must be equal. Therefore, $\frac{1}{2} \times \frac{2}{3} = \frac{2}{6}$:

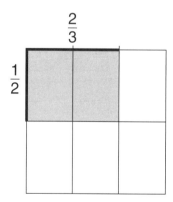

Now, let's consider a second example using the area model. To find the answer to $\frac{4}{5}$ and $\frac{2}{3}$, we begin with a unit square and show $\frac{4}{5}$ on one side and $\frac{2}{3}$ on the other side:

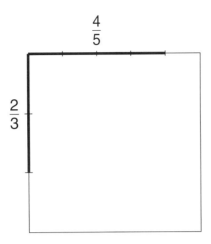

We subdivide the square and shade the rectangle that is $\frac{4}{5}$ on one side and $\frac{2}{3}$ on the other side:

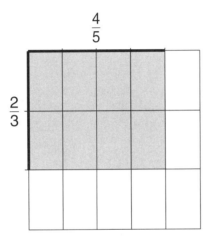

The area of this rectangle is $\frac{4}{5} \times \frac{2}{3}$. The area is also $\frac{8}{15}$. So, $\frac{4}{5} \times \frac{2}{3} = \frac{8}{15}$.

This method of modeling fraction multiplication requires the students to use the area concept. Before expecting them to understand this method, the teacher must ensure that they know that the product of the length and the width of a rectangle equals the area of that rectangle.

The third method for modeling fraction multiplication is occasionally recommended, but it is included here only to alert you to a problem that is inherent in its use. *This method is not recommended.* It is quick and easy to use, but it is not a meaningful way to multiply fractions. Suppose we want the answer to $\frac{3}{4} \times \frac{2}{3}$. In this approach we begin by using hatch marks in a fraction square to show one of the fractions:

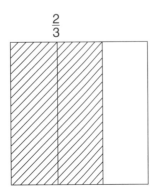

Then, we divide the square horizontally to show the other fraction. The hatch marks for this fraction are diagonal in the opposite direction. The part of the square that is cross-hatched is the answer to the multiplication. So, $\frac{3}{4} \times \frac{2}{3} = \frac{6}{12}$:

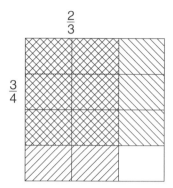

This process produces the correct answer. It is quick and relatively easy to use, but it is not a meaningful method because the students cannot understand why the part that is cross-hatched is the answer. The rationale for the answer—because it is cross-hatched—is meaningless. It would be just as meaningful (to the student) to say that the answer is the part that is not cross-hatched. That is also the correct answer for this example.

To the students, the real reason the part that is cross-hatched is the answer is that the teacher said it is. So, with this method, we have merely created a rote rule that involves drawing a picture. Even though this method still appears in some teacher materials, *research has shown it to be ineffective.*

Either of the first two methods works well. Both of them are meaningful to the students and provide effective modeling of fraction multiplication. The methods supply answers that students believe to be correct, because the process used to get those answers makes sense.

Dividing Fractions

Division of fractions is a topic that is often developed poorly. Sometimes the development is based on a set of examples drawn from a couple of special cases and then the procedural rules are generalized from those special cases—for example, $\frac{8}{9} \div 4$, $2 \div \frac{1}{3}$, and $\frac{3}{4} \div \frac{1}{8}$. Therefore, remediation is often necessary.

For $\frac{8}{9} \div 4$, start with $\frac{8}{9}$ and divide it into four equal parts:

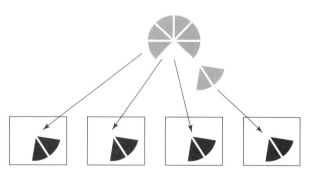

$$\frac{8}{9} \div 4 = \frac{2}{9}$$

For $2 \div \frac{1}{3}$, start with 2 and see how many times $\frac{1}{3}$ is contained in 2. One third is contained in 2 six times. So, $2 \div \frac{1}{3} = 6$:

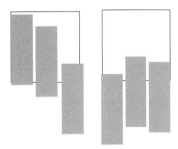

For $\frac{3}{4} \div \frac{1}{8}$, start with $\frac{3}{4}$ and see how many times $\frac{1}{8}$ is contained in $\frac{3}{4}$. The fraction $\frac{1}{8}$ is contained in $\frac{3}{4}$ six times. So, $\frac{3}{4} \div \frac{1}{8} = 6$:

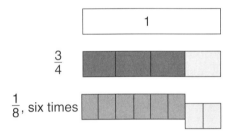

It would appear that we have a good mix of examples, but actually these are all examples of special cases. In every example, we divided a whole number by a fraction and had a *whole-number* answer, or we divided a fraction by a fraction and had a *whole-number* answer, or we divided a fraction by a *whole-number* and it came out "even." The most common case is avoided. In these examples, we did not divide a fraction by a fraction to get a fraction answer. Because many mathematics educators consider this last type to be difficult to model, there is seldom any attempt to include this most common type of fraction division in the development. Instead, the computational rule for division of fractions is generalized from those easier special cases. Remember: *Generalization from special cases is bad mathematics and should be avoided.*

We now examine a developmental sequence that includes examples when a fraction is divided by a fraction to get a fraction answer. We begin with simpler examples to establish the modeling procedures and then proceed to include all types before generalizing the computational rule.

The first thing we do is review *measurement division*, the kind of division that we will be using. If we want to find the answer to $8 \div 2$, we need to find out how many 2s are contained in 8:

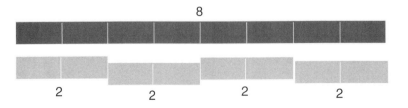

There are four 2s in 8, so $8 \div 2 = 4$.

We continue by using the same type of division and by following the same modeling procedures to find answers to fraction-division examples (Nowlin, 1996). We progress from very easy examples to those that are more difficult to model:

So, $2 \div \frac{1}{3} = 6$.

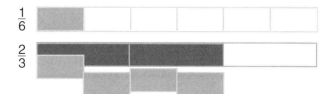

So, $\frac{2}{3} \div \frac{1}{6} = 4$.

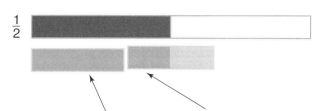

There are one $\frac{1}{3}$ and half of another $\frac{1}{3}$, so $\frac{1}{3}$ is contained $1\frac{1}{2}$ times in $\frac{1}{2}$.

So, $\frac{1}{2} \div \frac{1}{3} = 1\frac{1}{2}$.

How many times is $\frac{3}{4}$ contained in $\frac{1}{2}$?

$\frac{3}{4}$ is contained in $\frac{1}{2}$ less than one time.
What fraction of $\frac{3}{4}$ is contained in $\frac{1}{2}$? Only $\frac{2}{3}$ of $\frac{3}{4}$ is contained in $\frac{1}{2}$.

So, $\frac{1}{2} \div \frac{3}{4} = \frac{2}{3}$.

How many times is $\frac{4}{5}$ contained in $\frac{2}{3}$?

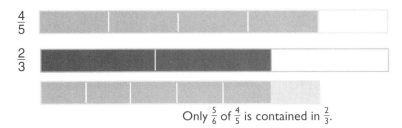

Only $\frac{5}{6}$ of $\frac{4}{5}$ is contained in $\frac{2}{3}$.

So, $\frac{2}{3} \div \frac{4}{5} = \frac{5}{6}$.

Now that we know how to use a model to get answers to fraction-division examples, we can use those results to discover the computation rule. By placing division examples beside related multiplication examples, we can help the student to recognize the pattern. For example, we can use the following pairs. In each pair we use the modeling procedure just discussed to find the division answers, and we allow students to use their previously learned ability to multiply fractions to get the multiplication answers:

$$\frac{2}{3} \div \frac{4}{5} = \frac{5}{6} \qquad \frac{2}{3} \times \frac{5}{4} = \frac{5}{6}$$

$$\frac{2}{5} \div \frac{1}{3} = \frac{6}{5} \qquad \frac{2}{5} \times \frac{3}{1} = \frac{6}{5}$$

$$\frac{3}{8} \div \frac{1}{5} = \frac{15}{8} \qquad \frac{3}{8} \times \frac{5}{1} = \frac{15}{8}$$

$$\frac{5}{6} \div \frac{5}{8} = \frac{4}{3} \qquad \frac{5}{6} \times \frac{8}{5} = \frac{40}{30} = \frac{4}{3}$$

The students should notice that the answers are the same for both examples of each pair and that the first fraction is the same for both examples in each pair. They should also see that in each pair, one example is division and the other is multiplication. They should notice that in the multiplication example, the second number is the reciprocal of the second number in the division example.

After they observe these patterns, the students can easily be led to the generalization that the answer to the division example is found by changing the divisor to its reciprocal and changing the division to multiplication. (This, of course, is the rule that all of us learned: *Invert the divisor and multiply.*)

As a point of interest, we now discuss a procedure for dividing fractions that is mathematically sound and easy to use. This is a standard procedure in algebra that is seldom included in the elementary school mathematics curriculum. Understanding this procedure depends on how well students understand comparison division.

One way to compare a group of 12 students to a group of 4 students is to divide. Since $12 \div 4 = 3$, we know that the larger group is three times bigger than the smaller group. If we reverse the groups and compare the group of 4 students to the group of 12, we have $4 \div 12 = \frac{1}{3}$. This tells us that the smaller group is $\frac{1}{3}$ as big as the larger group.

Suppose we want to compare eggs. In one group, we have 8 eggs, and in the other group, we have two dozen eggs. We cannot just divide the two numbers, $8 \div 2 = 4$, and then say that one group is four times bigger than the other. We must remember the big idea of comparison: *Always compare like units.* If we rename the two quantities so that the same unit is used for both, we can divide to make the comparison. We need to rename the two dozen eggs as 24 eggs. Now we can easily compare 8 eggs to 24 eggs. Since $8 \div 24 = \frac{1}{3}$, we can say that 8 eggs is $\frac{1}{3}$ as much as 24 eggs.

Now, we think of fraction division as comparison. To find the answer to $\frac{2}{3} \div \frac{4}{5}$, we compare the two fractions. But we have a problem: The fractional units are not the same.

Before we can make the comparison, we must rename the fractions using the same unit (a common denominator):

$$\frac{2}{3} \div \frac{4}{5} = \frac{10}{15} \div \frac{12}{15}$$

Now that the units are the same, we compare the two fractions, $\frac{10}{15}$ and $\frac{12}{15}$. We compare 10 of those units with 12 of the same units. The comparison is 10 to 12, or $\frac{10}{12}$. So, $\frac{2}{3} \div \frac{4}{5} = \frac{10}{12} = \frac{5}{6}$.

To state the process simply, we rewrite the fractions with a common denominator and compare the two numerators. This process appears in algebra as simplification of complex fractions. In the algebra texts, it would look more like this:

$$\frac{\frac{2}{3}}{\frac{4}{5}} = \frac{\frac{2 \times 5}{3 \times 5}}{\frac{4 \times 3}{5 \times 3}} = \frac{\frac{10}{15}}{\frac{12}{15}} = \frac{\frac{10}{15} \times 15}{\frac{12}{15} \times 15} = \frac{\frac{10}{1}}{\frac{12}{1}} = \frac{10}{12}$$

Multiplication and Division Activities

The following set of activities illustrates ways that a teacher might teach multiplication and division of fractions.

Activity 6.21   What Fraction Is in the Box?—Multiplication

Write a fraction on the board. Using fraction pies (fraction circles), have a student select the fraction pieces that represent that fraction and place the fraction pieces in a box. Have another student come forward and use the fraction pieces to represent the same fraction and then place those fraction pieces in the box with the first representation. Then have a third student do the same thing.

Ask the class how many times the fraction was placed in the box. Point out that since the fraction was placed in the box three times, the number in the box is three times the original fraction. Ask what number is in the box.

Repeat the activity with other examples.

Activity 6.22   Length Times Width Is Area

Show the students a rectangle separated into squares. Ask what the length and width of the rectangle are. Ask what the area is. Point out that the length is the same as the number of squares in one row, and the width is the same as the number of rows. The area is the number of rows times the number in each row: 3 × 6.

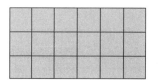

Show several rectangles with length and width given. Write each of the areas as a product (5 × 2, 5 × n, a × 4, or $\frac{4}{5} \times \frac{1}{2}$).

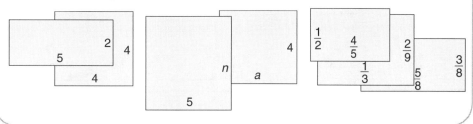

Activity 6.23   Two Names for the Area

Show a unit square with its sides subdivided as shown. Ask how many parts each side is divided into.

Highlight fractional lengths on each side as shown. Ask what fraction of each side is highlighted. Label the fractional lengths.

Subdivide the square and then shade the rectangle with the sides highlighted as shown.

Remind the class that you multiply the length and width of a rectangle to get the area. Write $\frac{2}{3} \times \frac{1}{2}$. Point out that this is the area of the shaded rectangle.

Ask how many parts the square was divided into. Ask how many parts are shaded. What is the fraction name for the shaded part of the square?

We now have two names for the shaded rectangle, $\frac{2}{3} \times \frac{1}{2}$ and $\frac{2}{6}$, so they must be equal: $\frac{2}{3} \times \frac{1}{2} = \frac{2}{6}$.

Repeat the process with several other examples. Keep a record of all the results.

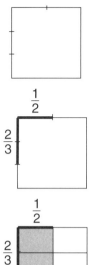

Activity 6.24   Match Me

Prepare pairs of cards with one card of each pair showing a fraction-multiplication example and the other card in the pair showing the answer to the example:

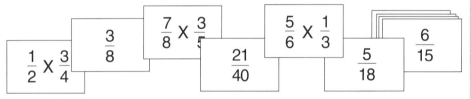

Pass out cards to the students. If there is an odd number of students, the teacher should keep a card and participate so everyone will have a partner. Have the students find their partners. Partners should have problems and matching answers.

When everyone has found a partner, have the partners hold their cards so that all students can see and check the answers.

Collect the cards, shuffle them, and repeat the activity.

Activity 6.25   Measuring with Fractions

Prepare strips of colored paper that are the indicated lengths and label them with the indicated labels. Make five of each green strip.

Red Paper	Label	Green Paper	Label
6 inches	6 inches	2 inches	2 inches
8 inches	8 inches		
4 inches	4 inches	8 inches	8 inches
30 cm	1	10 cm	$\frac{1}{3}$
15 cm	$\frac{1}{2}$	6 cm	$\frac{1}{5}$
10 cm	$\frac{1}{3}$	20 cm	$\frac{2}{3}$

Show the class how to measure the 6-inch red strip by using the 2-inch green strip as the unit. Show that three of the green strips equal the length of the red strip. Have students measure the 8-inch red strip by using the 2-inch green strips. Have them measure the 4-inch red strip with the 8-inch green strip. Fold the green strip so they can see what fraction of the green strip it takes.

Also measure a red strip with the label 1, using the green $\frac{1}{3}$. Measure the red $\frac{1}{2}$ with the green $\frac{1}{5}$, and measure the red $\frac{1}{3}$ with the green $\frac{2}{3}$.

Activity 6.26 Dividing by Measuring

Create a set of fraction strips and label each strip. Make several copies of each fraction strip. Measure the strips carefully, using the lengths that follow:

$\frac{1}{2}$	15 cm	$\frac{1}{3}$	10 cm	$\frac{2}{3}$	20 cm
$\frac{1}{4}$	7.5 cm	$\frac{3}{4}$	22.5 cm	$\frac{1}{5}$	6 cm
$\frac{2}{5}$	12 cm	$\frac{3}{5}$	18 cm	$\frac{4}{5}$	24 cm
$\frac{1}{6}$	5 cm	$\frac{5}{6}$	25 cm		

Also prepare a 12-inch strip of paper and three 4-inch strips. Begin with a whole-number division example. Write $12 \div 4$ on the board. Demonstrate how to find the answer to a division example by measuring. Show that since three 4s are contained in 12, we know that $12 \div 4 = 3$.

Use the fraction strips to demonstrate that since there are four $\frac{1}{6}$ strips in $\frac{2}{3}$, we know that $\frac{2}{3} \div \frac{1}{6} = 4$.

Show that $\frac{1}{2} \div \frac{1}{5} = 2\frac{1}{2}$. Show that $\frac{1}{2} \div \frac{3}{4} = \frac{2}{3}$.

Have the students come forward and find the answers to several examples.

Activity 6.27 Related Multiplication and Division

Following the procedures of Activity 6.26, find the answers to several fraction-division examples. Record the examples in a column with their answers. Then have the students find the answers to multiplication examples that are related to the completed division examples as follows:

$$\frac{1}{2} \div \frac{3}{4} = \frac{2}{3} \qquad \frac{1}{2} \times \frac{4}{3} = \frac{2}{3}$$

$$\frac{1}{3} \div \frac{1}{5} = \frac{5}{3} \qquad \frac{1}{3} \times \frac{5}{1} = \frac{5}{3}$$

Point out that the answers are the same for the division example and the related multiplication example. Ask how you could get the answer to the division without dividing. [You could do the related multiplication.]

Have the students find some answers to division examples by doing the related multiplication. Divide using the fraction strips to check the answers.

Activity 6.28 Find Three

Prepare sets of three cards. One card shows a division example, the second shows the related multiplication example, and the third shows the answer. There should be enough sets of cards so there will be a set for every two students plus one extra set to use as an example. Shuffle these cards and tape them to the walls around the room.

Point out the cards to the class. Select one of the division cards. Take it off the wall and hold it up so everyone can see. Tell them that there is a card with a related multiplication example. Have the students help you find it. Then tell them that the answer is also somewhere on the walls. Have them help you find it.

Pair all the students with partners. Have each pair of partners find a division card and take it off the wall. When they have done this, tell them to find the multiplication card and the answer card that go with their division card.

When everyone is finished, have the partners show their cards to the rest of the class. Is everyone correct? Have the class decide.

Activity 6.29 Division the Easy Way

Review what the class has learned about fraction division and the related multiplication examples. Have students help you verbalize a rule for changing division to multiplication. (The rule might be something like "Invert the divisor and multiply," but try to use the students' words as much as possible.)

Use the rule to do a division example.

Choose a student to come to the front and demonstrate using the rule to do another example. Keep emphasizing how easy it is.

Group the students with partners. Write division examples on the board. Have each student use the rule to find the answer. Then have the children check answers with their partners. If they do not agree on the answer, they should figure out who is correct.

Keep emphasizing how easy it is to divide fractions.

Adapting a Lesson on Fractions

We consider now another lesson plan, beginning with a traditional lesson based on suggestions like those that would be found in the teacher's guide. This lesson, which teaches equivalent fractions, is similar to lessons found in fifth-grade textbooks.

LESSON OBJECTIVE

The learner will write equal fractions using fraction models.

Lesson Opener

Have students name the fraction that is shaded:

Show the students that there are many ways to name the same number. Ten is the same number as $15 - 5$ or $8 + 2$. Have them write the number 10 using as many different names as possible.

Development

Direct the attention of the class to the example on the first page of the lesson. Point out that the child in the picture is placing two fraction pieces for sixths on top of one fraction piece for thirds. Draw their attention to the fact that the 2 sixths fit exactly on top of the third, so two sixths is the same amount as one third. Write $\frac{2}{6} = \frac{1}{3}$.

Have the students look at the second picture on the page. Point out that the 6 eighths fit exactly on top of the 3 fourths. Ask what number should be placed in the box to make the fraction equation true.

Monitoring Learning

Have the students do the three examples in the *Checking Learning* section at the bottom of the page. Identify students who do not understand.

Practice

Assign the practice exercises on the second page of the lesson. Remind the students that they should look at the picture of the fraction strips if they have difficulty. Assign the *Reteaching Worksheet* to students who had difficulty with the examples in the *Checking Learning* section.

Closure

At the end of math time, remind the class that today they learned how to use the fraction model to find equal fractions. Tell the class that their homework is to complete the rest of the assigned exercises.

Following is a revised plan that expands the developmental portion of the lesson. The lesson provides more visual input, is more kinesthetic, and has more opportunities for communication from and among students. Learning will be monitored regularly throughout the lesson. These adaptations make the lesson appropriate for most students. But, remember that some students may require further instructional adaptations.

LESSON OBJECTIVE

The learner will write equal fractions using fraction models.

Lesson Opener

Have students name the fraction that is shaded:

Direct the attention of the students to the last two examples. Ask if they can see how the two pictures are related. [The same amount is shaded.] If no one notices that the same amount is shaded, ask them what they would see if the shaded part of one picture were placed directly on top of the shaded part of the other picture. [They would fit exactly.]

After the students see that the same amount is shaded in both pictures, point out that the two fractions name the same amount. These two fractions are just two names for the same amount. Whenever two numbers name the same amount, they are equal. **Monitor understanding.** Observe the students closely. If any appear not to understand, show an example using prepared overhead transparencies for $\frac{1}{2}$ and $\frac{2}{4}$. Place one transparency on top of the other to help the students see that exactly the same amount is shaded in both fractions.

Explain that in today's lesson, they will learn how to use this idea to find equal fractions.

Development

Tape the following pictorial models of fractions on the board. Leave about 10 inches of board space below them.

Point to the first fraction. Ask someone to name the fraction. Then have her or him write the fraction on the board below its picture. Ask if anyone can find another fraction that has the same amount shaded. Have that person name that fraction and write it below the picture. Ask, "Since these two fractions name the same amount, what can we say about them?" [They are equal.] Write $\frac{2}{8} = \frac{1}{4}$.

Direct the attention of the students to the example on the first page of the lesson. Point out that the child in the picture is placing two fraction pieces for sixths on top of one fraction piece for thirds. Draw the students' attention to the fact that the 2 sixths fit exactly on top of the third, so two sixths is the same amount as one third. Write $\frac{2}{6} = \frac{1}{3}$.

Continue this process until all the equal fractions have been paired and identified as equal. **Monitor understanding.** Continue observing to see that everyone understands. Give particular attention to students with a history of poor comprehension. Actively involve these students in the discussion of results.

Hand out cards showing pictorial models of fractions. Every fractional quantity used should be on two cards, each illustrating a different fraction name for the same

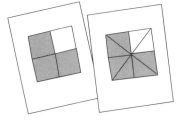 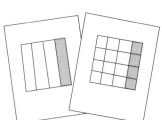

quantity. Have each student locate the other person who has the same amount pictured. **Monitor understanding.** Notice if students are having trouble finding others with the same amount shaded. Provide individual help as needed.

When the students are paired correctly, call on them, one pair at a time, to write the equation on the board that says that their fractions are equal. **Monitor understanding.** Provide help to students who are likely to have trouble so that they can complete this part of the activity correctly and avoid embarrassment.

Have the students look at the picture on the first page of the lesson in the textbook. Point out that the pictures show children using fraction pieces to do what we have been doing. Tell them to notice that, in the second picture, the 6 eighths fit exactly on top of the 3 fourths. Ask what number should be placed in the box to make the fraction equation true:

$$\frac{3}{4} = \frac{\square}{8}$$

Pair the students with partners. Have them complete the three examples in the *Checking Learning* section at the bottom of the page. When they are finished, they should compare answers with their partners. If their answers disagree, they are to discuss them and figure out together what the correct answers are.

Monitoring Understanding

Move around the room and observe students, work. Identify students who do not understand. Provide assistance as needed.

Practice

Have the students continue to work with their partners to complete practice exercises 2, 3, 7, and 9 on the second page of the lesson. Remind the students that the pictures can help them if they have difficulty with any exercise.

Closure

When enough time has been allowed to complete the exercises, ask the students what they learned today about equal fractions. If necessary, ask these questions: "How can you tell that two fractions name the same amount? If two fractions name the same amount, what can we say about those two fractions?"

Follow-Up

Hand out copies of the *Extra Practice Worksheet*. Have the students take the sheet home and show a parent how to do exercise 6.

Solving Problems Using Fractions

There is little difference between problem solving using fractions and problem solving using whole numbers. It is still necessary to visualize what is happening to quantities, whether they are quantities named by whole numbers or quantities named by fractions. A single quantity can be measured, or it can be separated. If there is more than one quantity, those quantities can be combined, or they can be compared.

Suppose we start with a single quantity that is being separated. Subtraction can probably be used to solve the problem. If the quantity is being separated into equal-sized groups, then division can probably be used.

Or, we might start with more than one quantity. If those quantities are being combined, addition can probably be used to solve the problem. If the quantities being combined are of equal size, multiplication can probably be used. If quantities are being compared to find a difference, subtraction can probably be used. If quantities are being compared to find how many times bigger one quantity is than another quantity, division can probably be used.

Problem-Solving Strategies

Of course, many problems are complex, and they might require a series of steps to arrive at a solution. These successive steps may even require different operations. Because of this complexity, the period since the 1980s has seen a shift in problem-solving emphasis from a focus that was almost exclusively on the solution of word problems toward a strong focus on problem-solving strategies. These strategies are, in effect, coping strategies for complex problem solving. They are ways of attacking problems. They are problem-solving patterns. In a very real sense, they are the big ideas of problem solving.

One problem-solving strategy that is included in almost all elementary school mathematics programs is: *Solve part of the problem or separate the problem into easier parts.* Another strategy that appears in many programs is: *Work backward.*

We examine an example of a problem that makes use of both of these strategies. We separate the problem into easier parts and complete those parts one step at a time, but we work backward, beginning with the last step:

> Beth brought some almonds to school one day and decided to share them with three friends. She asked her first friend how many almonds she would like. Her friend asked for three almonds, so Beth gave her three. Her second friend asked if she could have one third of the almonds that were left, so that's how many Beth gave her. Beth's third friend asked for one half of the remaining almonds, so Beth gave her that many. Beth ate the five almonds that were left. How many almonds did Beth bring to school?

We begin with the last step:

> Beth's third friend asked for one half of the remaining almonds, so Beth gave her that many. Beth ate the five almonds that were left.

Beth gave away half and had five left. This means that she was left with as many as she gave away. She must have given away five. So, before that she must have had 10 almonds. Now, we will back up to the previous step:

> Her second friend asked if she could have one third of the almonds that were left, so that's how many Beth gave her.

In this step, Beth gave her friend one third, so she must have been left with two thirds. Since one third is half as much as two thirds, she gave away half as many as she kept. Remember that, at the end of this step, Beth had 10 almonds. She must have given 5 to her second friend. That means that before doing this, she had 15 almonds. Now, we back up to the step where she shared with her first friend:

> She asked her first friend how many almonds she would like. Her friend asked for three almonds, so Beth gave her three.

She gave this friend 3 almonds and had 15 left. Before giving these 3 almonds away, she must have had 18 almonds. This is the number that she brought to school.

Another strategy that appears in most elementary school mathematics programs is: *Use a picture or diagram.* In the following problem example, we illustrate the use of this strategy combined with one of the strategies discussed earlier—*Separate the problem into easier parts*:

> Ms. Spiffey, a middle school art teacher, arranged for her students to paint one wall of her classroom. They first divided the wall into three equal sections. Then they divided the first of those sections into three equal parts and painted one part red, one part white, and one part blue. They divided the second section into two equal parts and painted one part green and one part yellow. Finally, they divided the third section into four equal parts and painted one part blue, one part red, one part green, and one part yellow. When they had finished, what fraction of the wall was painted each color?

To simplify the problem, we consider one section of the wall at a time. To help us visualize the problem, we draw a picture for each section of the wall. The first section looks like this:

We can easily see that, so far, $\frac{1}{9}$ of the wall is red, $\frac{1}{9}$ of the wall is white, and $\frac{1}{9}$ of the wall is blue. Now we look at the second section:

We can see, by examining the picture of this section, that $\frac{1}{6}$ of the wall is painted green and $\frac{1}{6}$ of the wall is painted yellow. Next, we consider the third section of the wall:

In this section, as we can see from the picture, $\frac{1}{12}$ of the wall is blue, $\frac{1}{12}$ of the wall is red, $\frac{1}{12}$ of the wall is green, and $\frac{1}{12}$ of the wall is yellow.

The last thing that we need to do to solve the problem is to add together all the red parts, the white parts, the blue parts, the green parts, and the yellow parts. To be sure that we have not overlooked any parts, we will use another commonly taught strategy—*Use a table*:

	Section		
Colors	**1**	**2**	**3**
Red	$\frac{1}{9}$		$\frac{1}{12}$
White	$\frac{1}{9}$		
Blue	$\frac{1}{9}$		$\frac{1}{12}$
Green		$\frac{1}{6}$	$\frac{1}{12}$
Yellow		$\frac{1}{6}$	$\frac{1}{12}$

What part of the wall is red? $\frac{1}{9} + \frac{1}{12} = \frac{4}{36} + \frac{3}{36} = \frac{7}{36}$

What part of the wall is white? $\frac{1}{9}$

What part of the wall is blue? $\frac{1}{9} + \frac{1}{12} = \frac{4}{36} + \frac{3}{36} = \frac{7}{36}$

What part of the wall is green? $\frac{1}{6} + \frac{1}{12} = \frac{2}{12} + \frac{1}{12} = \frac{3}{12} = \frac{1}{4}$

What part of the wall is yellow? $\frac{1}{6} + \frac{1}{12} = \frac{2}{12} + \frac{1}{12} = \frac{3}{12} = \frac{1}{4}$

Exercises and Activities

1. Adapt activities 6.01 to 6.03 to develop the concept of *three fourths*.

2. Develop a learning activity that has children find other fractions equivalent to given fractions by using the first equivalent fractions procedure described in this chapter.

3. Develop a learning activity that has children find other fractions equivalent to given fractions by using the second equivalent fractions procedure (grouping the objects) described in this chapter.

4. Develop an instructional activity to teach children how to find a fraction with a particular denominator that is equivalent to a given fraction. The activity should use the fraction-squares pictorial model.

5. Choose a lesson on fractions or mixed numbers from a published elementary school mathematics textbook series.

   a. Write a lesson plan that follows the teaching suggestions in the teacher's guide.

   b. Identify the parts of the lesson that provide visual information about the concept(s) or skill(s) being taught and expand the lesson by adding activities that provide more visual information about the concepts or skills being taught.

   c. Identify kinesthetic activity, if any is included in the lesson, and add more kinesthetic activity to the lesson.

   d. Identify parts of the lesson that include student communication about the concept(s) skill(s) taught in the lesson and add more opportunities for communication from or among students to the lesson.

   e. Identify the parts of the lesson designed to assess the learning of the students and add more continual assessment (monitoring of learning) to the lesson plan.

6. In this chapter, a process for adding unlike fractions is presented that involves finding a common denominator. Develop a lesson using the laboratory approach to teach this process for adding unlike fractions.

7. Develop a lesson using the laboratory approach to develop multiplication of fractions. Use the "fraction of a fraction" approach to model fraction multiplication.

8. Develop a lesson using the laboratory approach to teach multiplication of fractions. Use the area model to model fraction multiplication.

9. Consider the problem given next. Use the work-backward strategy to break the problem into easy parts. Then, explain to a friend how to solve the problem.

   > Beth brought some almonds to school and shared them with five friends. The first friend was given one fourth of the almonds. Then the second friend was given eight. The third friend was given one half of the remaining almonds, and then the fourth friend was given three. Beth gave the fifth friend one half of what she had left, and had four almonds leftover for herself. How many almonds did Beth bring to school?

10. The following fraction-division results illustrate an error pattern like the error patterns that were related by Robert Ashlock in his 2002 book, *Error Patterns in Computation: Using Error Patterns to Improve Instruction*:

    $$\frac{6}{8} \div \frac{3}{8} = \frac{2}{1} \qquad \frac{4}{9} \div \frac{2}{3} = \frac{2}{3} \qquad \frac{9}{17} \div \frac{3}{4} = \frac{3}{4} \qquad \frac{7}{2} \div \frac{2}{5} = \frac{3}{2}$$

    a. What is this student's error pattern? What is the student doing to produce the incorrect answers?

    b. Plan a mini-lesson to correct this student's error pattern.

11. The error pattern illustrated in Exercise 10 was almost a correct procedure. The procedure described in the following equation always produces a correct answer. Use fraction multiplication to demonstrate that this procedure is correct.

    $$\frac{a}{b} \div \frac{c}{d} = \frac{a \div c}{b \div d}$$

12. Find a lesson in a published elementary school mathematics textbook series that teaches subtraction of mixed numbers with regrouping.

   a. Describe a class activity that you can observe to determine which students have learned the lesson objective.

   b. How would you check whether an individual student has learned the lesson objective?

References and Related Readings

Ashlock, R. B. (2002). *Error patterns in computation: Using error patterns to improve instruction* (8th ed.). Upper Saddle River, NJ: Prentice Hall.

Nowlin, D. (1996). Division with fractions. *Mathematics Teaching in the Middle School, 2,* 116–119.

Thornton, C. A., Tucker, B. F., Dossey, J. A., & Bazik, E. F. (1983). *Teaching mathematics to children with special needs.* Menlo Park, CA: Addison-Wesley.

Tucker, B. F. (1989). Three methods for modeling multiplication of fractions. *Virginia Mathematics Teacher, 15*(2), 7–9. (Reprinted from *The Illinois Mathematics Teacher, 37*(4), 7–12.)

Wu, Z. (2001). Multiplying fractions. *Teaching Children Mathematics, 8,* 174–177.

Websites

www.corestandards.org/the-standards/mathematics
The Common Core State Standards for Mathematics can be found at this site.

http://mathforum.org/
Math forum links to math discussions and ideas.

http://teachers.net/lessons/posts/262.html
Fractions of a set.

http://teachers.net/lessons/posts/17.html
Fractions of a region.

proteacher.com/100014.shtml
Lesson plans, by teachers, on fractions, decimals, and ratios.

http://mathforum.org/paths/fractions/
Links to fraction sites and lessons.

seven

DECIMALS AND PERCENTS

Working with Base-Ten Units Smaller Than One and Using Hundredths as a Common Denominator

CHAPTER OUTLINE

Decimals

Place Value for Decimals

Comparing Decimals

Adding and Subtracting Decimals

Multiplying Decimals

Dividing Decimals

Multiplication and Division Activities

Fraction Comparison Revisited

Defining Percent

Adapting a Lesson on Decimals

Using Decimals to Solve Problems

Exercises and Activities

Decimals

Decimals can be thought of as fractions and sometimes as mixed numbers. They are fractions or mixed numbers with denominators that are always equal to the base-10 whole-number units. The whole-number base-10 units are ones, tens, hundreds, thousands, ten thousands, and so on. The *decimal fraction units* are tenths, hundredths, thousandths, ten thousandths, and so on. The number 1 can be thought of as the denominator for the decimal units that are greater than or equal to 1. The properties that control what we can do with decimals are the same ones that govern our use of whole numbers and decimals.

As with other numbers that we have considered earlier, we want our students to recognize and name decimal quantities using appropriate terminology, to use appropriate models to show decimal quantities, and to write decimals using appropriate notation. These learning objectives require that we have effective models for decimals. The minimum requirement for a decimal model is the ability to represent the basic units. This means that the chosen model should allow for the representation of ones, tens, hundreds, and so on, as well as tenths, hundredths, thousandths, and so on, or at least the units from this list that are being used in the current lesson.

The *base-10 block set* is a model that fits this description. The large cube would represent 1, the flats (each 1 tenth of the large cube) would represent tenths. The longs, or the rods (each 1 tenth of a flat and 1 hundredth of a large cube), would represent hundredths. The small cubes (each equal to 1 tenth of a long, 1 hundredth of a flat, and

1 thousandth of a large cube) would represent thousandths. The following illustration uses base-10 blocks to represent the decimal 1.324:

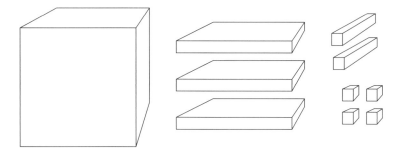

Another option is the *decimal square model*. This is a two-dimensional model that lends itself to the printed page, and it is frequently used in textbooks. A square represents 1. If the square is cut into 10 equal-sized strips, the strips represent tenths. If a strip is cut into 10 equal squares, these smaller squares represent hundredths. Sometimes the large square is divided into 100 smaller squares and part of the subdivided square is shaded to represent a decimal.

The number 2.47 is represented next by both models:

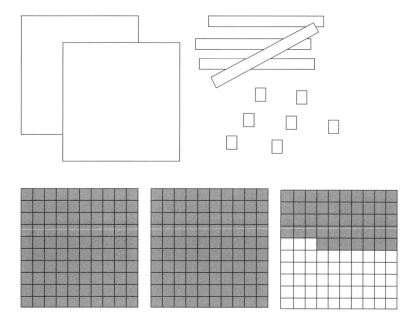

Another model that is sometimes used is the *metric-length model*. A meter represents 1, a decimeter represents 1 tenth, a centimeter represents 1 hundredth, and a millimeter represents 1 thousandth. This model is not often useful in instructional settings. In instructional settings, one of the other models is invariably more effective.

The *money model* is another model frequently used to represent decimals. Along with using one-, ten-, and hundred-dollar bills to represent ones, tens, and hundreds, this model also uses dimes to represent tenths and pennies to represent hundredths. Since the various pieces of money are capable of being combined, separated, and compared, this model is useful for teaching a wide variety of decimal topics.

The final model that we mention is the *pocket chart*, which is useful when the teacher is stressing place value. This model is relatively abstract and probably should not be used in the early introduction of decimals. Decimals are represented by markers placed in various positions, and the units associated with those positions must be identified in some way:

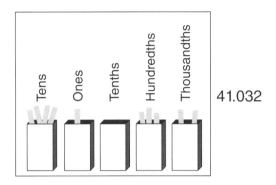

41.032

Place Value for Decimals

When decimal notation is used to write decimal fractions, the denominators are not written. Rather, they are indicated by the position of the number. One important task for the teacher, then, is to help students to be able to determine the decimal units from their position. *It is important to first communicate that decimal notation is really an extension of whole-number notation.* When we move from one position to another from right to left, the value of numbers in each position is 10 times the value of numbers in the previous position:

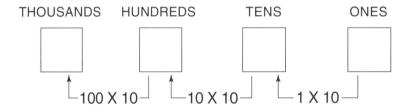

Similarly, when we move from one position to another from left to right, the value of numbers in each position is the value of numbers in the previous position divided by 10:

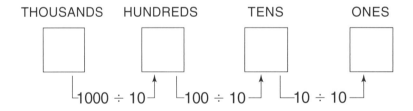

This pattern holds when we are adding the decimal units that are less than 1:

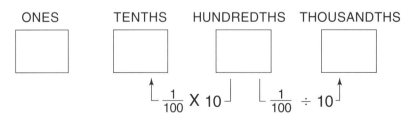

Students also need to understand that there is symmetry in the decimal numeration system (Thornton, Tucker, Dossey, & Bazik, 1983). A common misconception is that the system is symmetric around the decimal point. Actually, *the system is symmetric around the ones:*

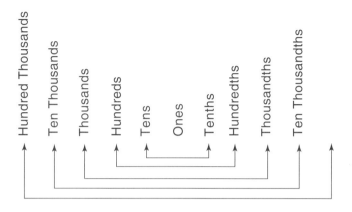

Once we are familiar with the nature of the symmetry, we have the ability to find the value of each place, starting from any known position. For example, if we know that the 7 is in the tens place of this number, we can figure out the value of the other places.

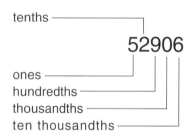

If we know that the 2 in this number is in the tenths place, we can figure out the value of all the other places.

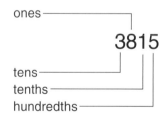

If we know that the 8 in this number is in the ones place, we can figure out the value of every other place.

A device called the *decimal point* helps us identify the place values. The decimal point is always placed to the right of the ones place. Once we know which position is the ones place, we use our knowledge of the symmetry of the system to identify the value of all the other positions:

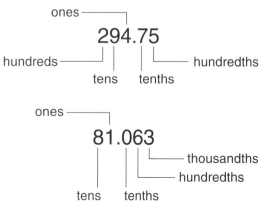

Students should be taught in a meaningful way to read decimals. If the instructional focus is on rote reading procedures, we might appear to gain fast results. However, because so much subsequent reteaching is necessary, we should question the value of such fast results. Remember, it is always harder to remember things that are meaningless. There are, however, several connections that can be developed that improve retention of the rules for reading decimals in a standard way.

Let's begin by looking at two simple, related examples from our work with fractions and mixed numbers:

$4 + \frac{2}{3}$ is usually written as $4\frac{2}{3}$ and read as "4 and $\frac{2}{3}$."

$6 + \frac{1}{2} + \frac{1}{4}$ would usually be simplified by adding the two fractions together to get $6 + \frac{3}{4}$. This would be read as "6 and $\frac{3}{4}$."

The decimal 5.27 literally means $5 + \frac{2}{10} + \frac{7}{100}$. This can be read as "5 and $\frac{2}{10}$ and $\frac{7}{100}$." We can simplify the reading by adding the two fractions. Then we can just read it as a mixed number. To add the two fractions together, we need to rewrite them using a common denominator:

$$5 + \frac{2}{10} + \frac{7}{100} = 5 + \frac{20}{100} + \frac{7}{100} = 5 + \frac{27}{100}$$

Then, we can read it as "5 and 27 hundredths." If we look at 5.27 using the decimal square model, we can arrive at the same result:

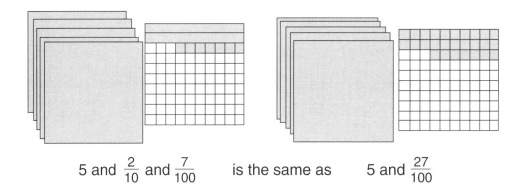

In the same way, we can show that 24.96, which is 24 and $\frac{9}{10}$ and $\frac{6}{100}$, is the same as "24 and $\frac{96}{100}$."

From examples like these, students can be led to understand why a decimal like 207.435 is read as "207 and 435 thousandths." They understand that they are simply reading a mixed number:

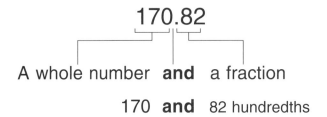

When learning decimals, the students should be able to complete six tasks correctly:

1. When shown a decimal quantity (represented by a decimal model), the students should be able to name (say) the decimal.
2. When shown a decimal quantity (represented by a decimal model), the students should be able to write the decimal.
3. When the students hear a decimal named, they should be able to show the decimal quantity (using a decimal model).
4. When the students hear a decimal named, they should be able to write the decimal.
5. When the students see a written decimal named, they should be able to name the decimal.
6. When the students see a written decimal named, they should be able to show the decimal quantity (using a decimal model).

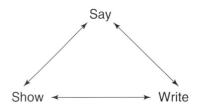

Instruction should include activities that help the students learn to do these tasks. The following activities illustrate how this can be done.

Activity 7.01   Show and Write

From a roll of receipt paper, cut nine strips that are 1 meter long, nine strips that are 10 centimeters long, and nine pieces that are 1 centimeter long. Explain that the 1-m strips each represent 1. The 10-cm strips each represent 1 tenth, and the 1-cm pieces each represent 1 hundredth.

Show the class some combination of strips of each size. Have each student write the decimal that is represented. Then ask someone to tell you how many of each unit is included. Write the correct decimal. Ask how many students got it right.

Repeat several times with different quantities.

Activity 7.02   Show, Write, and Tell

Use decimal squares to show a decimal quantity. For example, you might show the quantity at the right.

Have every student write the decimal that is represented. Then ask someone to read the decimal. If necessary, discuss why the written decimal shows 4 tenths and 6 hundredths, but we read it as 46 hundredths.

Repeat several times with different quantities.

 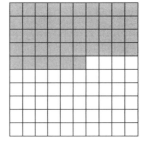

Activity 7.03   I'll Tell; You Show

Hand out copies of the decimal square worksheet shown at the right.

Read aloud a decimal (ones, tenths, and hundredths), and have the students color a representation of that decimal.

Repeat several times with different decimals.

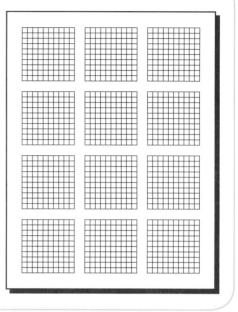

Activity 7.04   I'll Tell; You Write and Show

Hand out copies of the decimal square worksheet shown at the right.

Read aloud a decimal (ones, tenths, and hundredths), and have the students color a representation of that decimal.

Then have the students write the decimal.

Repeat several times with different decimals.

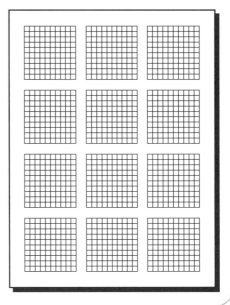

Activity 7.05   I'll Tell; You Write and Show Me the Money

Make 8 to 10 packages of play money. Include in each package 4 ten-dollar bills, 6 one-dollar bills, 5 dimes, and 9 pennies.

Form groups of three students, and give each group a package of money.

Explain that when you read a decimal, one person in the group will get the money to show that quantity, one person will write the decimal, and the third person will check the other two to see if they are right. Tell the students that they are to take turns doing each job.

Read aloud a decimal (tens, ones, tenths, and hundredths). Be sure that there are no more than 4 tens, 6 ones, 5 tenths, or 9 hundredths.

Repeat several times with different decimals. Be sure to monitor the students' work to catch and correct misconceptions.

Comparing Decimals

Comparison of decimals is not difficult. Virtually every error pattern related to comparing fractions results directly from lack of appropriate mental imagery for the numbers being compared. The student who thinks .98 must surely be greater than 1.2 because 9 and 8 are both more than 1 or 2 is not visualizing the numbers. The student who thinks 6.21 must be greater than 7.3 because three-digit numbers are bigger than two-digit numbers is not visualizing the numbers.

Almost invariably, error patterns like these can be eliminated by providing mental imagery for the numbers. It seems reasonable, then, that development of appropriate mental imagery should be an integral part of the initial teaching of this topic. Experiences with models that allow students to literally see when one decimal is greater than another can be used to develop meaningful rules and procedures for comparing decimals.

To compare .2 and .09, we begin by representing both decimals:

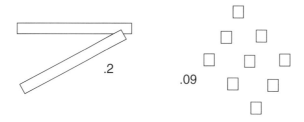

The students can easily see that 2 tenths is greater than 9 hundredths. If unsure, they can place the hundredths pieces on top of one of the tenths pieces to determine that 9 hundredths is even less than 1 tenth. Then we could ask the students to figure out how many hundredths it would take to equal 2 tenths. This helps to reinforce the comparison.

We use the model to make a lot of comparisons. For example, we might compare 3 and .3, 7.2 and .72, and 1.2 and .98:

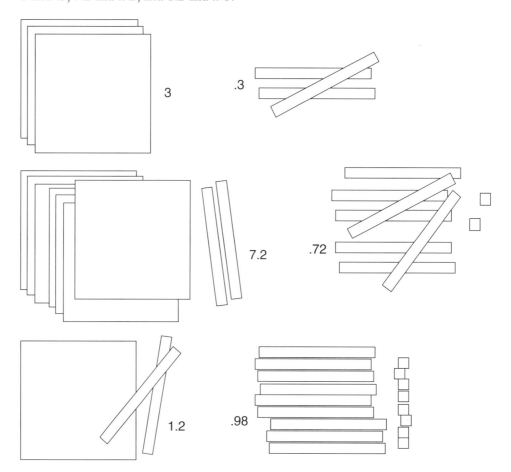

After recording these and other similar results, the teacher can lead the students to discover a number of helpful patterns:

The value of the number varies according to the position of the digits relative to the decimal point.	3 > .3
	7.2 > .72
	.06 < .60
The size of the digits is less important than the position of the digits relative to the decimal point.	.2 > .09
	.086 < .34
	1.2 > .98

Compare numbers by comparing the values of the first nonzero digit.	.206 > .094 (2 tenths is greater than 9 hundredths) .061 < .059 (6 hundredths is greater than 5 hundredths) 6.93 < 20.1 (6 ones is less than 2 tens)
If the values of the first nonzero digits are equal, then compare the values of the next digits.	.519 < .523 (1 hundredth is less than 2 hundredths) 6.43 > 6.29 (4 tenths is greater than 2 tenths) 32.4 < 38.1 (2 ones is less than 8 ones)

These patterns can then be fashioned into meaningful rules and procedures for comparing decimals. The rules will be meaningful to the students because they are generalizations from the students, own discoveries rather than just "what the teacher said to do."

The following sequence of activities demonstrates how a teacher can develop decimal comparison concepts and skills.

Activity 7.06   Comparing Decimals

Write two decimals on the chalkboard. Have two students come forward. Have each student represent one of the numbers using squares, strips, and small squares like those illustrated at the right.

2.47

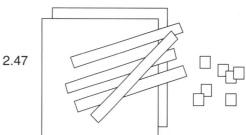

After the numbers have been represented with the model, have two other children come forward and check to make sure the numbers were represented correctly.

Then have another child come forward and look at the model representations and decide which number is greater. Have this student write < or > between the two numbers.

Repeat this activity with several pairs of decimals.

Activity 7.07   Partner Comparison

Pair students with partners. Give each pair a set of decimal pieces consisting of 5 ones, 9 tenths, and 9 hundredths.

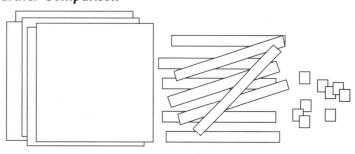

Write two decimals on the board. Have the partners each use the model to represent one of the numbers. After the numbers have been represented, have the partners decide which number is greater. Then choose a student to come forward and write < or > between the two numbers.

Repeat this activity with several pairs of decimals.

Activity 7.08   Comparison Prediction

Write two decimals on the board. Tell the students that they will be figuring out which number is greater. Have them predict which number is greater. If the students agree, call on someone to explain why he or she thinks that number is greater. If the students disagree, have those who disagree explain their thinking.

Next, have two students come forward and represent the numbers and check to see if their prediction is correct. Have another child come forward and write < or > between the two numbers.

If a student suggests a clear and correct way to decide which number is greater, write the method on the board and have the class use that method for the next example.

Repeat this activity with several pairs of decimals. Have the students sometimes decide which number is less.

Activity 7.09   Comparison Prediction

Prepare a set of about 50 cards showing decimals.

Form a group of two to four students. Give the group a set of decimal pieces. Shuffle the deck and place it facedown on the table.

On each play, all the players take a card from the deck and place it faceup on the table. The player with the greatest decimal takes the cards from that play. Play continues in this way until there are not enough cards for another play. The player who has taken the most cards is the winner.

If the players disagree about which decimal is greater, the disputing players explain their reasoning to try to convince the other players. If they cannot reach agreement, they should then represent the decimal with the model to check the comparison.

Adding and Subtracting Decimals

The teaching of addition and subtraction of decimals is almost identical to the teaching of addition and subtraction of whole numbers. The same big ideas that govern addition and subtraction of whole numbers are used for adding and subtracting decimals:

For addition:	Always add like units.
	When there are too many to write (in standard form), make a trade.
For subtraction:	Always subtract like units.
	When there are not enough, make a trade.

The only real difference between addition and subtraction of decimals and that of whole numbers is that with decimals, there are more units. We start the instruction by re-establishing the big ideas using a physical model. Using squares, strips, and small squares as a decimal model is an excellent way to illustrate addition and subtraction.

When adding, we model the two numbers, combine them, and record what is there after combining. When subtracting, we model the subtrahend, take away the minuend, and record the remainder:

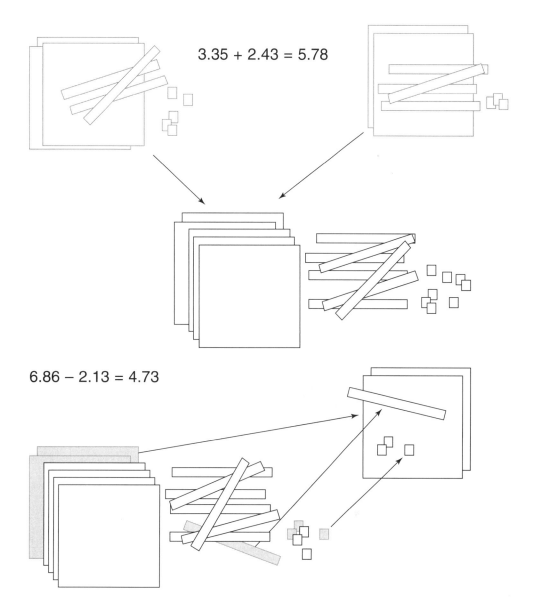

$$3.35 + 2.43 = 5.78$$

$$6.86 - 2.13 = 4.73$$

Another easy-to-use model for addition and subtraction of decimals is play money. When ten-dollar bills are used to represent tens, one-dollar bills to represent ones, dimes to represent tenths, and pennies to represent hundredths, this representation of decimals can be combined and separated, and, when necessary, equal trades can be made.

A Remediation Note. The most common error pattern in addition and subtraction of decimals comes from a rote rule learned when the students were working with whole numbers: The columns must be lined up. The problem with rote rules is that they are seldom true beyond certain narrow conditions. And students (even those who have memorized the rules correctly) tend to apply them in inappropriate circumstances. In particular, this rule, when correctly applied in whole-number addition, would not produce errors:

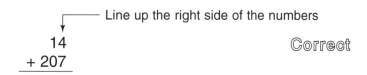

Line up the right side of the numbers

$$14$$
$$+\ 207$$

Correct

However, when the rule is applied to addition of decimals, the computation is not correct:

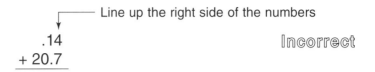

Line up the right side of the numbers

.14
+ 20.7

Incorrect

When the teacher identifies this error pattern, it is important that the student not merely be given a new rule (line up the decimal points) to replace the old rule. The reader should not misinterpret this statement. We are not saying that students should not learn to line up the decimal points when they are adding or subtracting decimals. Lining up the decimal points actually makes the addition or subtraction easier.

What we are suggesting is that when the teacher uses the model to show that if like units are lined up (remember that we *always add like units*), the result is that the decimal points will also be lined up. And, when we line up the decimal points, it turns out that like units are lined up. This is helpful because lining up like units makes it easier to *add like units.* The students still learn the same rule, but the rule is now meaningful. Not only does it make sense to the students, but the students also understand why they should follow the rule.

Adding and Subtracting Activities

The activities that follow can be used to develop the concepts related to addition and subtraction of decimals.

Activity 7.10   Adding Money

Using play hundred-, ten-, and one-dollar bills, have students come to the front of the room and illustrate this addition. Be sure that all children understand that they need to add like units and make a trade when there are too many to write.

628
+165

Then add some dimes and pennies to the money and have a student come forward and illustrate this addition. Emphasize to the class that they add exactly the same way when they are adding decimals.

24.73
+ 3.84

Have several other students come forward and use the money to illustrate other decimal addition examples.

Then write a decimal addition example on the board and have the students do the addition at their seats. When they are finished, have a student come forward and use the money to do the same example. Did everyone get it right?

Activity 7.11   Subtracting Money

Follow the procedures described for Activity 7.10, except use subtraction examples.

Activity 7.12   Be Careful What You Add

Write 42.03 + 615.6 on the board in horizontal form as shown here. Tell the students that you want to do this addition. Ask what decimal units you will have in the answer. [Hundreds, tens, ones, tenths, and hundredths] Ask how many ones there will be in the answer. Write 7 on the board with a decimal point after it. Ask how many tens will be in the answer. Record the 5 tens. Ask how many tenths. Record the 6 tenths. Ask how many hundredths. Record the 3 hundredths. Point out that to get the answer, the students must *add like units.* Model the same addition using play hundred-dollar bills, ten-dollar bills, one-dollar bills, dimes, and pennies to verify that the answer is correct.

Next, add 123.4 + 4.567 + 21.02 as a second example. After completing the addition, explain that even though decimal addition is easy, sometimes students really have to be careful to add only like units (ones to ones, hundredths to hundredths, and so on). Explain that it will be easier to add like units if the like units are written in columns. Rewrite the last example by lining up the like units. Add to demonstrate how much easier it is to add the like units when they are lined up.

Finally, do 107.64 + 5.193 as a third example, but this time line up the like units. When you have completed this example, point out that when like units are placed in columns, the decimal points are also lined up. Do another example by lining up the decimal points.

Activity 7.13   If There Aren't Any, Write Zero

Write 42.03 + 615.6 on the board in horizontal form as shown here. Ask what the smallest unit is in either number. [Hundredths] Ask how many hundredths there are in the second number. [There are none.] Ask how a person might write the number to show that there are no hundredths. [Write a zero in the hundredths place.] Rewrite the addition example as 42.03 + 615.60 and add.

Write 123.4 + 4.567 + 21.02 as a second example. Ask what fractional decimal units there are. [Tenths, hundredths, and thousandths] Rewrite the addition example using 0 to indicate when a number has none of some unit. Then add. Emphasize that decimal addition is just like whole-number addition: *Always add like units* and *when there are too many to write, make a trade.*

Write 107.64 + 5.193 as a third example. Have the students rewrite the numbers using zeros as they were used in the previous examples. Have the children add to get the answer.

Activity 7.14   If There Aren't Any, Write Zero–Subtraction

Write 38.2 − 5.78 on the board. Ask what units we have to take away. [Ones, tenths, and hundredths] Point to the subtrahend. Ask how many hundredths we are starting with. [There are none.] Ask how we can rewrite the number to show that there are no hundredths. [Use a zero.]

Rewrite the subtraction example as 38.20 − 5.78. Rewrite it again in vertical form and complete the example. Emphasize that decimal subtraction is just like whole-number subtraction: *Always subtract like units* and *when there are not enough to subtract, make a trade.*

Multiplying Decimals

Multiplication of decimals is also much like multiplication of whole numbers. It is still necessary to use partial products to find answers, but the other big idea of multiplication, multiplication by 10, must be expanded to include multiplication by .1. Once this has been accomplished, there really is little that is new.

The best overall model for multiplication of decimals is the *area model*. We have already used the area model when learning to multiply whole numbers and fractions. So, it is a small step to use this model to help the students learn to multiply decimals. The essence of the area model is that the length of a rectangle times its width equals the area:

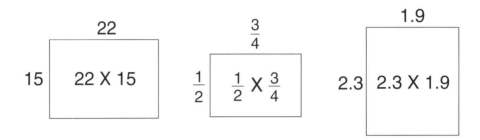

We use the area model to discover answers to some decimal-multiplication examples:

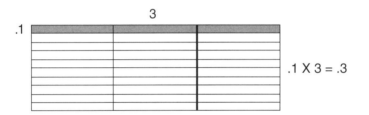

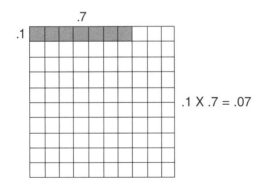

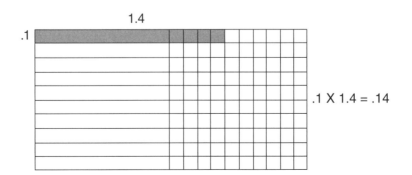

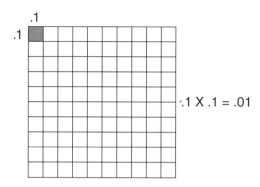

The pattern that you want the students to discover is that when they are multiplying by .1, the effect on the other number is that the decimal point is moved one place to the left. Once this pattern is discovered, they can use the generalization to find other answers. For example, for .1 × 3.9,

.1 X 3.9 =.39

> Move the decimal point one place to the left.
> 3.9

After the students give an answer using the generalization, the next step is to go back to the model to verify that the answer is correct. This confirms that the generalization really works:

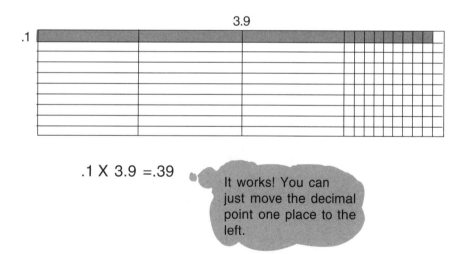

.1 X 3.9 =.39

> It works! You can just move the decimal point one place to the left.

We also need to establish the relationship between multiplication by .1 and multiplication by .01. From the previous generalization about multiplication by .1, we can see that

$$.1 \times .1 = .01$$

In other words, multiplication by .01 is equivalent to two multiplications by .1. This translates into moving the decimal point one place to the left twice, which is, of course, moving the decimal point two places to the left. Similarly,

$$.1 \times .1 \times .1 = .001$$

Multiplication by .001 is equivalent to multiplication by .1 three times—that is, move the decimal point three places to the left.

Now, let's see how this information can be used to help us multiply other decimals. Consider the example .7 × .34:

$$.7 \times .34 = (.1 \times 7) \times (.01 \times 34)$$ We do not need the parentheses here.

$$= .1 \times .01 \times 7 \times 34$$ We can rearrange the numbers when multiplying.

We are left with a whole-number multiplication and three multiplications by. 1. We know how to multiply the whole numbers:

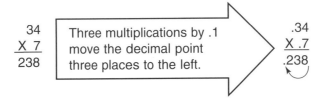

$$
\begin{array}{r}
34 \\
\times\ 7 \\
\hline
238
\end{array}
$$

Three multiplications by .1 move the decimal point three places to the left.

$$
\begin{array}{r}
.34 \\
\times\ .7 \\
\hline
.238
\end{array}
$$

From examples like this, the students should generalize that they multiply as if the numbers were whole numbers and then count the multiplications by .1 to place the decimal point.

After development of the rule, the students should test it by doing some examples and then using the area model for multiplication to verify that the rule does produce the correct results. For example, suppose we want to multiply 3.5 × 2.7. Using the rule, we get:

$$
\begin{array}{r}
3.5 \\
\times\ 2.7 \\
\hline
2\ 4\ 5 \\
7\ 0\ 0 \\
\hline
9.4\ 5
\end{array}
$$

Two multiplications by .1

Using the area model, we get:

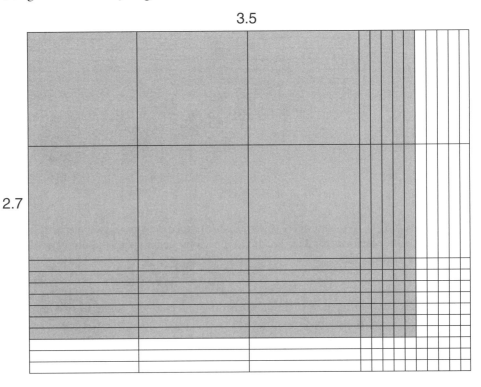

In the following piece, we have 6 ones—that is, (2 × 3) ones:

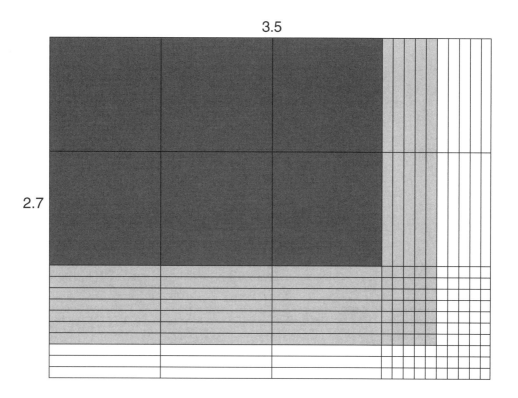

In the following piece, we have (2 × 5) tenths, or 10 tenths. That's the same as 1.

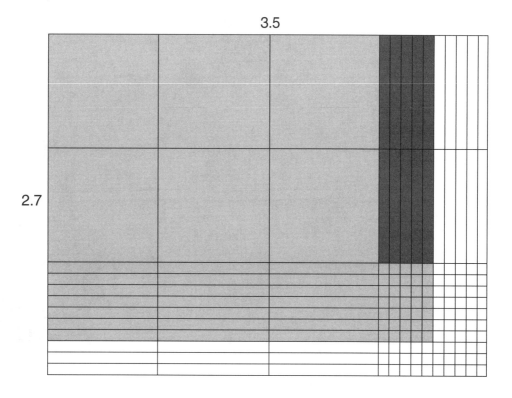

In the following piece, we have (7×3) tenths, or 21 tenths. That's the same as 2.1.

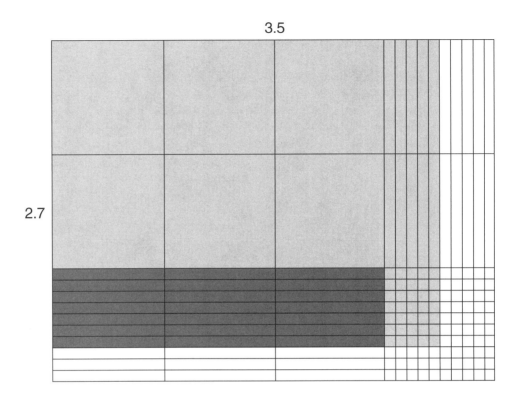

In the following piece, we have (7×5) hundredths, or 35 hundredths:

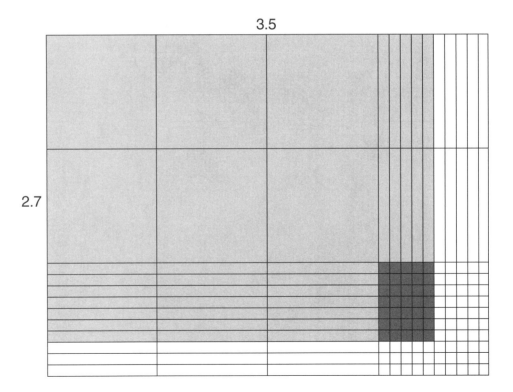

If we add these partial products together, we get:

$$
\begin{array}{r}
6. \\
1. \\
2.1 \\
.35 \\
\hline
9.45
\end{array}
$$

This is the same answer that was produced by applying the rule, which verifies that the rule did produce a correct answer. Two or three verifications like this thoroughly convince students that the rule is a quick, efficient, and correct way to get answers. The rule is meaningful because it was developed out of their own experiences. They used the model to verify that the rule is correct; they can literally see that their answers are correct. It will be viewed as an easy way to multiply decimals, so it will be perceived to be helpful, not just something that the teacher makes them do. They will be confident in the use of the rule. Retention will be outstanding. Remember that *it is always easier to remember things that are connected to other things that you know.*

Dividing Decimals

Division of decimals depends almost entirely on using the same two big ideas that were identified for division of whole numbers: *Divide one unit at a time* and *trade remainders for smaller units*. Compare these two divisions, one a division of a whole number by a whole number and the other a decimal by a whole number:

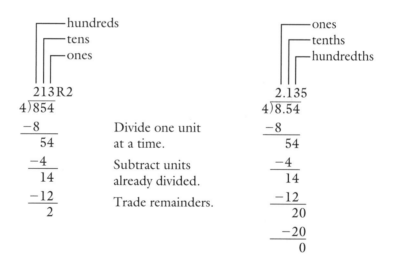

The procedures are precisely the same. The only difference is that there are some additional units. In the first example, we had a remainder of 2. There were 2 ones left over that could not be traded for smaller units because there were no smaller units. In the second example, the 2 hundredths that were left over could be traded for thousandths and then divided up.

Division of a decimal by a whole number is easy to teach. Using a physical model, we can demonstrate that the process is the same as for whole number division. Division by a decimal, however, is different. Division of a decimal by a whole number—for example, 4—can easily be modeled by separating the decimal units into four equal parts. Division by .4 cannot be modeled so easily. It does not make sense to separate decimal units into 4 tenths of an equal part. So, we need to develop a way to cope with decimal divisors.

Middle school students should see an interesting pattern that arises out of examples like these:

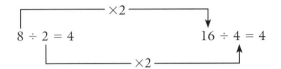

$$8 \div 2 = 4 \qquad\qquad 16 \div 4 = 4$$

$$45 \div 15 = 3 \qquad\qquad 9 \div 3 = 3$$

multiply by $\frac{1}{5}$

$$18 \div 9 = 2 \qquad\qquad 72 \div 36 = 2$$

multiply by 4

$$48 \div 16 = 3 \qquad\qquad 6 \div 2 = 3$$

divide by 8

When we multiply or divide both the divisor and the dividend by the same number, the quotient is unchanged. Sometimes division can be made much easier if we multiply or divide both the divisor and the dividend by the same number. For example, consider $450 \div 25$. If we multiply the divisor and the dividend by 4, we have $1800 \div 100$.

Division by 100 is easy. Instead of dividing $414 \div 18$, we can divide 414 and 18 by 2 and be left with $207 \div 9$. Division by a one-digit number is usually easier than division by a two-digit number.

This technique can be used to turn any decimal division example into a whole-number division example. The example, $8.21 \div .7$, can be changed to $821 \div 70$ when we multiply both the divisor and the dividend by 100. The example, $439 \div 3.6$, can be changed to $4390 \div 36$ when we multiply both the divisor and the dividend by 10. Likewise,

$2.7\overline{)4.98}$ can be changed to $27.\overline{)49.8}$ when we multiply by 10

$.36\overline{)21.8}$ can be changed to $36.\overline{)2180.}$ when we multiply by 100

We can change any division example with a decimal divisor into an example with a whole-number divisor:

$.23\overline{)6.9}$ To make the divisor in this example a whole number, we must multiply by 100. So, we will multiply both the divisor and the dividend by 100.

$.23\overline{)6.90}$ Multiplying by 100 moves the decimal point two places to the right.

$58.9\overline{)4.932}$ To make the divisor in this example a whole number, we must multiply by 10. So, we multiply both the divisor and the dividend by 10.

$58.9\overline{)4.932}$ We move the decimal point in both the divisor and the dividend one place to the right.

Multiplication and Division Activities

The following sequence of activities illustrates how a teacher can develop the decimal-multiplication and decimal-division concepts.

Activity 7.15   What's in the Box?

Write 4 × 23 on the board. Ask the students what it means. [23, four times] Have four students come forward and use bundled sticks to represent the number 23. Then have each of them put the number into a box. Ask the class how many 23s are in the box. [4] Next, ask who knows what is in the box altogether. How many ones are in the box? [12] Point out that is too many to write in the ones place. Ask what to do. [Make a trade.] Make the required trade and then ask how many ones are left in the box. [2] Ask how many tens are in the box after the trade. [9] Record the answer to the multiplication.

Write 3 × 1.62 on the board. Follow the same procedures to have the students find the answer. Use dollars, dimes, and pennies to model the decimal.

Repeat with 6 × 21.9, 2 × 3.76, and 7 × 5.8. Emphasize that multiplication of decimals is almost exactly like multiplication of whole numbers.

Activity 7.16   The Product Is the Area

Draw a rectangle on the board and label the sides 3 and 6. Sketch in the squares to show the area.

Remind the students that they can multiply the length times the width of the rectangle to get the area. Write the product, 3 × 6, on the rectangle.

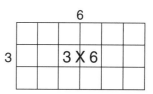

Draw another rectangle and label the sides 7 and n. Tell the students that n is the length of the side but you don't know what number n is equal to. Ask how they could find the area if they know what n is equal to. Label the interior of the rectangle with the product, 7 × n.

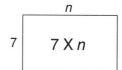

Show other rectangles and have the students tell what product will be equal to the area. Have them label the interiors of the rectangles with the products.

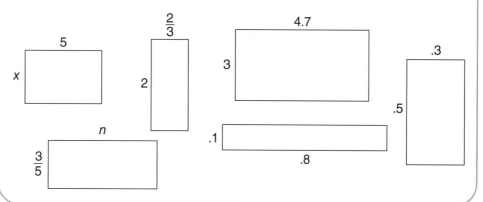

Activity 7.17 Area Match

Prepare pairs of cards with one card showing a rectangle with its sides labeled and the other showing the product of the two sides.

Pass out the cards to the students and have them find their partners.

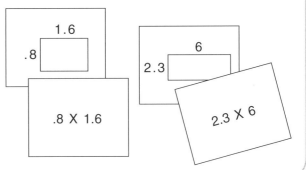

Activity 7.18 Easy Tenths

Use the area model shown at the right to demonstrate that .1 × 2 = .2

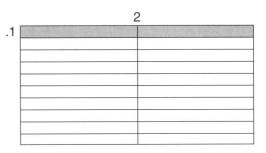

Use the following area model to demonstrate that .1 × 3.7 = .37:

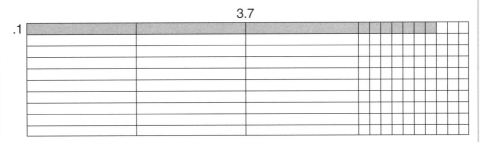

Repeat with .1 × 1.4 and .1 × 3.76. Ask what always happens when you multiply by .1. [The decimal point "moves" one place to the left.] Have the students tell what they think the answer to .1 × 4.5 will be. [.45] Use the area model to verify the answer.

Activity 7.19 More Easy Tenths

Write 46 × .1 on the board and then write "46 tenths" below it. Ask if these statements say the same thing. [Yes.] Next, write "40 tenths + 6 tenths." Ask if this is the same thing. [Yes.]

Ask what 10 tenths is equal to. [1] Ask what 40 tenths is equal to. [4] So, 46 tenths must be equal to 4 and 6 tenths. Write 46 × .1 = 4.6.

Write 92 × .1 and ask what is it equal to. If necessary, point out that 90 tenths is 9, so 90 tenths and 2 more tenths is 9 and 2 tenths. Write 92 × .1 = 9.2.

Ask for the answers to 74 × .1, 21 × .1, and 123 × .1.

Ask what always happens when someone multiplies by .1. [The decimal point moves one place to the left.]

Activity 7.20   Hundredths and Thousandths Are Easy, Too

Ask what always happens when someone multiplies by .1. [The decimal point moves one place to the left.] Write .1 × .1 on the board. Ask what the answer is. [.01] Write .1 × .1 = .01.

Point out that since .01 is the same as .1 × .1, multiplying by .01 is the same as multiplying by .1 twice. Write 86 × .01 = 86 × .1 × .1.

Ask again what always happens when someone multiplies by .1. [The decimal point moves one place to the left.] Ask what would happen if you multiplied by .1 twice. [The decimal point would move two places to the left.]

Write 86 × .01 and ask for the answer. [.86] Ask for the answers to 235 × .01, 45.3 × .01, and 7.98 × .01.

Write .1 × .1 × .1 and ask for the answer. [.001] Write 86.3 × .001 = 86.3 × .1 × .1 × .1. Point out that multiplying by .001 is the same as multiplying by .1 three times. So, the student would move the decimal point three places to the left.

Write 86.3 × .001 and ask for the answer. [.0863] Ask for the answers to 235 × .001, 4.53 × .001, and 79.8 × .001.

Activity 7.21   Two-Step Multiplication

Write 23 × 4.5 on the board. Then rewrite the multiplication as 23 × 45 × .1.

Ask if this is the same thing. Why? [Yes, because 45 × .1 equals 4.5.] Have the students multiply 23 × 45 and then multiply the answer by .1. Remind them that when you multiply by .1, the decimal point moves one place to the left.

Write 35 × 2.14 and then rewrite it as 35 × 214 × .01. Ask if they are equal. Why? Have the students multiply 35 × 214 and then multiply the answer by .01. Remind them that when you multiply by .01, that's the same as multiplying by .1 twice, so the decimal point moves two places to the left.

Write 37 × 3.9 and have the students find the answer. Remind them that they can multiply as though the numbers are whole numbers and then move the decimal point. *Multiply and then place the decimal point.*

Then have them do 21 × .64, 1.36 × 45, and 24 × .061.

Activity 7.22   More Two-Step Multiplication

Write 2.3 × 4.5 on the board. Then rewrite the multiplication as 23 × .1 × 45 × .1. Ask if this is the same thing. Why? Ask how to rearrange the numbers so that you end up with a whole-number multiplication and multiplications by .1. [23 × 45 × .1 × .1] Have the students multiply 23 × 45 and then multiply the answer twice by .1. Remind them that when you multiply by .1, the decimal point moves one place to the left. Since there are two multiplications by .1, the decimal point moves two places to the left.

Write 3.5 × 2.14 and ask what two whole numbers are multiplied. [35 and 214] Ask how many multiplications by .1 there are. [3] Remind them that each multiplication by .1 moves the decimal point one place to the left.

Write 3.7 × 3.9 and have the students find an answer. Remind them that they can multiply as though the numbers are whole numbers and then move the decimal point. *Multiply and then place the decimal point.*

Also have them do .21 × .64, 1.36 × 4.5, and 2.4 × .061.

Activity 7.23 Get the Point?

Have the students work with partners. Each pair of partners should have a calculator. Give them a list of decimal-multiplication examples. The partners should take turns using the calculator.

For each example, one partner uses the calculator to multiply the related whole numbers. (For example, if the example is 2.76×5.4, the student multiplies 276×54.) Then the other partner writes the product on a sheet of paper and places the decimal point in the correct position. Finally, the first partner uses the calculator to multiply the original decimals to check the answer.

The partners should then switch roles and continue until all the examples have been completed.

Activity 7.24 Dividing Is Dividing

Tell the students that you want to review division. Write $4\overline{)856}$ on the board. Have a student come forward and use base-10 blocks to represent the number 856. Ask how many equal parts we are to divide this number into. [4] Work through the example, separating the number into four equal parts. Record the steps as you go. Emphasize that you *divide one unit at a time* and *trade remainders for smaller units*.

Then, beside the first division example, write $4\overline{)8.56}$. Have someone come forward and use dollars, dimes, and pennies to represent the number 8.56. Work through this example, separating the number into four equal parts. Record each step. Emphasize that you *divide one unit at a time* and *trade remainders for smaller units*.

Point out how decimal division is like whole-number division.

Next, do the two examples $5\overline{)657}$ and $5\overline{)65.7}$. The first has a remainder of 2 ones. In the second example, you also have a remainder, this time 2 tenths. Point out that when you are working with decimals, there are always smaller units to trade for. In the first example, 2 ones can be traded for 20 tenths, which can be separated into five equal parts. In the second example, the 2 tenths (dimes) can be traded for 20 hundredths (pennies), which can be separated into five equal parts.

Activity 7.25 Same Answer

Write $18 \div 3$ on the board and ask for the answer. Record that answer.

Then ask what you get if you multiply 18 by 3. What if you multiply 3 by 3? Record these new numbers below the 18 and the 3.

$$18 \div 3 = 6$$
$$\times 3 \quad \times 3$$
$$54 \div 9$$
$$54 \div 9 = 6$$

Have the students divide 54 by 9. Be sure that they notice that the answer is the same as the answer to the original example.

Do other examples in the same way. Start with $14 \div 2$. Multiply by 5 to get $70 \div 10$. Find both answers. The answers are the same.

Start with $280 \div 35$. Multiply by 2 to get $560 \div 70$. Have the students compute the answer to $280 \div 35$. [8] Ask them to give the answer to $560 \div 70$ without computing.

Activity 7.26   Making Division Easier

Write 135 ÷ 5 on the board. Then tell the class that you are going to multiply both numbers by 2. Write 270 ÷ 10 directly below the original example. Ask the students what they know about the answers to these two divisions. [They are the same.] Ask which division they would rather do.

Write 144 ÷ 18 on the board. Then tell the class that you want to multiply both numbers by $\frac{1}{2}$. Ask what the new numbers would be. [72 and 9] Write the new division, 72 ÷ 9. Ask the students what they know about the answers to these two divisions. [They are the same.] Ask which division they would rather do.

Tell the students that you can sometimes make division easier if you multiply both the divisor and the dividend by the same number.

Write 112 ÷ 16 on the board. Have the students suggest what we could multiply by to get an easier problem. Try out each suggestion to see if it gives an easier division. [Some good numbers to multiply by are 5 and $\frac{1}{2}$.]

Activity 7.27   Always Divide by a Whole Number

Write $2\overline{)68.96}$ on the board. Remind the students that this means that they are to divide 68.96 into two equal parts. Write $6\overline{)7.38}$ and remind them that means they are to divide 7.38 into six equal parts. Write $.2\overline{)3.406}$ and ask what this means. Point out that they cannot divide 3.406 into two tenths of an equal part. That doesn't make sense.

Remind the class that they can sometimes change a hard division into an easier one by multiplying both the divisor and the dividend by the same number. Ask what number they could multiply by to change the divisor into a whole number. [Possible answers are 5, 10, . . .] Choose 10, because multiplication by 10 is easy. Multiply the divisor and the dividend by 10 to change the division to $2\overline{)34.06}$.

Also do $.9\overline{)34}$. Multiply by 10 to change the division to $9\overline{)340}$. Do $.12\overline{)6.092}$. Multiply by 100 to change the division to $12\overline{)609.2}$. Do $4.32\overline{).7592}$. Multiply by 10 to change the division to $432\overline{)7.592}$. Do $.024\overline{)1.92}$. Multiply by 1000 to change the division to $24\overline{)1920}$.

Fraction Comparison Revisited

Recall that one big idea—*always compare like units*—was identified for comparison. To compare unlike fractions (fractions with different denominators), we normally rename the fractions using a common denominator. Then the comparison is easy. If there are several fractions to compare, finding a common denominator is more complicated. But we must still rename the fractions using the same unit. It is possible to decide ahead of time what fractional unit (denominator) you will use and then "force" the fractional quantities into those units. For example, suppose you decide to compare three fractions using the fractional unit thirds. Suppose, further, that the fractions are the following:

$$\frac{1}{2} \qquad \frac{3}{4} \qquad \frac{2}{3}$$

The last of these fractions is already in thirds. You need to rename the other two fractions in thirds. Begin by multiplying numerator and denominator of each of these fractions by 3:

$$\frac{1 \times 3}{2 \times 3} = \frac{3}{6} \qquad \frac{3 \times 3}{4 \times 3} = \frac{9}{12}$$

Then divide the numerator and denominator of each fraction by the original denominator:

$$\frac{3 \div 2}{6 \div 2} = \frac{1.5}{3} \qquad \frac{9 \div 4}{12 \div 4} = \frac{2.25}{3}$$

You now have three fractions, all named in thirds, and any comparison that the students want to make is easy:

$$\frac{1.5}{3} \qquad \frac{2.25}{3} \qquad \frac{2}{3}$$

Let's look at another example. This time, rename all the fractions in fifths:

$$\frac{1}{2} \qquad \frac{1}{4} \qquad \frac{3}{8}$$

Multiply the numerator and the denominator by 5:

$$\frac{1 \times 5}{2 \times 5} = \frac{5}{10} \qquad \frac{1 \times 5}{4 \times 5} = \frac{5}{20} \qquad \frac{3 \times 5}{8 \times 5} = \frac{15}{40}$$

Then divide the numerator and the denominator by the original denominator:

$$\frac{5 \div 2}{10 \div 2} = \frac{2.5}{5} \qquad \frac{5 \div 4}{20 \div 4} = \frac{1.25}{5} \qquad \frac{15 \div 8}{40 \div 8} = \frac{1.875}{5}$$

The resulting fractions are all in fifths.

Or, rename unlike fractions using the fractional unit hundredths. Multiply both the numerator and the denominator by 100 and then divide the numerator and the denominator by the original denominator:

$$\frac{5 \times 100}{8 \times 100} = \frac{500 \div 8}{800 \div 8} = \frac{62.5}{100}$$

$$\frac{3 \times 100}{5 \times 100} = \frac{300 \div 5}{500 \div 5} = \frac{60}{100}$$

$$\frac{2 \times 100}{3 \times 100} = \frac{200 \div 3}{300 \div 3} = \frac{66.666\ldots}{100}$$

Defining Percent

The numerators of fractions with a denominator of 100 are called *percents*. Seventeen percent of a quantity is precisely the same as 17 hundredths of that quantity. The symbol for percent is %:

$$24\% = .24 = \frac{24}{100}$$

$$273\% = 2.73 = \frac{273}{100} = 2\frac{73}{100}$$

$$.7\% = \frac{.7}{100} = \frac{7}{1000}$$

Adapting a Lesson on Decimals

Next, we examine a lesson plan that follows suggestions that might be found in the teacher's guide of an elementary school mathematics program. Note that it is a good plan. However, it does have some weaknesses that are typical of traditional lesson plans for teaching elementary school mathematics. Notice that:

1. The focus is on teaching the textbook pages.
2. The developmental part of the lesson is minimal.
3. A large amount of practice using the rule for placement of the decimal point is recommended.

Note that when there is a minimum of development, a maximum of practice is always required.

LESSON OBJECTIVE

The learner will multiply a decimal by a whole number.

Lesson Opener

Have students find each of these products:

$$8 \times 7 \qquad 6 \times 13 \qquad 16 \times 14 \qquad 28 \times 34$$

Ask: "If your grandmother gave you $2.10 every week for 3 weeks, how much money would she have given you?" Use dollar bills and dimes to show $2.10 three times. Count the money to see how much she would have given.

Development

Direct the students' attention to the first page of the lesson. Have them read problem 1. Tell them to look at the money in the picture. This is what Mrs. Sanchez paid Lucita on Monday. Ask how many days Lucita worked for Mrs. Sanchez. [3] Ask how much money Lucita was paid on Tuesday and how much she was paid on Friday. Point out that since she was paid the same amount all 3 days, multiplication can be used to find how much she was paid altogether. Write the multiplication. Complete the multiplication steps.

$6.24	2 decimal places
× 3	0 decimal places
$18.72	2 decimal places

Point out that the number of decimal places in the answer is the same as the number of decimal places in the multiplicand. Lead the class through a similar discussion of problem 2. Point out that in both problems the number of decimal places in the answer is the same as the number of decimal places in the multiplicand.

Monitoring Learning

Have everyone do the four *Check Understanding* examples. Have students who are having difficulty imagine money for the decimal.

Practice

Ask the students to complete the 48 examples on the practice page. Remind them to place the decimal point. Have them think about correct placement of the decimal point.

Closure

At the end of math time, remind the children that they have learned how to multiply a decimal by a whole number.

Now, we will adapt this lesson to increase the amount and depth of the developmental part of the lesson. To do this, we will make the lesson more visual and more kinesthetic, make assessment a continual process that provides feedback about the effectiveness of instruction while that instruction is going on, and increase communication about what is being learned from the students and among the students. These adaptations make the lesson appropriate for almost all students. But, remember that some students with severe needs may require further instructional adaptations.

LESSON OBJECTIVE

The student will multiply a decimal by a whole number.

Lesson Opener

Group students with partners and have each set of partners find the first of these products:

$$6 \times 13 \qquad 28 \times 34$$

When they have finished, have them exchange their work with another set of partners, who check their work for accuracy. If the two sets of partners disagree about whether the work of either set is correct, they should discuss the steps in the computation to resolve their differences. Then have the partners do the second example. **Monitor understanding.** As the sets of partners are working, carefully observe to identify individuals who do not seem to understand how to do the multiplication. Have the sets of partners that include those individuals use a base-10 model, such as base-10 blocks or bundled sticks, so that they can see what is happening in the multiplication.

Ask, "If your grandmother gave you $2.10 every week for 3 weeks, how much money would she have given you?" Using dollar bills and dimes, have three students come forward and show $2.10. Have these three students combine the money to show how much she would have given in 3 weeks. Have the class tell you, step by step, how to figure out how much money there is. Have a student count the money to check the answer. **Monitor understanding.** Carefully observe those students who had difficulty with the two preceding multiplication examples. Be sure they understand the process.

Development

Ask the class, "If you put some rocks, some crayons, and some paper clips into an empty box, who can tell me what would be in the box?" [Some rocks, some crayons, and some paper clips] Emphasize that the only things that could be in the box would be those things that were put into it. Place 10 rocks, a box of crayons, and a box of paper clips on the desk. Write "2 rocks, 5 crayons, and 3 paper clips" on the board. Have a student come to the front and place those objects into an empty box. Ask what is in the box. Empty the box.

Write $\times$ 3 under the list of objects on the chalkboard:

$$\begin{array}{r} 2 \text{ rocks, 5 crayons, and 3 paper clips} \\ \underline{\times\ 3} \end{array}$$

Have each of three students come forward and place 2 rocks, 5 crayons, and 3 paper clips in the box. Then ask the class what is in the box. [6 rocks, 15 crayons, and 9 paper clips] Emphasize that 2 rocks were placed in the box three times, 5 crayons were placed in the box three times, and 3 paper clips were placed in the box 3 times.

Write this multiplication example on the board. Remind the class that we can use money to represent decimals. Ask how you could use the money to show the decimal 3.82. [3 dollars, 8 dimes, and 2 pennies] Have a student come forward and represent the number 3.82 two times. Have the student

$$\begin{array}{r} 3.82 \\ \underline{\times\ 2} \end{array}$$

place the two representations of the number together in a box. Ask what is in the box altogether. Emphasize that since 3.82 was placed in the box two times, each part of that number was placed in the box two times. Two hundredths were placed in the box two times. Eight tenths were placed in the box two times, and 3 ones were placed in the box two times. Have someone count the money in the box to check the answer. He or she will need to trade the 10 extra tenths for a one. **Monitor understanding.** Continue to observe individuals who do not understand. Be sure to involve them in the procedures.

Following the same steps, lead the class through 6×2.37. For this example, emphasize that since we put ones, tenths, and hundredths into the box, that's what we will find in the box. We just have to decide how many of each there are altogether. Point out further that when there are too many to write, we trade for larger units. **Monitor understanding.** Continue to observe to identify individuals who are having difficulty understanding. Provide extra help as it is needed.

Direct the students' attention to the first page of the lesson. Have them read problem 1. Tell them to look at the money in the picture. This is what Mrs. Sanchez paid Lucita on Monday. Ask how many days Lucita worked for Mrs. Sanchez. [3] Ask how much money Lucita was paid on Tuesday and how much she was paid on Friday. Point out that since she was paid the same amount all 3 days, multiplication can be used to find how much she was paid altogether. Write the multiplication. Complete the multiplication steps. Point out the relationship between fractional parts of the multiplicand and the product.

$$
\begin{array}{rl}
\$\ 6.24 & \text{tenths and hundredths} \\
\underline{\times\ 3} & \\
\$18.72 & \text{tenths and hundredths}
\end{array}
$$

Point out that because both the multiplicand and the product include tenths and hundredths, both numbers have two decimal places.

Lead the class through a similar discussion of problem 2. Point out again that the number of decimal places in the answer is the same as the number of decimal places in the multiplicand. **Monitor understanding.** Continue to observe as these two problems are completed to identify individuals who are having difficulty understanding. Provide extra help as it is needed.

Monitoring Learning

Pair students with partners. Have one of the partners do the first *Check Understanding* example. That student should explain to the partner what is being done and why at each step. For each new example, the partners should switch roles, taking turns working out the solution. While the partners are working, move around the room to monitor their work. Have students who are having difficulty use money to help them visualize multiplication of the decimal. Remind them that the answer will have the same fractional units as the multiplicand (hence the same number of decimal places).

Practice

From the 48 examples on the practice page, choose 4 representative examples and assign them for practice. Be sure that at least 1 example requires no regrouping (trading), at least 1 requires regrouping (trading) once, and at least 1 requires regrouping (trading) twice.

Remind the students that you want every example to be correct. Tell them that you have the answers on a sheet of paper on your desk. Have them come to your desk when they are finished and check their answers. If they have errors, have them show their work to another student and have that person help them find and correct the error.

Monitoring Learning

While the students are working to correct their problems, move around the room to monitor the discussions and provide help as needed.

Closure

Near the end of math time, ask the students what kind of multiplication they learned to do today. [They have learned how to multiply a decimal by a whole number.]

Follow-Up

Identify an example from the practice page that requires regrouping (trading) one time. For homework, have the students explain to their parents (or some other older person) how to do the example. Tell them to have that person sign the paper and indicate whether or not the explanation was clear.

Using Decimals to Solve Problems

When teaching problem solving using decimals, teachers should apply the same basic principles as when they teach problem solving using other kinds of numbers. The teacher should emphasize that the choice of operation depends on what is happening to the quantities in the problem. For example, if quantities are being combined, then addition can probably be used. If the number names of the quantities are decimals, then those decimals should be added. If the quantities in the problem are being separated into equal parts, then division can probably be used. If the number names of the quantities are decimals, then those decimals should be divided.

As previously noted in Chapter 6, a current instructional emphasis for problem solving in mathematics is developing and providing experience using a wide variety of problem-solving strategies. We have already seen examples using the following strategies:

Solve part of the problem.
Separate the problem into easier parts.
Work backward.
Use a picture or diagram.
Use a table.

We now examine a problem appropriate for children at about the fifth-grade level. The solution employs one of the strategies demonstrated in Chapter 6 (use a table), and it also uses three additional strategies: *Solve a simpler problem, try and check* (sometimes called *trial and error*), and *list the possibilities*.

Juan works at a small store in the mall called "Nuts to You." The store normally sells nuts by the scoop. The price is listed for one scoop of each kind of nuts. For the Christmas season, the store decided to sell prepackaged nuts at $3.00 per package. Juan was asked to figure out how many different mixtures there would be that would sell for $3.00 each if the mixtures were made by combining full scoops of different kinds of nuts.

Price per Scoop	
Peanuts	$ .25
Walnuts	.50
Almonds	.75
Cashews	1.00
Pecans	1.25

We begin by solving several simpler problems. First, suppose the package contained only peanuts. How many scoops would it take?

Since each scoop of peanuts costs 25 cents, the package would have to include 12 scoops of peanuts.

A second simpler problem is: If Juan made a mixture of cashews and peanuts but included only one scoop of cashews, how many scoops of peanuts would be needed?

Since one scoop of cashews costs $1.00, Juan needs to include enough peanuts to make up the other $2.00. The package would have to include eight scoops of peanuts.

A third simpler problem might be: Suppose Juan included two scoops of cashews. In how many different ways could he complete the package?

Since two scoops of cashews costs $2.00, Juan needs to include enough nuts to make up the other $1.00. This can be done in several ways. Juan could use four scoops of peanuts. Juan could use two scoops of walnuts. Juan could use one scoop of almonds and one scoop of peanuts. Juan could use one scoop of walnuts and two scoops of peanuts.

As we discover the different ways to make a $3.00 package of mixed nuts, we need to have an organized way to keep track of the information. To do this, we use a table something like the following one. By *try*ing out different combinations *and check*ing how much each would cost, we can finally arrive at the solution to the problem. There are 46 possibilities.

Pecans $1.25	Cashews $1.00	Almonds $.75	Walnuts $.50	Peanuts $.25
2	0	0	1	0
2	0	0	0	2
1	1	1	0	0
1	1	0	1	1
1	1	0	0	3
1	0	2	0	1
1	0	1	2	0
1	0	1	1	2
1	0	0	3	1

Exercises and Activities

1. Placement of the decimal point during multiplication of decimals can be taught by using the following fractions approach:

$$3.5 \times 2.7 = \frac{35}{10} \times \frac{27}{10} = \frac{35 \times 27}{10 \times 10}$$

This approach depends on students' understanding that division by 10 moves the decimal point one place to the left. Develop an instructional sequence to teach students that division by 10 moves the decimal point one place to the left.

2. Develop an instructional sequence to show the meaning of percents as described in this chapter. Include visuals and kinesthetic activity.

3. Develop an instructional sequence to teach students how to find percents equivalent to given fractions or decimals.

4. Develop an instructional sequence to teach children how to change percents like $\frac{1}{2}\%$, $\frac{3}{4}\%$, or $\frac{5}{8}\%$ to decimals.

5. Complete the preceding table to verify the number of $3.00 mixtures of nuts.

6. Choose a lesson on decimals or percents from a published elementary school mathematics textbook series.

   a. Write a lesson plan that follows the teaching suggestions in the teacher's guide.

   b. Identify parts of the lesson that include student communication about the concept(s) or skill(s) taught in the lesson. Add to the lesson more opportunities for communication from or among students.

   c. Identify the parts of the lesson designed to assess the learning of the students. Add more continual assessment (monitoring of learning) to the lesson plan.

   d. Adapt the lesson plan by adding concept and/or skill development and by adding more kinesthetic activity.

7. Suppose you have a student who thinks that $\frac{1}{4}\%$ is equal to 0.25. Use the definition of percent that is given in this chapter to develop an explanation of why $\frac{1}{4}\% = 0.0025$.

8. Pose this problem for a sixth-grade class.

   Friends are coming to visit and watch a football game. You want to make a snack that requires cheese, salsa, and tortilla chips. The cheese costs $3.99, the salsa costs $1.69, and the chips cost $3.49. There is a 9.72% tax on the groceries. Can you buy what you need with a $10 gift card?

   a. Plan a step-by-step teacher-led solution of the problem.
   b. What questions would you ask as you lead the class to the solution?

9. Pose this problem for a seventh-grade class.

   A store is having a sale on several items of clothing. Jeans that originally cost $28.99 are marked down 20%. Sweaters that originally cost $30.99 are marked down 33%. There is also a sales tax of 6.25%. Can you buy a pair of jeans and a shirt with a $50 gift card?

   a. Plan a step-by-step teacher-led solution of the problem.
   b. What questions would you ask as you lead the class to the solution?

References and Related Readings

Bennett, A. B., & Nelson, L. T. (1994). A conceptual model for solving percent problems. *Mathematics Teaching in the Middle School, 1,* 20–25.

Thornton, C. A., Tucker, B. F., Dossey, J. A., & Bazik, E. F. (1983). *Teaching mathematics to children with special needs.* Menlo Park, CA: Addison-Wesley.

Websites

www.corestandards.org/the-standards/mathematics
The Common Core State Standards for Mathematics can be found at this site.

www.mathforum.org/
Math forum links to math discussions and ideas.

http://mathforum.org/library/topics/fractions/
Links to decimal and fraction sites.

eight

MEASUREMENT

Assigning a Number to a Quantity

Measurement and Geometry

This text deals with measurement and geometry separately. However, the middle school mathematics curriculum typically integrates these two content areas. In fact, middle school geometry content can hardly be discussed without continual references to measurements of some sort. This chapter shows how measurement concepts are developed. More-advanced measurement concepts depend on understanding and use of more-advanced geometric concepts.

Defining Measurement

Before discussing the teaching of measurement, we first consider the meaning of measurement. We measure many different kinds of things, including the size of a set of objects, the length of an object, the capacity of a container, the value of an object, or the likelihood of an occurrence. Not only are the things we measure different, but also the processes used to measure them vary from type to type. But, in every case, we are assigning a number to some quantity. In fact, this is precisely what measurement is: *Measurement* is the process of assigning a number to a quantity.

For example, suppose there is a set of children consisting of Ann, Mark, Carlos, Denise, Tyler, and Morgan. A set of children has many attributes that can be measured. We might be interested in how intelligent the group of children is. We might be interested in how long the group is if the individuals were laid end to end. We might be interested in how heavy the group is. We might be interested in how fast the group can run. We might be interested in how nice the children are. All of these things can be measured by assigning a number to the group that represents the attribute being measured. Frequently when a set of objects is being measured, the attribute that we are most interested in is the "numerousness" of the set: How many objects are in the set? In this case, how many children are in the group? If we count the children in the group, we find that there are six. The number that tells how many is 6. We have measured the set.

An important idea in all measurement is the notion of *unit*. When we measure the set of children, the unit is *child*. To find the size of the set, we count to see how many units there are (that is, we count to see how many *children* there are) in the set. The unit of measurement used to measure the set of children is an example of a direct unit. In non-formal language, a *direct unit* is a piece of the attribute that is being measured. When measuring with direct units, we count how many of those units are contained in the thing being measured.

The Piagetian concept of conservation is another consideration when teaching measurement. *Conservation*, as a prenumber mathematical concept, typically involves children experiencing the notion that a quantity does not change when it is spread out or rearranged, as long as nothing is added or removed from the quantity. This awareness supports the important understanding that there are many ways to name a given quantity. For example, when considering the measurement concept of area, students can rearrange a complex figure into several simpler figures and be confident that the area of the resulting figures is the same as the original figure.

In addition to a more complete understanding of conservation, an intentional awareness of precision, as it relates to measurement, is important for students to recognize. *Precision* depends on the size of the unit used to measure. It can be improved by using smaller units to measure. The smaller the unit, the more precise the measurement will be. For example, when measuring a pencil, a child might recognize that the pencil is less than a foot long. However, a more precise measurement would be to identify it as being 6 inches long.

Measuring Length

Length is measured in direct units. For example, when we measure the length of a desk, we decide on a unit of length (a piece of length) and figure out how many of those units equals the length of the desk. If we decide to use a crayon as the unit of length, we lay crayons end to end on top of the desk to see how many crayons equals the length of the desk.

The length is 11, 11 crayons.

When a measurement is communicated to another person, there must be agreement regarding the unit that is used to make the measurement. Furthermore, the process of agreeing on the length of the units is called the *standardization of the units*.

The following key ideas related to the measurement of length should be emphasized:

- **When a length is being communicated, the number is meaningless without the unit**. The length of an object might be 2 pencils long or it might be 8 paper clips long. If one object has a length of 3 and another object has a length of 7, we do not know which is longer unless we know which units were used to measure the two objects.

- **The number of units depends on the size of the unit.** If we use a short unit to measure the length of something, it will take more units than if we use a longer unit.

Whatever system of standard units of length is to be used (whether it be inches, feet, and miles or centimeters, meters, and kilometers) it can be effectively taught by following these five steps:

1. **Justify the need for the system of standard units**. This is best accomplished by stressing the need for clear communication of measurements.

2. **Develop mental imagery for each unit**. Students should be able to show a reasonable approximation of each unit. This step is essential if they are to have any success in estimating lengths.

3. **Help students develop the ability to estimate lengths using each of the units**.

4. **Aid students in discovering, understanding, and learning the relationships among the units within the system**.

5. **Help students become familiar with and proficient in the use of measurement tools that make use of the units in the system.** Examples of such tools include 12-inch rulers, yardsticks, meter sticks, and tape measures.

The most common mistake made in teaching length measurement is to begin with the fifth step without spending sufficient time on the previous four steps. Emphasizing steps 1 through 4 helps students become proficient in (1) using measurement both inside and outside the classroom, (2) completing measurement exercises, and (3) in solving problems that involve measurement. This emphasis allows students to gain such proficiency in both common and unusual settings as well as when the need to measure is anticipated and when unexpected needs require measurement or estimation.

If measurements are made with measuring tools that provide clear imagery of the unit being used, that mental imagery can then be used to make subsequent estimates. The activity provides immediate feedback on the accuracy of each estimate, which allows students to make corrections in their mental imagery before making the next estimate. Accuracy of estimates typically improves dramatically. Effective estimation activities typically follow these four steps:

1. An object is identified.
2. The measurement is estimated.
3. The length is measured to check the estimate.
4. Another object is identified.

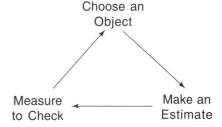

Measuring Area

Area is different from length in that we do not, for the most part, actually measure area. In most cases, we measure some combination of lengths and use them in a formula to compute the area. So, the study of area can be separated into two parts. The first part consists of developing the concepts of *area* and *unit of area* and using the units to determine the area. The second part consists of the development of the area formulas. Problem solving, using the level of understanding and skill that has been developed, is found throughout.

A coherent development of area concept would follow these four steps:

- The *concept of area* should be developed first by making gross comparisons of the areas of different objects.

- The *concept of a unit of area* as a piece of area should be developed.

- The *concept of measurement of area* as the number of units it takes to cover the area being measured should be developed. Mental imagery for the units should be developed. Students should be able to show a reasonable approximation of the unit.

- Students should develop the *ability to estimate areas* using each of the units.

Although we provide a brief development here, creating teaching and learning activities for developing area concepts is left as exercises for the reader.

Comparisons of area are more complex than comparisons of length. When comparing areas, we must take into account length, width, and shape. When the following shapes are compared, children have very little problem deciding which has the bigger area. Shape B is bigger in every way. Students would probably choose shape B even if they did not know what area is:

The next two shapes are considerably more difficult because one shape is longer but the other is wider. This forces the child to think beyond one dimension:

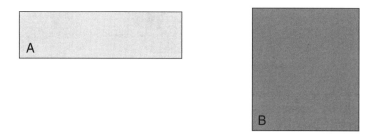

An appropriate way to check the comparison is to cut shape A into parts and rearrange them. Then it can easily be seen that B has a bigger area than A does:

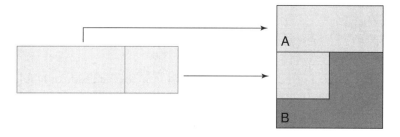

The next pair of figures is even more difficult because, in addition to length and width, the shapes of the figures have an impact on their areas:

Once again, by cutting and rearranging one of the figures, we can easily check the comparison. Figure C has the greater area:

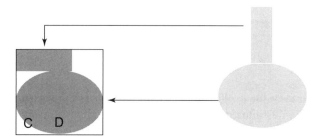

As figures get more complex in shape, look-see comparisons become more difficult, and so we need to introduce the use of units to help with the comparisons. A good way to start is to have students cover the shapes with some common objects, like pennies, in order to help with the comparisons. We want to see how many pennies can be placed inside each shape. We do not want any to go outside the boundary of the shape. Fourteen pennies are required to cover Figure A, and 18 pennies are required for Figure B. This can help us to decide that Figure B has the greater area:

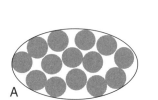 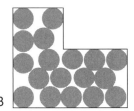

This process breaks down with complex shapes. Consider the following two figures. We can place seven pennies on Figure C but only six pennies on Figure D. But does figure C really have the greater area?

 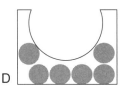

The student will quickly point out that more of the inside of D is left uncovered. The problem is that the pennies do not fit together well. There is space between them that does not get counted. We need to use a unit with a shape that *tessellates* (a shape that fits together with copies of itself without any space in between). Among the many shapes that tessellate are a triangle, a parallelogram, a hexagon, and a plus sign:

Although there is value in allowing students to explore the measurement of area with the tessellating units just illustrated, the majority of student time should be spent using *square units* of area. These are the units that are commonly used in area-computation formulas. When introducing students to the use of square units, emphasize that the area of a figure is the number of square units it takes to cover the inside of the figure:

The area of this figure is 12 square units.

To cover this area, we use 12 whole squares and 3 half squares. Altogether, the area is $13\frac{1}{2}$ square units.

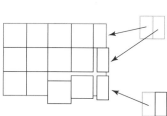

After students are comfortable measuring areas by placing and counting squares, area-computation formulas can be taught. The first of these is the area formula for rectangles. This formula can be developed from a series of discoveries made when the students are placing squares on rectangles and determining how many squares there are.

First, because rectangles are the same length from the bottom all the way to the top, every row of squares contains the same number of squares:

In this rectangle, every row has six squares. We can find the total number of squares by multiplying the number in each row times the number of rows.

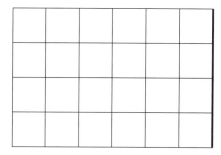

Area = 6 X 4 = 24 squares

In this rectangle, there are three rows of five squares. The area is $5 \times 3 = 15$ square units.

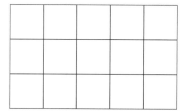

In this rectangle, there are six squares in the first row, so there must be six squares in every row. There are three rows. The area is $6 \times 3 = 18$ square units.

So, we see that we can compute the area by multiplying the number of squares in each row times the number of rows:

Area of rectangle = Number of squares in each row × Number of rows

Second, if the length and width of the rectangle are given in inches and the area units are square inches, then the number of squares in the first row is the same as the length of the rectangle. The length of this rectangle is 8 inches, so 8 square inches fit in the first row:

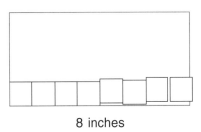

8 inches

Third, if the width is given in inches and the area units are square inches, then the number of rows is the same as the width:

The width of this rectangle is 4 inches, so the area will be four rows of square inches.

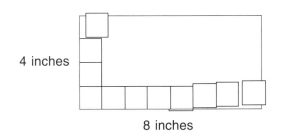

4 inches

8 inches

The formula for the *area of a rectangle* can then be written as:

Area = Length of the rectangle × Width of the rectangle

or   A = L × W

The Big Idea for Developing Area Formulas

There is one big idea that constantly recurs as the area-computation formulas are developed. This big idea is related to the concept of conservation of area: The amount of area is not changed if the area is rearranged. So, *when we have a figure for which there is no area formula, we rearrange the shape to get a figure for which we have an area formula.* This big idea is used to develop the rest of the area-computation formulas.

We now examine how we can rearrange the areas of several common shapes to find the areas. First, consider a parallelogram. We call the base of the parallelogram *b* and call the height *h*:

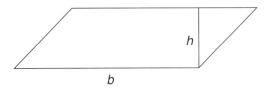

We do not have a formula for area of a parallelogram, but we do have a formula for area of a rectangle. We rearrange the area of the parallelogram into the shape of a rectangle. First, we cut one end of the parallelogram off, leaving square corners:

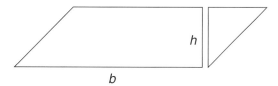

Then we move the piece that we cut off to the other end:

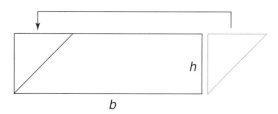

We now have a rectangle with length b and width h. The area of this rectangle is $A = b \times h$, where b is the length of the original parallelogram and h is its height. But this is also the area of the parallelogram because we did not add or take away any area. We just rearranged the area. The *area of a parallelogram* is:

$$A = b \times h$$

Next, we consider a triangle. The base of this triangle is b and its height is h:

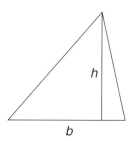

We do not have a formula for area of a triangle, but we do have formulas for areas of rectangles and parallelograms. We need to rearrange the area into the shape of either a rectangle or a parallelogram. To accomplish this, we begin by making a copy of the triangle. When we have done this, we will have twice as much area as we started with:

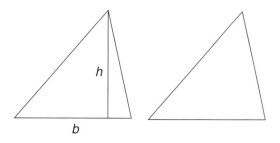

We then rotate the copy and place it on the other side of the original triangle:

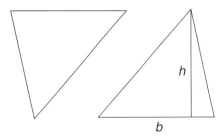

Then we join the two triangles together to form a parallelogram. The area of this parallelogram is A = $b \times h$, where b is the base of the original triangle and h is the height of the original triangle:

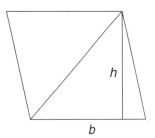

But, remember that because we included a copy of the original triangle, we have twice the original area. To get the actual area, we multiply by $\frac{1}{2}$. The formula for the *area of a triangle*, then, is:

$$A = \tfrac{1}{2} \times b \times h$$

Now, consider a trapezoid. Trapezoids have two bases, which are parallel sides. The height is the distance between the bases. We label the bases b_1 and b_2 and label the height h:

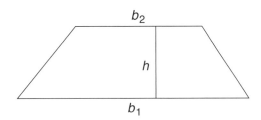

As we did with the triangle, we copy the trapezoid. Remember that this doubles the area:

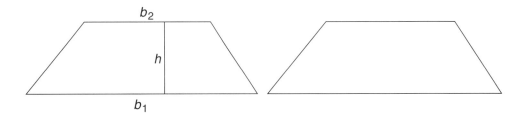

We rotate the copy and join it to the original trapezoid. Together, the two trapezoids form a parallelogram:

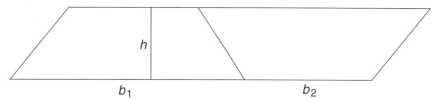

We can find the area of this parallelogram by multiplying the base times the height: $A = (b_1 + b_2) \times h$.

But, remember that we doubled the area, so this area is twice what we want. We need to multiply by $\frac{1}{2}$ to get rid of the extra area. That leaves us with the formula for the *area of a trapezoid*:

$$A = \frac{1}{2}(b_1 + b_2)h$$

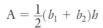

To discover the formula for the area of a circle, the students already need to know the relationship between the *diameter* of a circle (the width of the circle) and the *circumference* of the same circle (the perimeter or the distance around the circle).

This relationship can be discovered through an exploratory activity where students measure the diameter and circumference of several round things—some big, some small, and some in between. Then, for each circle, the student divides the circumference by the diameter. In every case, the distance around the circle is a little bit more than three times the distance across. Although, because of measurement error, the quotient of the circumference and diameter will vary slightly from circle to circle, the ratio is the number that we call *pi* (π). The relationship between the circumference and the diameter is given by this formula:

$$C = \pi d$$

Since the diameter (d) is twice the radius, another way to express this relationship is given by these formulas:

$$C = \pi \times 2r \qquad \text{or} \qquad C = 2\pi r$$

Now, consider this circle. We want to find the area but do not have a formula for the area of a circle. We try to rearrange the area into a shape for which we have one.

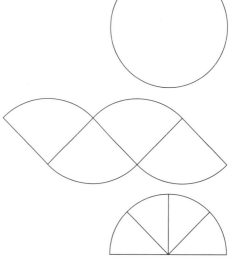

Notice that if we cut the circle into fourths and rearrange them, the area is in a shape with two straight sides, but the shape does not resemble a shape for which we have an area formula.

We cut the circle into eighths and separate it into two equal parts.

Then we arrange the pieces as pictured. We can see that the shape is very much like a parallelogram.

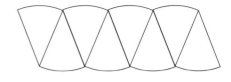

If we cut the circle into twelfths and rearrange the pieces in the same way, the shape looks even more like a parallelogram.

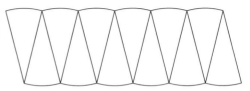

The more parts the circle is cut into, the more the rearrangement of the pieces looks like a parallelogram. So, we can imagine 100 parts and a shape that is almost exactly in the shape of a parallelogram. Regardless of the number of pieces, the base of this "parallelogram" is half the cir-

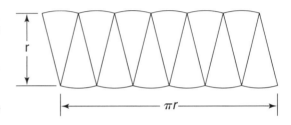

cumference (πr), and the height of the "parallelogram" is the radius (r). To find the area of this "parallelogram," we multiply the base times the height:

$$A = (\pi r)r$$

This result is the formula for the *area of a circle*:

$$A = \pi r^2$$

When students have learned to find areas of unfamiliar shapes in this way—*when the shape is unfamiliar, change it into a familiar shape*—area problems involving composite shapes are typically not difficult. For example, suppose we want to find the area of the following figure:

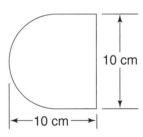

10 cm

10 cm

The figure consists of half of a circle with a radius of 5 cm

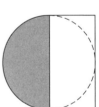

and a rectangle that is 5 cm by 10 cm. The areas of these two parts can be added to find the area of the original figure.

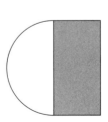

No instructional activities for developing the area formulas are included here, but they are left to the reader as exercises.

Measuring Volume

Strong parallels exist between area concepts and volume concepts. Units of area are pieces of area. Units of volume are pieces of volume. We measure area by finding how many units it takes to cover the interior of the shape. We measure volume by finding how many units it takes to fill the interior of the shape. We do not normally actually measure area; we measure linear dimensions and compute the area using formulas. We do not normally actually measure volume; we measure linear dimensions and compute the volume using formulas. The one big idea when we are developing area formulas is: *When we have a shape for which we do not have an area formula, we rearrange the area into a shape for which we do have a formula.* The one big idea when we are developing volume formulas is similar: *When we have a shape for which we do not have a volume formula, we rearrange the volume into a shape for which we do have a formula.*

We begin the development of volume concepts by establishing meaning for the term *volume*. We talk about the size of the inside of the shape and make gross comparisons. For example, we can see that box A will hold more than box B, so we say that the volume of box A is greater than the volume of box B:

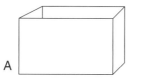
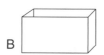

On the other hand, because they are shaped differently, it is harder to tell which of the following two boxes, C or D, would hold more:

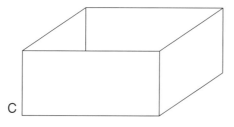
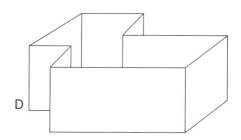

If we fill both shapes with marbles, we can count the marbles to see which shape holds more:

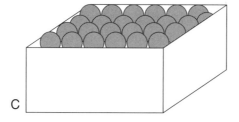
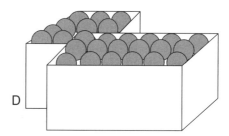

But, now we can see a problem similar to the one we saw when we used circular units of area. There is space between the marbles that is not being measured. So, we want to use a unit of volume that completely fills the shape without leaving space between the units. There are actually a lot of shapes that would work, but the volume-computation formulas require the use of units in the shape of a cube. We begin experimenting with *cubic units* to measure the volume of rectangular prisms (or boxes).

As students fill boxes with cubes and count the cubes, they learn that the measure of the volume of the box is the number of cubes it takes to fill the box:

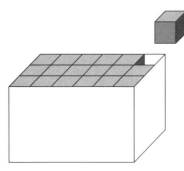

Students can also easily discover that since the box is the same size and shape from the bottom all the way to the top, every layer of cubes contains the same number:

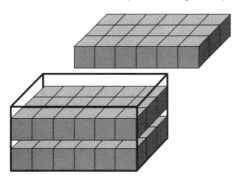

So, the volume will be the number in each layer times the number of layers:

Volume = Number of cubes in the first layer × Number of layers

In this transparent box, we see that the first layer contains 18 cubes and that there are three layers. The volume is 3 × 18, or 54 cubes:

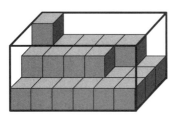

If the area of the base (bottom) of the box is marked off in squares, then in the first layer of cubes, a cube will be on top of every square. So, the number of cubes in the first layer is equal to the area of the base of the box:

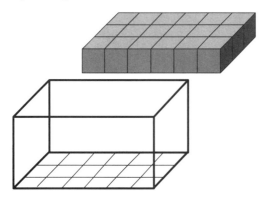

The number of layers is the same as the height of the box. In this example, the height is 3 units and there are three layers:

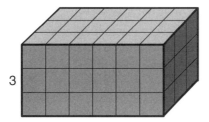

3

The volume is equal to the number of cubes in the first layer times the number of layers. But, since the number of cubes in the first layer is equal to the area of the base and the number of layers is equal to the height, we let B represent the area of the base, let *h* represent the height, and write the formula for the *volume of a box* (rectangular prism) as:

$$V = Bh$$

The same formula works for any box as long as the box is the same size and shape from the bottom to the top:

A round box (a circular prism, or cylinder)

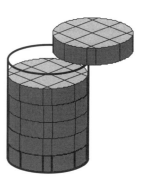

A triangular box (a triangular prism)

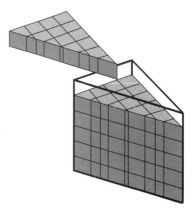

Or, even a strangely shaped box (an unusual prismlike figure)

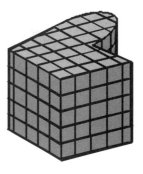

For any box that is the same size and shape from the bottom to the top (called a *prism* or *prismlike figure*), the same volume formula will work:

$$V = Bh$$

There is another formula for the volume of a cylinder: $V = \pi r^2 h$. However, the area of the base of a cylinder is πr^2, so the cylinder formula is exactly the same as the formula for all the other prismlike figures: $V = Bh$. If students know all the situations when the formula for prismlike figures can be used, they will, in effect, have fewer formulas to remember.

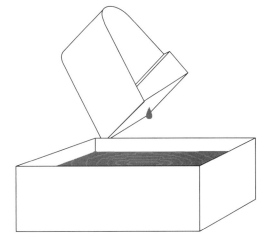

Suppose we have a set of water containers that have prismlike shapes. If one of the shapes is unusual and it is difficult to find the volume, we could fill the unusual container with water and then pour that water into a rectangular, box-shaped container.

We then have rearranged the shape of the water (which is the volume) into a shape for which we have a volume formula.

We can use this technique to discover a volume formula that works for an entire class of three-dimensional shapes.

Consider the following two figures. One is a rectangular prism. The other is an inverted pyramid. We do not have a volume formula for pyramids, but we do have one for prisms. These figures have identical bases; that is, the base of the prism is the same size and shape as the base of the pyramid. Also, the height of both figures is the same:

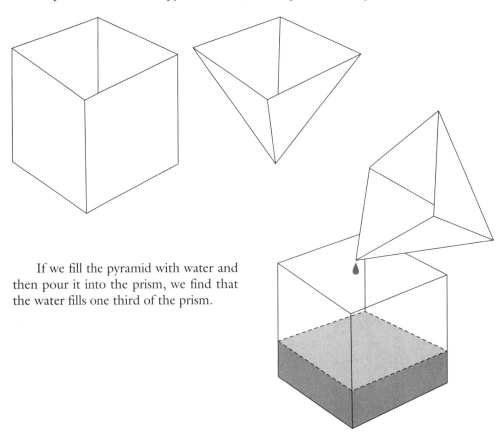

If we fill the pyramid with water and then pour it into the prism, we find that the water fills one third of the prism.

Now, consider the following figures. One is a triangular prism. The other is a triangular pyramid. Again, both figures have the same base and the same height:

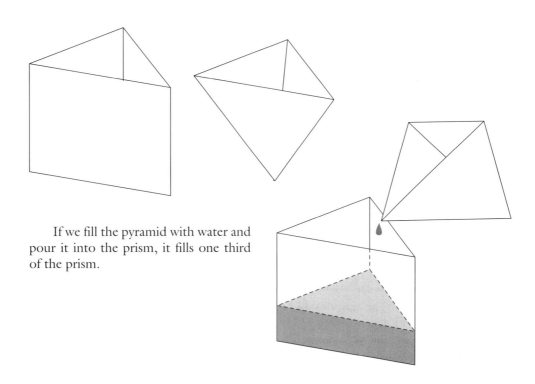

If we fill the pyramid with water and pour it into the prism, it fills one third of the prism.

The next two figures are a prismlike figure and a pyramidlike figure with the same base and the same height:

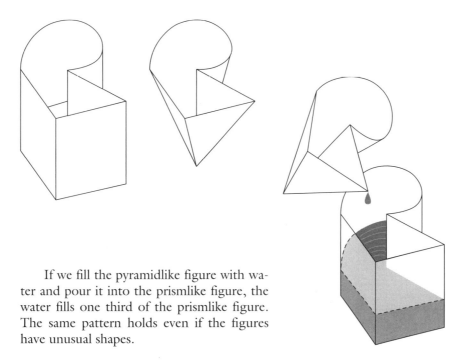

If we fill the pyramidlike figure with water and pour it into the prismlike figure, the water fills one third of the prismlike figure. The same pattern holds even if the figures have unusual shapes.

As we expect, we see the same relationship between cones and cylinders. This cylinder has the same base and height as the cone:

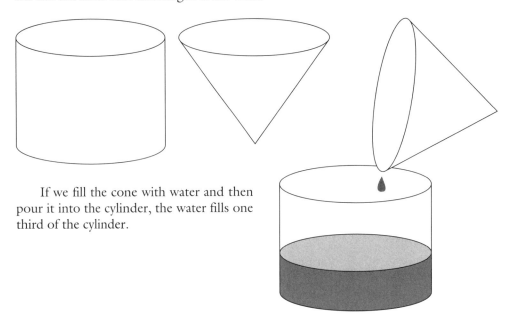

If we fill the cone with water and then pour it into the cylinder, the water fills one third of the cylinder.

The relationship between the volume of pyramidlike figures (including cones) and prismlike figures with the same base and height gives us the volume formula for all pyramidlike figures. For the same base and height, the volume of the pyramidlike figure is always one third the volume of the prismlike figure. Since the volume of a prismlike figure is B × h, the *volume of a pyramidlike figure* is one third of that:

$$V = \frac{1}{3}Bh$$

The following are activities that a teacher might use to develop volume concepts.

Activity 8.01   Pick the Big Box

Assemble a variety of boxes of different sizes and shapes.

Choose two of them and ask the students which will hold the most. Repeat this process with several pairs of boxes. If the students are unable to decide which of a pair of boxes is bigger, set that pair of boxes aside.

Activity 8.02   How to Decide?

Point out one of the pairs of boxes for which the students were unable to identify the biggest.

Conduct a brainstorming session, asking students to think of ways to decide which box is bigger. Remind them that the bigger box is the one that would hold more.

Write every suggestion on the chalkboard, regardless of how good or how practical it is. Then ask the students to decide which methods are most reasonable (make the most sense, are easy to use).

Then, try some of the suggested methods to see how they work.

Activity 8.03 How Can You Fill It Full If There Aren't Enough Cubes?

Construct six small boxes that have the following interior dimensions:

5 in. by 8 in. by 3 in.	6 in. by 6 in. by 4 in.
5 in. by 7 in. by 6 in.	4 in. by 9 in. by 7 in.
7 in. by 6 in. by 5 in.	4 in. by 8 in. by 5 in.

Form six groups of students. Give each group one of the boxes and about 300 inch-cubes. Have each group fill its box with cubes to see how many cubes are needed.

Take away all but 60 cubes from each group. Then have the groups exchange boxes. Point out that the group no longer has enough cubes to fill the boxes. Tell the students that you want each group to try to use the cubes that they have to figure out how many cubes it would take to fill the box.

Have each group report to the class how the group was able to complete the task. Emphasize that every layer of cubes will contain the same number of cubes.

Activity 8.04 Even Fewer Cubes

Form six groups of students. Give each group one of the boxes prepared for Activity 8.03. (Be sure that no group has a box that it previously worked with.) This time, give each group just 22 cubes. Have the group members see if they can figure out the number of cubes needed to completely fill the box when they have only 22 cubes.

After each group is finished, have the groups report how the group members figured out the answer. During the discussion, ask how they figured out how many cubes would be in the first layer. Also ask how they figured out how many layers there would be.

Activity 8.05 The Bottom of the Box

Cut a piece of white paper to fit exactly on the bottom of the inside of each of the boxes prepared for Activity 8.03. Draw lines to make 1-inch squares on each piece. Place the papers inside the boxes.

Form six groups of students and give a box to each group. Also give each group about 50 inch-cubes.

Point out that the groups may look at the paper on the bottom of the box and see the area of the bottom. Ask each group to figure out the area of the bottom of its box.

Next, have the students place a cube on top of every square in the area. Ask how the area of the bottom is related to the number of cubes it takes to make one layer.

Collect all but 10 cubes from all the groups and have the groups exchange boxes. Tell the groups to use what they have to find how many cubes will fit in their boxes.

When they are finished, ask how to find how many cubes it takes to fill the box. Emphasize that the number of cubes in the first layer times the number of layers is the number needed to fill the box.

Activity 8.06   Using a Ruler

Form six groups of students. Give each group one of the boxes prepared for Activity 8.03. (Be sure that no group has a box that it previously worked with.) This time, give each group a ruler. Tell the students that you want each group to see if it can use the ruler to figure out how many inch-cubes will fit in the box.

After each group is finished, have the group members report how they figured out the answer. Ask how you can tell how many cubes will be in the first layer. Ask how you can tell how many layers there will be.

Write the formula for the volume of a box on the chalkboard:

$$V = lwh$$

Place parentheses around the *lw*:

$$V = (lw)h$$

Explain that when you multiply these numbers, you have the area of the bottom of the box. Remind the students of a few things: This area is the same as the number of cubes in the first layer, the height tells how many layers of cubes you have, and a ruler can be used to obtain the measurements (length, width, and height).

Activity 8.07   Odd Boxes

Construct several boxes with unusual shapes like the following. Draw squares showing the area of the bottom of each box:

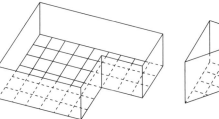 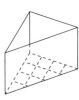 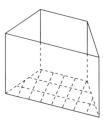

Have the students figure out the volume of each box. Let them use a ruler to measure the height of the boxes. Emphasize that the area of the base tells how many cubes are in the first layer and the height tells how many layers there are.

Activity 8.08   Build a Box and a Pyramid

Construct a box and a pyramid out of stiff cardboard. The base of the box and the base of the pyramid must be identical. The height of the box must also be the same as the height of the pyramid.

Have a student fill the pyramid with beans and then pour the beans into the box. She or he will find that the beans will fill the box one third full.

Ask how the volume of the pyramid is related to the volume of the box.

> ### Activity 8.09   Build a Cylinder and a Cone
>
> Construct a cylinder and a cone out of stiff cardboard. The base of the cylinder and the base of the cone must be identical. The height of the cylinder must also be the same as the height of the cone.
>
> Have a student fill the cone with beans and then pour the beans into the cylinder. He or she will find that the beans will fill the cylinder one third full.
>
> Ask how the volume of the cone is related to the volume of the cylinder.

Measuring Angles

Teaching measurement of angles is easy if sufficient time is spent helping the student to conceptualize the unit of measure for angles. To understand the need for the careful conceptualization of angle measurement, consider these angles. Although the sides are longer on angle *A*, we say that angle *B* is greater. The explanation might be that angle *B* is "open wider."

Now consider these two angles. Remember that, from the previous example, the student has a sense that the angle that is open wider is the bigger angle. But, even though angle *D* appears to be open wider, the student is told that angle *C* is actually the greater angle.

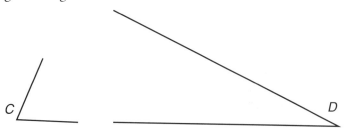

These apparent inconsistencies can be explained in various ways, but the need for such explanations can be reduced or even eliminated by a careful development of what is being measured (Van de Walle, 2004; Wilson & Adams, 1992).

We begin by helping the students think of an angle as indicating an amount of rotation. One side of the angle represents a beginning position, and the other side represents an ending position. The size of the angle is thought of as the amount of rotation needed to get from the initial position to the terminal position:

The size of angle *X* is one fourth of a turn.

The size of angle *Y* is less than one fourth of a turn. So, angle *X* is greater than angle *Y*.

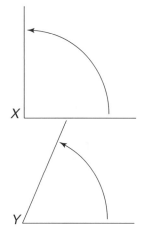

A folded piece of waxed paper can be used to help students begin to measure angles. Fold the sheet of waxed paper into eighths as pictured first. Then place the paper on top of the angle to measure how many eighths of a rotation are indicated by the angle. The angle shown is about three eighths of a rotation. The angle can easily be seen through the waxed paper, and the folds are easy to see. The waxed paper also works well with an overhead projector.

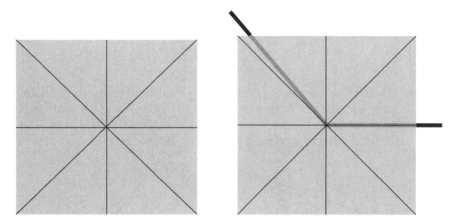

To measure angles with more precision, fold the waxed paper into sixteenths. Angles of about three sixteenths and five sixteenths are shown next:

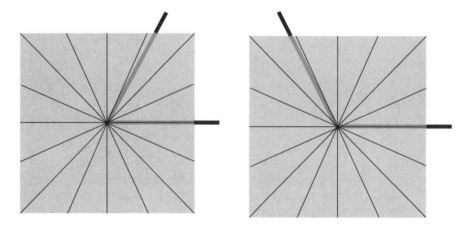

We could fold the paper into smaller parts to gain more precision in our measurement, but there are measuring tools called *protractors* that let us measure angles to the nearest $\frac{1}{360}$ of a rotation. Such a rotation is called a *degree*. An angle with a measure of 45 degrees shows $\frac{45}{360}$ of a rotation.

The following sequence of activities shows how a teacher might develop the concept of angle measurement.

Activity 8.10   Rotation

Attach an object to the bulletin board using a single thumbtack in the center.

Draw the students' attention to the object. Turn the object and tell the students that you are rotating it. Tell them that you are going to do one complete rotation. Then turn the object 360 degrees. Tell them that you are going to do one fourth of a rotation. Then turn the object 90 degrees.

Have students come to the bulletin board and show a full rotation, one half of a rotation, and three fourths of a rotation.

Activity 8.11 Point and Turn

Call on a student to come to the front and stand with one arm pointing straight out to the side. Tell the class that the student is going to do one complete rotation. Ask where he or she will be pointing after the rotation. Help the student demonstrate one complete rotation.

Have other students come forward and demonstrate one fourth, one half, and three fourths of a rotation.

Activity 8.12 Two Strings

Attach a white string and a red string to a thumbtack in the center of the bulletin board. Use a thumbtack to secure the other end of the white string so that it is stretched straight out to the right. Tie the other end of the red string around a pushpin and stretch it out on top of the white string:

Show rotation by moving the pushpin to a new position to show an angle with one fourth of a rotation (90°):

Move the white string back to the initial position and then move it to show angles with one half, and then three fourths, of a rotation.

Activity 8.13 Measuring with Waxed Paper

Fold a sheet of waxed paper into eighths as shown. Draw several angles on transparencies and use the waxed paper on the overhead projector to measure the angles to the nearest eighth of a rotation.

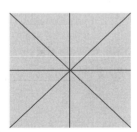 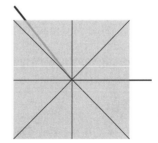

Activity 8.14 Measuring with More Precision

Fold a sheet of waxed paper into sixteenths as shown. Draw several angles on transparencies and use the waxed paper on the overhead projector to measure the angles to the nearest sixteenth of a rotation.

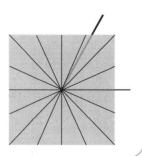

Measuring with Indirect Units

The measurements that we have examined so far have all used direct units of measure. The unit has been a piece of what was being measured. For example, we measured length with pieces of length—inches, centimeters, and so on. We measured area with pieces of area—square inches, square meters, and so on. We measured volume with pieces of volume—cubic centimeters, cubic feet, and so on. We introduced the concept of angles as showing an amount of rotation and then learned to measure angles with parts of rotation called degrees. Some attributes are not measured with direct units, but with *indirect units*. We examine this kind of measurement next.

Measuring Weight

Weight is not typically measured with direct units. Rather, we usually measure weight with a spring scale. The object being weighed is placed on the scale. Gravity pulls down on the object, which causes the spring to stretch. The stretching spring causes a pointer to move along a number line (which is often curved around a circle). We read the number to get the weight in pounds, ounces, kilograms, grams, or some other measurement.

Students need to weigh many things to gain a "sense of heaviness." They need to estimate weights of objects and then weigh those objects to check their estimates. They should experience weight measurement in many situations to learn when and how weight is used.

Note that the mass of an object can be measured with direct units of mass and a balance scale. When the mass of an object is being measured, the object is placed on one side of the scale. Weights are placed on the other side of the scale until the object is balanced. By adding up the weights, we can find the mass of the object.

Measuring Temperature

Temperature is also measured with indirect units. A thermometer consists of a tube of mercury or another substance that reacts to heat and cold by expanding and contracting. As it expands and contracts, the top surface of the mercury reaches higher or falls lower. The numbers beside the tube of mercury indicate how hot or how cold it is.

Students need to measure the temperature of many things to gain a "sense of heat." They need to estimate temperatures and then use thermometers to check their estimates. Students should experience temperature measurement in many situations to learn when and how measurement of temperature is used.

Measuring Value

The value of things is also measured with indirect units. When we use money to determine what something is worth, we are measuring the value of that thing. The same 20 pieces of paper ($20) can be traded for bread, for meat, for a taxi ride, for a t-shirt, or for any number of things. We can buy things with money because we agree with others to let money represent the value of those things.

The concept that money has certain value because we have agreed to let it have that value must be developed. Without an acceptance of this agreement about the value of money, many things do not make sense to a child. Why are five pennies worth the same amount as one nickel? Only because we have agreed that they should. Why is a nickel worth less than a dime even though it is much bigger than the dime? Only because we have agreed that it is. Why is one dollar bill worth more than three nice shiny quarters? Only because we have agreed that it should be.

Adapting a Lesson on Volume

The following lesson plan is similar to one that might be taken from the fifth-grade teachers' book of a published elementary school mathematics textbook series.

LESSON OBJECTIVE

The learner will find volume by counting cubes.

Lesson Opener

Have the students find the area of these figures:

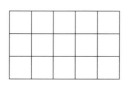 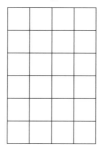 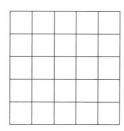

Development

Direct the attention of the students to the picture on the first page of the lesson in the student book. Point out that the student in the picture is filling the box with cubes. Explain that the number of cubic units something holds is called its *volume*. Ask how many cubes the box in the picture will hold. [8] Ask what the volume of the box is. [8 cubic units]

Monitoring Learning

Direct the attention of the class to the second example on the page. Have everyone find the number of cubes needed to fill the box. Ask how many cubes are needed. [9] Ask what the volume of the box is. [9 cubic units] Observe to identify children who do not understand.

Practice

Have children who had difficulties with the teaching examples complete the *Extra Practice Worksheet*. Have the rest of the class complete exercises 1 to 20.

Closure

At the end of the lesson, remind the students that the volume of a figure is the number of cubes needed to fill the figure.

This lesson focuses on completion of the textbook page. There is very little development—only two examples. The nature of the lesson requires the students to be still, listen to the teacher, and do "seatwork." There is little active involvement in learning.

We adapt the lesson by increasing the amount of developmental work and reducing the amount of practice. We increase the visual input in the lesson and include a substantial amount of kinesthetic learning activity. We have the students communicate about the lesson, and we monitor learning throughout every part of the lesson.

LESSON OBJECTIVE

The learner will find volume by counting cubes.

Lesson Opener

Prepare pairs of cards like these:

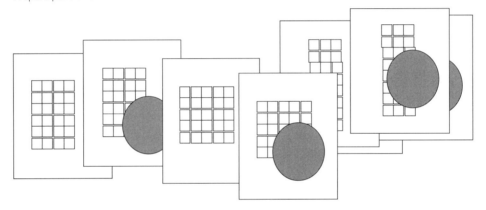

Shuffle the cards and give one to each student. Point out that some of the rectangles have part of the squares hidden. Have the students find partners whose rectangles are the same as theirs. One partner will have a rectangle with some squares hidden. The other partner will have an identical rectangle with no squares hidden. **Monitor understanding.** Pay particular attention to children who might have difficulty with this activity. Provide assistance as needed.

When everyone has found a partner, have the partners figure out how many squares are in their rectangles. Ask them how they could have figured out how many squares if they had only the rectangle with some squares hidden. Choose one of the cards that has some of the squares hidden. With the class telling you how to do it, figure out how many squares are in the rectangle. Emphasize that every row of squares has the same number. They can multiply the number of squares in one row times the number of rows.

Development

Have the partners from the previous activity stay together. Give each pair of partners a small box and some centimeter-cubes. Tell them to fill the boxes completely full of cubes and figure out how many cubes their boxes will hold. **Monitor understanding.** Observe to be sure that all the partners are stacking the cubes into the boxes so that there are no spaces between the cubes.

When everyone is finished, ask two or three students how many cubes fit in their boxes. Explain that the amount that a box can hold is called the *volume* of the box. The centimeter-cubes are the units used to measure volume. Choose one of the boxes. Ask how many cubes fit in that box. Write the volume of the box on the board. [For example, the volume might be 12 cubic centimeters.] Have each pair of partners write the volume of their box. **Monitor understanding.** Observe to be sure that all the students are writing the volume correctly. If any students are having difficulty, provide assistance as needed.

Ask which box has the greatest volume. Which has the least? Choose four boxes. Have the class help you line them up in order from least to greatest volume. **Monitor understanding.** Observe to be sure that all the students correctly understand volume.

Direct the attention of the students to the picture on the first page of the lesson in the student book. Point out that the student in the picture is filling the box with cubes. Remind the class that the child in the picture is doing exactly what they were doing, except that the cubes are bigger. Ask how many cubes the box in the picture will hold. [8] Ask what the volume of the box is. [8 cubic units] Write the volume on the board.

Direct the attention of the class to the second example on the page. Have everyone find the number of cubes needed to fill the box. Ask how many cubes are needed. [9] Have all the students write down the volume of the box. [9 cubic units] **Monitor understanding.** Check what the students have written to be sure they understand how to write the volume.

Practice

Have the students work with their partners to complete exercises 1 to 5 in the student book. Tell them to do one exercise at a time. Each student is to find the answer, then check with his or her partner to see if they agree. If their answers are not the same, they should do the exercise together. **Monitor understanding.** Move around the room, observing the students' work. Identify students who are having difficulty and provide assistance where needed.

Closure

After everyone is finished, ask the students what they learned today. Ask how to find the number of cubes that a box will hold. Ask what *volume* is.

Follow-Up

Tell the students that they are to take their books home and explain to their parents what volume is. Then they are to show their parents how to find the volume in exercise 6 on the practice page.

Using Measurement to Solve Problems

Remember that measurement is simply a process by which we assign a number to a quantity. When measurement is used in problem solving, computation is usually performed on those numbers (measurements). When teaching problem solving using measurements, the teacher should apply the same basic principles used when he or she is teaching problem solving using other kinds of numbers. The teacher should emphasize that the choice of operation depends on what is happening to the quantities in the problem. If quantities are being combined, then addition of the measurements can probably be used. If the measurements in the problem are being separated into equal parts, then division can probably be used.

The current instructional emphasis for problem solving in mathematics is to develop a wide variety of problem-solving strategies and provide experience using those strategies. The following problem-solving strategies are suggested:

Solve part of the problem.

Separate the problem into easier parts.

Work backward.

Use a picture or diagram.

Use a table.

Solve a simpler problem.

Try and check.

List the possibilities.

We now examine a problem appropriate for children at about the sixth-grade level. The solution employs separating the problem into easier parts, but it also uses a new strategy—*Use a formula*:

> Anna works for a hardware store, where she cuts glass into the sizes and shapes needed by customers. One day, a customer requested a circular piece of glass with a 10-inch diameter.
>
> The store manager had told Anna that she should always try to have the smallest possible amount of wasted glass. So, Anna began by cutting a circular piece of cardboard with a diameter of 10 inches. She compared the cardboard circle with several pieces of glass and found that she could cut the requested glass from any of the three pieces shown here.
>
> Which piece should she use in order to have the smallest amount of waste?

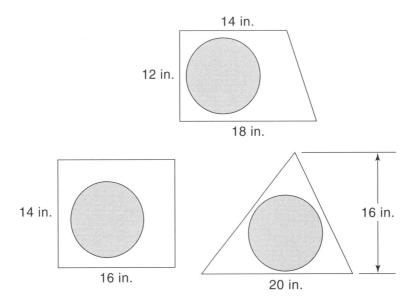

We want to choose the option that leaves us with the smallest amount of wasted glass. To do this, we *solve three easier parts* to the overall problem. We find the amount of waste for each of the three options.

First, we consider the piece of glass that is shaped like a trapezoid. We need to find the amount of glass in the trapezoid and the amount of glass that we will use in the circular piece. To do this, we *use the formulas* for the area of circles and trapezoids. Then, we subtract to find the amount of wasted glass:

> The formula for the area of a trapezoid is $A = \frac{1}{2}(b_1 + b_2)h$. The two bases of the trapezoid have lengths of 14 inches and 18 inches. The height of the trapezoid is 12 inches. When we use these values in the formula, we find that the area of the trapezoid is 192 square inches.
>
> The formula for the area of a circle is $A = \pi r^2$. Since the diameter of the circle is 10 inches, the radius is 5 inches. When we use this value in the formula, we find that the area of the circle is 78.5 square inches.
>
> When we subtract, we find that if we use the trapezoid-shaped piece of glass, we will waste 113.5 square inches of glass.

Second, we follow the same procedures with the rectangular piece of glass:

> The formula for the area of a rectangle is $A = bh$. The base of the rectangle is 16 inches and the height of the rectangle is 14 inches. Using the formula, we find that the area of the rectangle is 224 square inches.
>
> When we subtract the area of the circle, we find that we would waste 145.5 square inches of glass if we use this piece.

Third, we follow these procedures with the triangular piece of glass:

> The formula for the area of a triangle is $A = \frac{1}{2}bh$. The base of the triangle is 20 inches and its height is 16 inches. Using the formula, we find that the area of the triangle is 160 square inches. When we subtract the area of the circle, we find that we would waste 81.5 square inches of glass if we use the triangular piece.

Finally, we compare these three results and discover that we have the smallest amount of waste if we use the triangular piece of glass.

Exercises and Activities

1. Develop a learning activity that develops the concept of *area* by having the students make gross comparisons of the areas of different shapes.

2. Develop a learning activity that develops the concept of a *unit of area* as a piece of area. Use units of area that are not squares.

3. Develop a learning activity that develops the concept of *measurement of area* as the number of units it takes to cover the area being measured. Use square units.

4. Develop a learning activity that develops the *ability to estimate areas* by using some standard unit. For example, you might use square centimeters or square inches.

5. Write a sequence of developmental activities that can be used to teach the *area formula for rectangles.*

6. Write a sequence of developmental activities that can be used to teach the *area formula for parallelograms.*

7. Write a sequence of developmental activities that can be used to teach the *area formula for triangles.*

8. Write a sequence of developmental activities that can be used to teach the *area formula for trapezoids.*

9. Write a sequence of developmental activities that can be used to teach that the *circumference of a circle is π times its diameter.*

10. Write a sequence of developmental activities that can be used to teach the *area formula for circles.*

11. Choose a lesson on measurement from a published middle school mathematics textbook series.

   a. Identify parts of the lesson that provide visual imagery for the concept(s) or skill(s) taught in the lesson and add more activities to the lesson that will develop visual imagery for the concept(s) or skill(s) taught in the lesson.

   b. Identify the parts of the lesson that develop the concept(s) or skill(s) taught in the lesson and add more developmental activity to the lesson plan.

12. The following subtraction results illustrate an error pattern like the error patterns related by Robert Ashlock in his book, *Error Patterns in Computation: Using Error Patterns to Improve Instruction:*

$$
\begin{array}{rl}
{}^{7}\!\!\not{8}\text{ yards,} & {}^{1}1\text{ foot} \\
-5\text{ yards,} & 2\text{ feet} \\
\hline
2\text{ yards,} & 9\text{ feet}
\end{array}
\qquad
\begin{array}{rl}
{}^{8}\!\!\not{9}\text{ meters,} & {}^{1}4\text{ decimeters} \\
-4\text{ meters,} & 8\text{ decimeters} \\
\hline
4\text{ meters,} & 6\text{ decimeters}
\end{array}
$$

$$
\begin{array}{rl}
{}^{5}\!\!\not{6}\text{ feet,} & {}^{1}7\text{ Inches} \\
-2\text{ feet,} & 9\text{ Inches} \\
\hline
3\text{ feet,} & 8\text{ Inches}
\end{array}
\qquad
\begin{array}{rl}
{}^{5}\!\!\not{6}\text{ gallons,} & {}^{1}2\text{ quarts} \\
-2\text{ gallons,} & 3\text{ quarts} \\
\hline
3\text{ gallons,} & 9\text{ quarts}
\end{array}
$$

   a. What is this student's error pattern? What is the student doing to produce the incorrect answers?

   b. Plan a mini-lesson to correct this student's error pattern.

13. Choose a lesson on measurement from a published middle school mathematics text-book and identify the objective(s) that the students are to learn during the lesson.

   a. Write an objective test item that can be used to determine whether the students have learned the lesson objective(s).

   b. Design a small-group activity that you could observe to determine which children have learned the lesson objective(s) and which students have not.

References and Related Readings

Ashlock, R. B. (2002). *Error patterns in computation: Using error patterns to improve instruction* (8th ed.). Upper Saddle River, NJ: Prentice Hall.

Thompson, C. S., & Van de Walle, J. A. (1981). A single-handed approach to telling time. *Arithmetic Teacher, 28*(8), 4–9.

Thornton, C. A, Tucker, B. F., Dossey, J. A., & Bazik, E. F. (1983). *Teaching mathematics to children with special needs.* Menlo Park, CA: Addison-Wesley.

Van de Walle, J. A. (2004). *Elementary and middle school mathematics: Teaching developmentally* (5th ed.). Boston: Allyn & Bacon.

Wilson, P. S., & Adams, V. M. (1992). A dynamic way to teach angle and angle measure. *Arithmetic Teacher, 39*, 6–13.

Websites

www.corestandards.org/the-standards/mathematics
The Common Core State Standards for Mathematics can be found at this site.

www.proteacher.com/100023.shtml
Activities and lesson plans on measurement.

www.iit.edu/~smile/ma9705.html
Measurement activities.

nine

GEOMETRY

Using the Big Ideas to Study Geometric Shapes

CHAPTER OUTLINE

The Big Ideas of Middle School Geometry
    Straightness
    Congruence
    Similarity
    Parallelism
    Perpendicularity
    Symmetry
Using the Big Ideas to Study Geometric
Shapes
    Rectangles in Middle School

    Circles in Middle School
    Angles in the Fifth through Eighth Grades
    Prisms in Middle School
Adapting a Geometry Lesson
Using Geometry to Solve Problems
Exercises and Activities

For purposes of our discussion in this chapter, we consider *geometry* to be the naming of shapes and the study of their characteristics. This view of geometry is fairly limited. It departs somewhat from the more mathematical approach, which might be a study of points in space, or perhaps a logical development of a system of theorems from a beginning set of assumptions. However, the naming of shapes and the study of their characteristics is, more or less, what is done in middle school geometry. As noted at the beginning of Chapter 8, geometry is closely related to measurement. The study of characteristics of geometric shapes frequently calls for the application of skills that were developed in measurement lessons.

The Big Ideas of Middle School Geometry

The ability to identify and name shapes depends almost entirely on having a working understanding of some combination of geometric relationships (Clements & Sarama, 2000). When studying a geometric shape, we find that each of these relationships either exists or does not exist in that shape. Therefore, these relationships can be thought of

205

as the big ideas of middle school geometry (Lerch, 1981; Thornton, Tucker, Dossey, & Bazik, 1983). If we teach students to look for these big ideas, it is easier for them to classify, name, and use geometric shapes.

Straightness

The first big idea is the notion of *straightness*. It is important to know whether lines or line segments, or edges, or surfaces are straight when we are studying geometric shapes. For example, one of the following shapes is not a triangle. Why not? Figure C is not a triangle because all the sides of a triangle must be straight:

Knowing whether an object is straight is important; therefore, the students need simple methods for testing straightness. One simple way to check is to pick up the shape and look along the edge to see if the edge is straight. Another way to test straightness is to use a straightedge. Rather than using a ruler, children can be taught to fold a sheet of paper and use the folded edge as a straightedge. Examples of activities that can be used to develop straightness are included in this chapter.

The notion of straightness has a three-dimensional extension—*flatness*. A surface is flat if and only if it is "straight in all directions." The simplest way to test a surface to see if it is flat is to lay a straightedge on the surface in a lot of directions. If the straightedge always coincides with the surface, then the surface is flat:

Congruence

The second of the big ideas of middle school geometry is *congruence*. Two geometric figures are congruent if and only if they are exactly the same size and shape. In middle school geometry, we study congruence of simple figures such as line segments and angles. We also consider congruence of more-complex figures such as triangles and prisms. When we are classifying geometric figures, congruence is always important. For example, why is one of the following figures not a rectangle? Figure K is not a rectangle because the opposite sides of rectangles are always congruent:

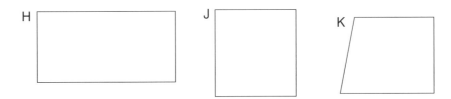

Consider the following two figures. Figure M is a prism, but figure P is not. How can you tell? The two bases of a prism are always congruent:

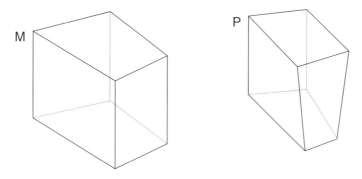

One of the following figures is a circle and one is not. How can you tell? Figure Y is not a circle. Every line segment from the center to the circle (all the radii) must be congruent:

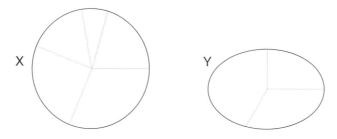

The easiest method for testing two plane figures for congruence arises from the fact that congruence is a transitive relation. Students can easily use the following procedure: The child traces one figure and then moves the tracing onto the second figure. If the tracing is an exact match for the second figure, then the two original figures are congruent. Children can understand that the two figures are congruent because they are both congruent to the tracing.

Similarity

The third of the big ideas for middle school geometry is the notion of *similarity*. Two figures are similar if they are the same shape. Whenever two figures are the same shape, two important relationships are present: First, every angle of one shape is congruent to the corresponding angle of the second shape. Second, the lengths of one figure are proportional to the corresponding lengths of the second figure. Another description of proportionality is that the ratio of a length in the first figure to the corresponding length in the second figure is always the same. For example, the two figures that follow are similar:

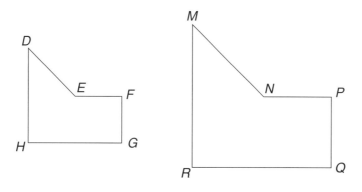

Corresponding angles of the two figures are congruent. For example, angle *D* is congruent to angle *M*. Angle *G* is congruent to angle *Q*. Angle *E* is congruent to angle *N*. Corresponding sides are proportional. For example, the length *DE* divided by the length *MN* is two thirds. *HG* divided by *RQ* is also two thirds and *EF* divided by *NP* is also two thirds.

Two examples of how the concept of similarity is used in classifying geometric figures are, first, all circles are similar, and, second, all squares are similar. In a more complex setting, consider the truncated pentagonal pyramid pictured at the right. If the top of the pyramid is cut off parallel to the base, the top surface of the remaining figure is similar to the base. (A pyramid is the same shape from the bottom to the top, but not the same size.)

A simple, easy-to-use method for testing plane figures for similarity is illustrated next. Note that a fairly complex shape is used in this example. Students need to be introduced to this method with simpler shapes such as triangles and rectangles.

Place the two shapes so they are oriented in the same direction. Begin by drawing a line through any point of the first figure and the corresponding point of the second figure.

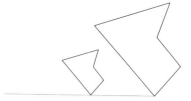

Then draw a line through another pair of corresponding points. Notice that these two lines intersect.

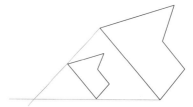

Draw lines through other pairs of corresponding points. All the lines intersect at the same point if the figures are similar.

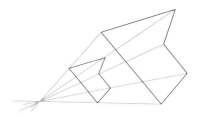

Parallelism

The fourth big idea of middle school geometry is *parallelism*. If two lines are parallel, we know that the lines do not intersect, no matter how far they are extended. We also know that the lines go in the same direction. The two lines are the same distance apart, no matter where we measure the distance. The first of these characteristics of parallel lines is not helpful because we cannot extend them forever. However, the other two notions provide ways to test for parallelism.

For example, parallel lines go in the same direction. Consider lines *a* and *b*, shown next. To determine the direction of the two lines, we draw a third line that crosses both of them:

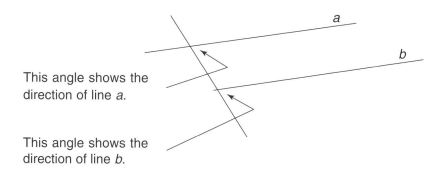

This angle shows the direction of line *a*.

This angle shows the direction of line *b*.

We can make a tracing of one of these angles and move it on top of the other angle to see if they are congruent. If the angles are congruent, then the direction of both lines is the same. The lines are parallel.

Parallel lines are also *equidistant*—the same distance apart wherever they are measured. Consider lines *j* and *k* in the following illustration. If we place a sheet of paper with its edge on line *j*, we can use a pencil to mark the distance between the two lines. By sliding the paper along the line, we can check to see if the distance is the same everywhere:

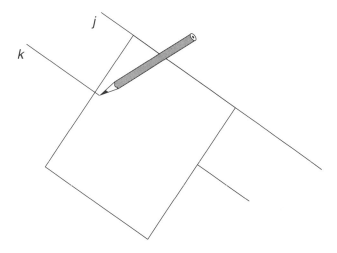

Whether lines are parallel can be used to identify and classify many figures. For example, one pair of opposite sides of a trapezoid is always parallel, but the other pair of opposite sides is not. On the other hand, both pairs of opposite sides of a parallelogram are parallel.

Perpendicularity

The fifth big idea of middle school geometry is *perpendicularity* (square corners). Students are able to look for square corners to help them recognize certain shapes. For example, a square has four square corners, and every vertical edge of a right prism is perpendicular to the bases. For students, the simplest test of perpendicularity is to create a square corner by folding a sheet of paper and then laying that square corner on top of other corners that are being checked:

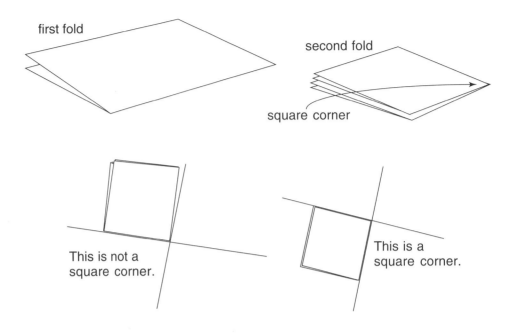

first fold

second fold

square corner

This is not a square corner.

This is a square corner.

Symmetry

The sixth big idea of middle school geometry is the notion of *symmetry*. There are actually several kinds of symmetry (line symmetry, slide symmetry, and rotational symmetry), but in middle school geometry, we are primarily concerned with line symmetry. Therefore, we limit the discussion here to line symmetry.

Many shapes studied by middle school students are symmetric. Many important characteristics of those shapes arise from that symmetry. Students need to be able to check figures to see if they are symmetric. The simplest test for line symmetry and the easiest for students to use is to fold the figure along the line of symmetry to see if the two halves are an exact match.

Using the Big Ideas to Study Geometric Shapes

We now trace the development of four geometric shapes as they might be developed in grades 5 through 8 within a middle school textbook series. The four shapes that we examine are rectangles, circles, angles, and prisms. As we look at the development of these four shapes, take note of how the six big ideas identified earlier are used, either informally or formally, to characterize or classify the shapes. Keep in mind, also, that other geometric shapes are being developed at the same time.

Rectangles in Middle School

Prior to fifth grade, students should have learned that rectangles are closed figures with four sides, four corners, and always two lines of symmetry. They should also know that square rectangles (squares) have four lines of symmetry. Students should also be able to recognize that the faces of some three-dimensional objects can be rectangles. In the fifth through eighth grades, students use more formal mathematical terminology to describe rectangles, but they continue to use the big ideas of geometry to describe and classify them. They learn that closed figures with straight sides are called *polygons*. (*Poly* means "many" and *gon* means "side.") They learn that polygons with four sides are called *quadrilaterals*. (*Quad* means "four" and *lateral* means "side.") They learn that trapezoids and parallelograms are special kinds of quadrilaterals and that *rhombi* (*rhombuses*) and rectangles are two special kinds of parallelograms. They also learn that squares are special rhombi and also special rectangles.

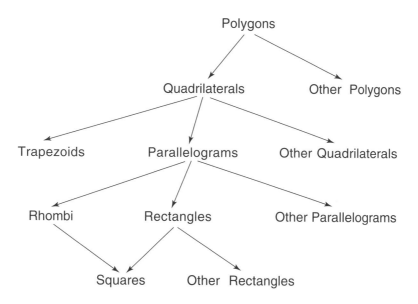

Activity 9.01 illustrates a standard procedure for testing whether or not a shape is a rectangle. This activity requires students to use characteristics of rectangles that have been learned in earlier grades.

Activity 9.01   Is It a Rectangle?

Cut out several large shapes from construction paper. Some of the shapes should be rectangles. Some of the shapes should have corners that are not square. Some of the shapes should be parallelograms. Some should not be closed figures. Some should be trapezoids. Some should be squares.

Point out one of the shapes. Ask if it is a rectangle. If the shape is a rectangle, ask why it is. If it is not a rectangle, ask why it is not. Repeat this procedure with each of the remaining shapes.

Circles in Middle School

Prior to fifth grade, students should have learned that circles are closed figures that are round, smooth, curved (no straight sides), the same size in all directions (all diameters are congruent), and symmetric. They should be able to explain why other shapes are not circles as well as to recognize circles in three-dimensional shapes like cylinders, cones, and spheres. In the middle grades, the study of circles becomes more formal, with greater emphasis on mathematical terminology. During these years, children are able to identify and use mathematical terminology to name the center, radius, diameter, and circumference of circles. They learn that all the radii are the same length (*congruent*), as are all the diameters. They learn about *chords* (*straight* lines with both endpoints on the circle), and central angles of circles, as well as angles inscribed in circles. They learn to use mathematical symbols and notation to write about these circle concepts.

Activity 9.02 All about Circles

Display several circles in front of the class. Explain that shapes like these are called *circles*. Ask the students to tell about the circles in their own words. Accept all descriptions that are offered. However, if a description is obviously not correct, ask the student to explain why he or she thinks the circles are like that. Ask what the other students think.

Activity 9.03 Circles, Circles, Everywhere

If necessary, place a variety of circular objects in sight around the room. Examples of objects that you might have in the room are a Hula Hoop, a Frisbee, a bicycle (for its wheels), a round-faced clock, a paper plate, a wastebasket (for its top and bottom), an oatmeal box, a drinking glass, a round picture frame, a pencil sharpener (circular holes for the pencils), a computer CD, or assorted circles cut from colored paper.

Point out one of those objects—for example, a clock with a circular face. Ask the children to tell you the shape of the clock. Do the same with a second round object. Then have the children look around and identify other objects that have the shape of a circle.

Angles in the Fifth through Eighth Grades

Prior to fifth grade, children should have learned that shapes with straight sides have corners (angles). They should know that the number of corners and the "sharpness" of the corners help them in classifying shapes (for example, if a shape has three angles, it is a triangle). Students should know that square corners are right angles and are formed by perpendicular lines. They should also be able to draw angles, compare angles, and identify which of two angles is greater. In addition, students should be able to classify angles as right angles, greater than right angles, or less than right angles.

Activity 9.04 Right Angle Search

Cut sheets of paper into fourths and draw angles on them. There should be 20 right angles, 8 angles that are very close to but not quite right angles, 10 angles that are obviously less than right angles, and 10 angles that are obviously more than right angles. Mix up the angles and tape them to the walls around the room.

Separate the students into four teams. Have each team find 5 angles that are right angles and find 5 angles that are not right angles. The students are to use the right angles that they made by folding a sheet of paper to decide whether or not the angles are right angles. Each team is to take its 10 angles back to its table. Every team member is to check every angle to be sure that the team has 5 right angles and 5 angles that are not right angles.

We expect children in grades 5 and 6 to use mathematical language as they describe and classify angles as right angles, acute angles, and obtuse angles. They learn to use a protractor to measure angles and discover that right angles have 90 degrees, acute angles have less than 90 degrees, and obtuse angles have more than 90 degrees. At this time, they also begin to develop the ability to estimate the measure of angles.

They use more formal mathematical language for angles (for example, angles are two rays with a common endpoint), and use more formal mathematical notation as they write about angles. They learn about *congruent* angles and angle *bisectors* (separating an angle into two *congruent* angles). They understand how to use a compass and a *straight edge* to construct an angle *congruent* to a given angle and to construct the bisector of a given angle. They learn about complementary and supplementary angles, as well as central angles of circles.

By seventh grade or eighth grade, students learn that the point of an angle is called the *vertex*. They learn that vertical angles are formed when two lines intersect and that vertical angles have the same measure (they are congruent), and that adjacent angles are two angles with a common side. They learn that the sum of the measures of the angles of a triangle is 180 degrees, and that an angle with a measure of 180 degrees is called a *straight angle*. The students study central angles of circles, angles inscribed in circles, and how their measures are related.

Students discover the relationships among angles formed when parallel lines are cut by a transversal. They learn about interior angles, exterior angles, alternate interior and alternate exterior angles, corresponding angles, and vertical angles and which of those angles are *congruent* and which of them are *supplementary*.

Prisms in Middle School

Prior to middle school, children should be able to identify and describe prisms as box-shaped objects with square corners formed by perpendicular edges and perpendicular faces. They should also know that the opposite sides of the box (prism) are the same size and shape (they are congruent). Students should also be able to distinguish prism-shaped objects from other three-dimensional objects. They should also know that box shapes with all edges being congruent are called *cubes*. They should also know the name for rectangular prisms.

Boxes are PRISMS

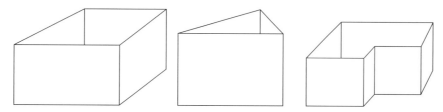

Unfortunately, the treatment of cubes and rectangular prisms often develops into the misconception that cubes are not rectangular prisms. Furthermore, from the limited variety of examples of rectangular prisms that they see in these earlier grades, children often think incorrectly that all rectangular prisms are right rectangular prisms, and that every face of a rectangular prism must be a rectangle.

The activities that follow are examples of the ways that middle school teachers can remediate the rectangular-prism misconceptions.

ACTIVITY 9.06 Tell Me about Boxes

Bring a variety of boxes to the classroom: big boxes, little boxes, cube-shaped boxes, boxes that are not rectangular. Place them at the front of the room where they are visible to the students.

Tell the students that you have brought some boxes for them to look at. Ask them to tell you all about the boxes that they see. Ask them how the boxes are alike and how they are different. Ask them what boxes are used for.

Select a cube-shaped box and another rectangular box and ask the students to tell you how these boxes are alike and how they are different.

Gather all the cube-shaped and rectangular-shaped boxes together. Have the students tell how all these boxes are alike.

Activity 9.07 All about Rectangular Prisms

Bring a variety of rectangular prisms to the classroom: big boxes, little boxes, cube-shaped boxes, wooden shapes that are rectangular prisms. Also bring some non-rectangular-prism shapes: boxes that are not rectangular, cans, cones, balls. Mix them up and place them at the front of the room where they are visible to the students.

Pick up one of the shapes that is a rectangular prism and show it to the class. Explain that a shape like this is called a *rectangular prism*. Explain the attributes of rectangular prisms as you point them out in the shape that you are holding. Then pick up another rectangular prism. Explain that it is also a rectangular prism. Point out the attributes that make it a rectangular prism.

Tell the students that you have brought some shapes for them to look at. Explain that some of the shapes are rectangular prisms and some are not. Select another rectangular prism and ask the students if it is a rectangular prism. Have them tell you why it is.

Select other shapes and ask if they are rectangular prisms. If they are rectangular prisms, ask why they are. If they are not rectangular prisms, ask why they are not.

In the earlier grades, students could develop the misconception that right angles are formed by the edges of rectangular prisms (that *all* the corners are square corners). This misconception arises out of the fact that most curriculum materials picture only rectangular prisms that are right rectangular prisms. Limiting the variety of rectangular prisms also results in the misconception that all faces of rectangular prisms are rectangles. In a right rectangular prism, all angles are right angles and all faces are rectangles. However, in general, the bases of a rectangular prism are rectangles and the rest of the faces are *parallelograms*. Angles formed by the edges of a rectangular prism may or may not be right angles, and the faces may or may not be rectangles. To remediate this misconception, the middle school teacher should show non-right rectangular prisms and discuss with the students the characteristics of right and non-right rectangular prisms.

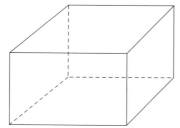 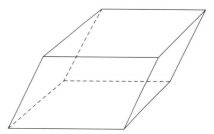

A right rectangular prism   A non-right rectangular prism

In the middle grades, the students learn to find the volume of a rectangular prism by counting cubes, and later they compute the volume by multiplying length times width times height. They create rectangular prisms by cutting out and folding paper patterns. They learn that the "top" and "bottom" faces of rectangular prisms are the same (they are *congruent*). They learn to recognize and name prisms by the shape of their bases and discover, therefore, that prisms are rectangular prisms when their bases are rectangles. They learn that prisms—cubes, rectangular prisms, and nonrectangular prisms—are all **polyhedrons.**

The following activity can be used by a middle-grade teacher when the students are learning about rectangular prisms.

Activity 9.08   Describe These Shapes

Assign students to work with one or two partners. Have one set of partners complete the activity at a time.

Give the partners three shapes: a cube, a rectangular prism that is not a cube, and a triangular prism. Tell them to find out everything that they can about the three shapes and write down everything that they discover. Allow them to use any measurement tools that are appropriate.

After all sets of partners have completed the activity, have the class discuss what they found out about the three shapes. Compile a list for each shape.

Also in the middle grades, students continue to use mathematical terminology related to rectangular prisms. They recognize that prisms are polyhedrons, and they name the parts of prisms as faces, edges, vertices, and bases. They use mathematical notation as they write about prisms. They learn the formula for the volume of a prism, and they compute the volume and surface area of prisms.

Adapting a Geometry Lesson

We now adapt a geometry lesson—one that would likely be found in grade 5. The lesson plan uses teaching procedures typical of those suggested in current fifth-grade teachers' guides. The lesson is an acceptable one. However, as is all too common, there is a minimal amount of concept development before the practice.

LESSON OBJECTIVE

The learners will classify polygons based on their sides and angles.

Lesson Opener

Direct the students' attention to the design at the top of the page in their textbooks. Point out the different shapes in the design. Point out the differences among those shapes. Explain that today's lesson is about classification of those different shapes.

Development

Tell the students to look at the first row of figures in the middle of the page and share with them that all of those figures are called polygons. Explain that *poly* means "many" and *gons* means "sides," so the word *polygon* means a shape with many sides. Explain that differently shaped polygons have names that are based the number of sides or the number or size of angles.

Explain that *tri* means "three," so polygons with three angles are called *triangles*. *Lateral* also means "sides" and *quadri* means "four," so polygons with four sides are called *quadrilaterals*. *Penta* means "five," so polygons with five sides are *pentagons*; *hexa* means "six," so polygons with six sides are *hexagons*; and *octa* means "eight," so polygons with eight sides are octagons.

Direct the students' attention to the third row of polygons. Point out that all the figures have four sides, so they are all quadrilaterals. Also point out that if a quadrilateral has two pairs of parallel sides it is called a *parallelogram,* and if a quadrilateral has exactly one pair of parallel sides it is called a *trapezoid.*

Explain that the bottom row of figures is all parallelograms. *Rect* means "right," so parallelograms with right angles are called *rectangles*. Rectangles with four equal sides are *squares*. A parallelogram with four equal sides is a *rhombus*, and a rhombus with right angles is a *square.*

Monitoring Learning

Have the students complete the top row of exercises on the second page of the lesson. After they have had enough time to complete the exercises, give them the correct answers, and ask if there are any questions.

Practice

For homework, assign the odd-numbered exercises on the second page of the lesson.

Closure

Point out that this lesson showed how different kinds of polygons are related.

To improve this lesson, we need to increase the amount of time spent developing the concepts. To make the lesson more complete, we need to increase the amount of visual information. We must make the lesson much more kinesthetic and plan for increased communication about the lesson concepts from and among the children. The plan needs more constant monitoring of learning throughout the lesson. These adaptations would make the lesson appropriate for almost all students. But, remember that some students with severe needs may require further instructional adaptations. The revision of this lesson plan is left to the teacher as an exercise at the end of the chapter.

Using Geometry to Solve Problems

Most problems involving geometry are really measurement problems. Although there are geometry concepts that must be considered, the solution frequently requires the application of measurement concepts, such as the problem in Chapter 8. The problem that follows is another example of a geometry problem that involves measurement:

George wants to build a rectangular corral for his horses beside a barn that is 50 feet long. He has 90 feet of fence, but because he wants the corral to have as large an area as possible, George decides to use the side of the barn as one side of the corral. If George makes the area of the corral as large as possible, what should its dimensions be?

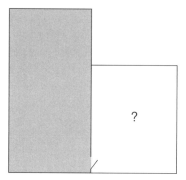

To solve this problem, we use two strategies that we used before: *Try and check* and *use a formula*. First, we try a couple of possibilities to see what the results are:

Suppose the corral used the barn for a 20-foot side and the fence for the other three sides. The corral would be 20 feet by 35 feet and would have an area of 700 square feet. Or, suppose the corral were square, with each side 30 feet long, the area would then be $30 \times 30 = 900$ square feet:

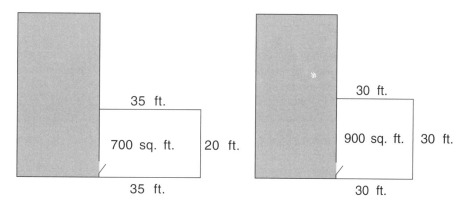

These two possibilities suggest that we can increase the size of the corral by making the barn side of the corral longer. We try other examples to see if this pattern holds:

If George would make the barn side of the corral 40 feet long, the corral would be 40 feet by 25 feet and would have an area of 1,000 square feet. If George would make the barn side of the corral 46 feet long, the corral would be 46 feet by 22 feet and would have an area of 1,012 square feet:

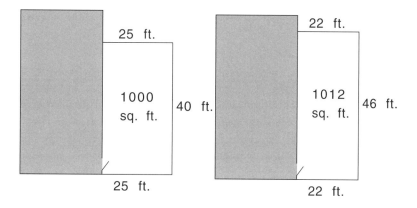

These two examples suggest that the pattern continues and that we can increase the area of the corral by making the barn side of the corral longer. So, it would make sense to use the full length of the barn as a side of the corral. We try that possibility and check to see if we are correct:

But, if George uses the full length of the barn for one side, the corral is 50 feet by 20 feet, and the area is 1,000 square feet:

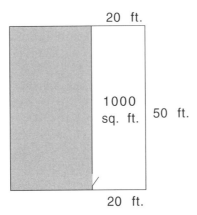

So, we can see that the area would be 1,000 square feet if the dimensions were 40 feet by 25 feet or if they were 50 feet by 20 feet. But the area is greater when the length is between 40 feet and 50 feet. We next try a corral with a length halfway between 40 feet and 50 feet:

If the barn side of the corral is 45 feet long, then the corral would be 45 feet by 22.5 feet, and its area would be 1,012.5 square feet. If we try other lengths between 40 feet and 50 feet, we would find the areas to be less than 1,012.5 square feet. George has the greatest area in his corral if he makes the barn side 45 feet long:

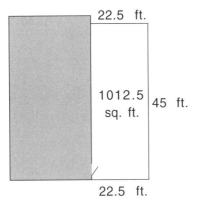

Exercises and Activities

1. Adapt the geometry lesson plan in this chapter to provide additional development of the ideas, additional visual representation of the ideas, additional kinesthetic activity, additional student communication, and additional monitoring of learning.

2. Consider the topic *parallelograms*. Create a list of the ways that each of the six big ideas of geometry (straightness, congruency, similarity, parallelism, perpendicularity, and symmetry) relate to parallelograms.

3. Consider the capital letter *W*:

Create a list of the ways that each of the six big ideas of geometry (straightness, congruency, similarity, parallelism, perpendicularity, and symmetry) relate to the letter.

4. Choose a lesson on geometry from a published middle school mathematics textbook series.

   a. Write a lesson plan that follows the teaching suggestions in the teacher's guide.

   b. Identify the parts of the lesson that develop the concept(s) of the lesson.

   c. Expand the lesson by adding more development of the concepts being taught. Use the big ideas of geometry and the ways that those big ideas relate to the lesson concepts to build understanding of those concepts.

   d. Identify kinesthetic activity that is included in the lesson and add more kinesthetic activity to the lesson.

   e. Identify parts of the lesson that include student communication about the concept(s) taught in the lesson and plan more opportunities for communication about the lesson concepts from or among the children.

   f. Identify the parts of the lesson designed to monitor the learning of the students and add more continual monitoring of learning to the lesson plan.

References and Related Readings

Ambrose, R. C., & Falkner, K. (2002). Developing spatial understanding through building polyhedrons. *Teaching Children Mathematics, 8,* 442–447.

Andrews, A. G. (1996). Developing spatial sense—A moving experience. *Teaching Children Mathematics, 2,* 290–293.

Battista, M. T. (2002). Learning geometry in a dynamic computer environment. *Teaching Children Mathematics, 8,* 333–339.

Clements, D. H., & Sarama, J. (2000). Young children's ideas about geometric shapes. *Teaching Children Mathematics, 6,* 482–487.

Lerch, H. H. (1981). *Teaching elementary school mathematics: An active learning approach.* Boston: Houghton Mifflin.

Thornton, C. A., Tucker, B. F., Dossey, J. A., & Bazik, E. F. (1983). *Teaching mathematics to children with special needs.* Menlo Park, CA: Addison-Wesley.

Websites

www.corestandards.ora/the-standards/mathematics
The Common Core State Standards for Mathematics can be found at this site.

www.proteacher.com/100021.shtml
Activities and lesson plans on geometry can be located on this site.

http://mathcentral.uregina.ca/RR/database/RR.09.96/archamb1.html
Lessons and activities on geometry can be located on this site.

www.sedl.org/1
Construction and geometry with a link to standards-based activity.

ten

DATA ANALYSIS AND PROBABILITY

Getting Information from Data and Measuring Likelihood

CHAPTER OUTLINE

Data Analysis and Probability: Two Distinct
  but Related Areas of Mathematics
Data Analysis
  Emphasizing the Big Ideas of Data Analysis
  Adapting a Data Analysis Lesson
  Using Data Analysis to Solve Problems

Probability
  Emphasizing the Big Ideas of Probability
  Adapting a Probability Lesson
  Using Probability to Solve Problems
Exercises and Activities

Data Analysis and Probability: Two Distinct but Related Areas of Mathematics

Statistics (or *data analysis*, as it is sometimes called) and *probability* are two distinct areas of mathematics, but the two fields are related. *Inferential statistics*—procedures used to make inferences about populations from representative data sets—is a field of study that is very dependent on probability. However, statistics in elementary and middle school is mostly descriptive, dealing with ways to gather, organize, describe, and present sets of data. The field of *descriptive statistics* relies very little on probability.

In elementary and middle school, probability and data analysis are normally developed independently. Although the elementary school mathematics textbook may present data analysis and probability in the same chapter, the two topics will generally appear as two distinct sections of the chapter. We will, therefore, follow the same pattern in this chapter. We will first examine data analysis (statistics), and then we will examine probability. We will emphasize the content and the approach to this content that one would expect to find in middle school mathematics.

Data Analysis

Emphasizing the Big Ideas of Data Analysis

As was done in the earlier chapters of this book, in this chapter we will identify big ideas—in this case, the big ideas of data analysis and probability. These big ideas are constantly recurring and can serve as a basis for developing students' understanding of data analysis and probability. Of course, the language used when the teacher is discussing the big ideas with students should be developmentally appropriate for them. With young students, the language should be informal and relate to specific situations that the children are experiencing. The language used with older children should be more formal and more precise.

The first big idea of data analysis is: *When appropriate data are gathered from a particular source, these data can inform you about that source.* With young students, data produced by counting might be used to describe the class or the students' families. Older students might gather data from a sample that has been selected from some larger group of people and then use those data to describe the larger group. At every level, however, this big idea should be emphasized. If you collect *appropriate* data, then those data are *useful information* and can be used to *answer questions.*

The second big idea of data analysis that we have chosen to emphasize is: *Well-organized data are more informative than data that are not well organized.* At every level, when data are gathered, students should be encouraged—and sometimes even required—to organize these data. As the students progress, they should learn to create tables to present the organized data. As this big idea is emphasized, students should learn to automatically think about *how data should be organized* to make it more useful for answering the questions that they wish to answer.

The third big idea of data analysis is: *Appropriate graphic representation can make data more understandable.* As students progress through the elementary school mathematics program, they learn to use a wide variety of graphs, each of which has advantages in particular situations. The simplest graphs are merely visual representations of organized data (see graphs below), whereas in middle school, the more complex graphs provide visual representations that use statistics that are descriptive of the data set. Throughout the development, the emphasis should be on *which graph is most appropriate* to present the information that we wish to convey.

The fourth big idea of data analysis is: *Descriptive statistics (numbers) can be used to describe a set of data.* The notion of *descriptive statistics* begins with simple descriptors such as the number of items in the set of data and the greatest or least number in the set of data. Older students should learn to use averages to describe sets of data. Still older students should use a variety of *measures of central tendency* (mean, median, and mode) and *measures of spread* (range and possibly even standard deviation).

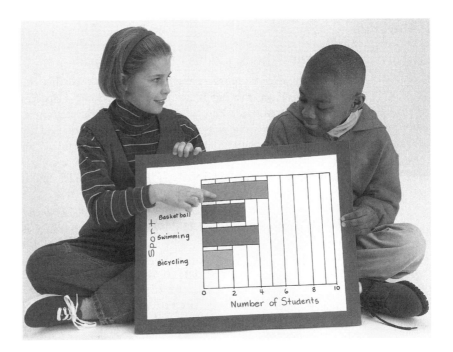

Data Analysis in Fifth Grade.   In fifth grade, students continue to collect data in natural settings and gain more experience in conducting surveys to answer questions. They may also begin to gather data from experiments and use their understanding of data organization to make sense of those results. The idea that organization of data makes the data easier to understand should be constantly reinforced. Students continue to learn to use more formal language to describe the data-gathering and data-organizing activities.

In the fifth grade, students will learn to interpret and construct broken-line graphs and circle graphs. As the students are introduced to these new kinds of graphs, they should develop a clear understanding that bar graphs and pictographs are used to show frequencies within categories, broken-line graphs are used to show changes over time, and circle graphs are used to show the relative sizes of the parts when some quantity is divided into parts.

The students will learn to read and interpret line graphs that show how two variables are related. They will be exposed to box-and-whisker plots and stem-and-leaf plots, both of which provide visual imagery of the spread within data sets. They will use information from tables and graphs to solve problems and use the mean, median, and mode to describe sets of data.

The following sequence of activities illustrates how some of these concepts might be developed.

Activity 10.01   In the Box

This activity requires a small cardboard box that is less than 8.5 inches by 12 inches but larger than 5 inches by 7 inches. The box should have an open top.

Use masking tape to make a line on the floor about 8 feet from a wall. Place the box against the wall. Explain to the children that you are going to have everyone in the class stand behind the line and try to toss a cube into the box. Point out how many students are in the class. Ask them to guess how many will toss the cube into the box. Write down their guesses. Ask how we can keep track of how many hit the box and how many miss the box. [We can use tally marks to record each hit and each miss.]

Choose a student to tally the results. Have that person toss first, record the outcome, then continue to record the rest of the outcomes. When everyone has had a turn, count the tallies.

Finally, have each student create a bar graph showing the results of the experiment.

Activity 10.02   Predicting and Checking

This activity requires two cubes. Write the numbers 1, 1, 1, 1, 1, and 2 on the six faces of one cube. Write 4, 4, 4, 4, 5, and 6 on the faces of the other cube.

Show the cubes to the class. Show the class the numbers on each cube. Ask the students what would be the least possible outcome if you tossed the two cubes and added the two numbers showing. What would be the greatest possible outcome? What other outcomes would be possible? Write all the possibilities in a column on the board.

Explain that the two cubes will be tossed 30 times. Ask which outcome will occur most often. Choose a student to record each outcome by placing a tally mark next to that number on the board. When all the tosses have been recorded, count the tallies. Whose prediction was the best one?

Have each student create a bar graph showing the results of the experiment.

Activity 10.03   Showing the Ups and Downs

Have the students record the outdoor temperature at the same time every day for a week. At the end of the week, show the class how to construct a broken-line graph.

Explain that this is called a *broken-line graph* and that it shows a change that takes place over time.

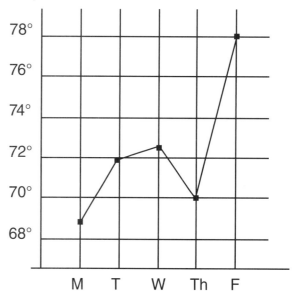

Activity 10.04   Another Week

Have the students record the outdoor temperature at the same time every day for a second week. At the end of the week, have the students work with partners to construct a broken-line graph showing the changes in the temperature for this week.

Activity 10.05   Selfish Sam

Tell the class this story:

> A boy named Sam was very selfish. One day, when he had 12 pieces of candy, he decided to share it with three friends: Deb, Jo, and Al. Sam gave each of his friends 2 pieces of candy, but he kept 6 pieces for himself. Sam thought he was being fair with his friends because, after all, it was his candy. But, for some reason, his friends were upset.

Ask the class to tell why his friends were upset. Tell the class that they are going to make a different kind of graph that will show how the candy was divided up. A graph like this might help Sam to see why the way he shared the candy upset his friends.

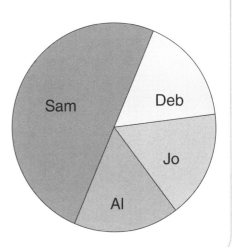

Draw a circle on the board. Ask what fraction of the candy Sam kept for himself. [one half] Draw a line separating the circle into two equal parts. Write "Sam" inside one of the two halves. Ask what part of the rest of the candy went to each of Sam's friends. [Each of them got one third of the remaining candy.] Divide the second half of the circle into three equal parts. Write "Al" in one part, "Jo" in one part, and "Deb" in' the last part.

Explain that this is called a *circle graph*.

Activity 10.06   Divide the Dollar

Draw a circle on the board, and draw lines from the center to separate the circle into sectors. Point to the angles in the circle and ask what the sum of these angles would be. [360°] Tell the students to remember this sum because we will use it later.

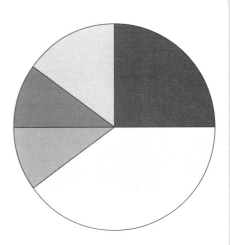

Show a dollar bill to the class. Ask how many cents are in a dollar. [100 cents] Ask the students to suppose they have a dollar and are going to save 25 cents. Ask what percent of the dollar will be saved. [25%] If 40 cents will be used to buy a snack, what percent of the dollar would that be? [40%] If 10 cents will be given to a little brother and another 10 cents will be given to a little sister, what percent of the dollar will each of them get? [10%] If the rest of the dollar will be given to grandma to pay her back what you owe her, what percent of the dollar would go to her? [15%]

Tell the students that they are going to make a circle graph to show how the dollar will be spent. Since we want part of the circle to represent the 40 cents that will be spent on a snack, that part must be 40% of the circle. All the angles add up to 360, so 40% of the circle would be .40 × 360° = 144°. Draw a circle and use a protractor to draw a sector with a central angle of 144°. Use the same process to determine the size and draw the rest of the parts of the circle graph. Label the parts of the graph.

Ask the students what the circle graph tells them.

Activity 10.07   Divide Your Own Dollar

Ask the students create circle graphs to show how each of them would spend a dollar.

Activity 10.08 Describe the Data

Write this set of numbers on the board:

3   4   7   6   4   5   4   9   4   4

Tell the students that you want each of them to use a single number to describe this set. Have them pick numbers that tell something about the set. Tell them that the number 10 describes the set. See if they can see why. [There are 10 numbers in the set.] Give the class time to think about the numbers and decide on a number that describes the set of numbers.

Have them tell what numbers they think describe the set and then tell why. Answers will vary. One might choose 3 because it is the first number listed. Another might choose 8 because it is not in the set. Others might choose 4 [there are more 4s], 3 [the smallest number], 9 [the largest number], 50 [the sum of the numbers], or other numbers for any reason at all. Do not make any judgments about which numbers are good choices or poor choices.

Activity 10.09 One Way to Describe the Middle

This is a follow-up to Activity 10.08

Using the same set of numbers that was used in Activity 10.08, tell the class that we would like to choose a number to describe where the middle of a set is. Point out that when you look at this set, you can immediately see that there are a lot more 4s than any other number. The *most frequent* number in the set is 4. Explain that the most frequent number is called the *mode* of the set. Write "mode" on the board. Write another set of numbers on the board. Have the students identify the mode.

Activity 10.10 A Second Way to Describe the Middle

This is a follow-up to Activity 10.08.

Using the same set of numbers that was used in Activity 10.08, tell the class that we would like to choose a number besides the mode to describe where the middle of a set is. Point out that we can find the average of the numbers by adding them all together and dividing by how many numbers we have. Have the students find the average. Explain that this "average" number is called the *mean* of the set. Write "mean" on the board. Write another set of numbers on the board. Have the students compute the mean.

Activity 10.11 A Third Way to Describe the Middle

This is a follow-up to Activity 10.08.

Write these 15 numbers on the board:

2   5   4   8   6   5   9   4   3   6   8   1   6   2   7

Tell the students that we would like to choose a number besides the mode or the mean to describe where the middle of this set is. Tell them that, first, we will rearrange the numbers so they are lined up from smallest to largest. Then, we will find the middle number:

1   2   2   3   4   4   5   5   6   6   6   7   8   8   9

This 5 is in the middle.

Explain that this "middle" number is called the *median* of the set. Write "median" on the board. Write a set of nine numbers on the board. Have the students find the median.

Data Analysis in Grades 6 through 8. In sixth through eighth grades, students will continue to gather and organize data. They will continue to interpret bar graphs, pictographs, circle graphs, and broken-line graphs. They will also use tables and bar graphs, pictographs, circle graphs, and broken-line graphs to display existing data as well as data that they have gathered. They will interpret and construct box plots and stem-and-leaf plots. The language used to describe these activities will become more formal and precise during these years. They will learn to interpret and construct double bar graphs that display two related data sets. Students may learn to interpret and construct histograms. They may learn to interpret scattergrams and box-and-whisker plots.

Students will use the mean, the median, and the mode to describe sets of data. They will learn to use the range to describe the amount of spread within a data set. Students will compute and interpret these descriptive statistics. They will gather data and use the resulting statistics to make estimates. They will also use data from existing tables and graphs to solve problems, and they may make tables or graphs to solve problems.

The following sequence of activities illustrates how these data analysis ideas might be developed.

Activity 10.12   Two . . . Two . . . Two Graphs in One

This activity requires two overhead transparencies. Your professor has copies of these transparencies in the instructor's manual.

Explain to the students that sometimes two bar graphs can be used to make comparisons between two groups. Tell them that Mrs. Jones and Mrs. Smith are the teachers of two classes, both of which made a bar graph showing how many boys and how many girls were in the class. Place the transparencies showing the two bar graphs on the overhead projector. Ask which class has more girls. Which class has more boys?

Explain that the comparisons would be a lot easier if all the information were on one graph. Place one transparency on top of the other and slide them together until the numbers and words coincide exactly. Explain that when two bar graphs are combined like this, the result is called a *double bar graph*. Point out that it is easier to compare the two classes with a double bar graph:

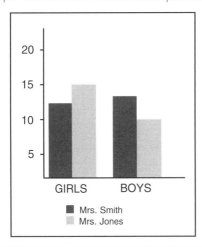
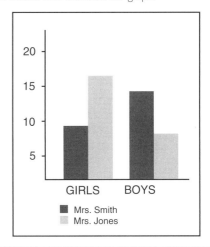

Activity 10.13   Survey Two Classes

This activity is a follow-up to Activity 10.12. Have the class survey the students in two other classes to find out how many prefer cats and how many prefer dogs. Then lead the class to complete a double bar graph that shows the results. Ask why a double bar graph might be preferred over two separate bar graphs.

Adapting a Data Analysis Lesson

We will now examine a typical data analysis lesson that would probably appear early in a middle grade textbook. Data are being gathered, analyzed, and graphed. However, to the students, the lesson appears to be about counting. We will begin by showing a lesson plan that is based on suggestions that you would likely find in the teacher's edition of the textbook.

LESSON OBJECTIVE

The learner will solve problems by making a bar graph.

Lesson Opener

Place some (fewer than 10) objects on a table. Choose a student to come to the table, count the objects, write the number of objects on the board, and stand next to the number. Repeat the process with two other students. Ask who counted the most objects. Who counted the fewest objects?

Ask the students what kinds of shirts they like to wear. When a type of shirt is described, ask who else likes that kind of shirt.

Development

Direct the attention of the class to the picture on the first page of the lesson. Ask what is pictured. [Shirts on hangers] Ask how they are different. [The colors are different.]

Have the students count the red shirts. Ask how many red shirts there are. [Six] Direct their attention to the columns of boxes below the picture. Have them use a red crayon to color the bottom six boxes in the first column—one for each red shirt. Tell the students do the same for shirts of each of the other colors pictured.

Monitoring Learning

Be sure that the students have counted correctly and have colored the correct number of boxes in each column:

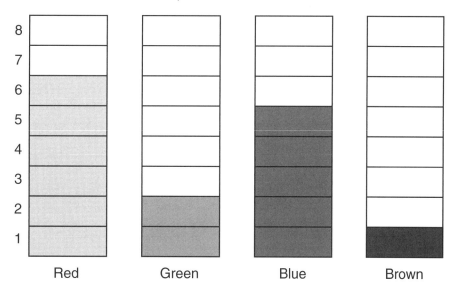

Direct their attention to the numbers next to the first column. Ask what those numbers tell us. [How many of each color] Explain that if we look at those numbers, we can tell how many without counting the boxes.

Practice

Have the students look at the picture on the second page of the lesson. Point out that this is another *graph*. Ask what has been counted. [Different kinds of shoes] Ask how we can tell how many of each kind there were without counting. [Look at the numbers beside the boxes.]

Explain that the graph shows what kinds of shoes the students in a class were wearing. The graph can help us answer questions. Tell the students that you are going to read some questions. Tell them to look at the graph to figure out the answers.

Read the questions one at a time. Give the students time to find the answer. Then tell them to write their answers in the answer boxes provided.

Closure

At the end of math time, remind the class that today we have used a graph to solve problems.

This lesson is a good lesson. There is some development of the new ideas and some kinesthetic activity. There is also visual representation of the ideas, communication from the children, and opportunities for the teacher to monitor the learning of the children.

However, we will revise the lesson plan to *increase* the amount of development. We will include *more* kinesthetic activity and more visual representations. We will plan for *even more* communication from and among the students, and for *more continual* monitoring of learning.

LESSON OBJECTIVE

The learner will solve problems by making a bar graph.

Lesson Opener

Scatter some (fewer than 10) counting chips on the floor at the front of the room. Choose a student to come pick up some, but not all, of the chips. Repeat the process with two other students. Ask the class who they think has picked up the most chips.

Have one of the students line up his or her chips in a row on the overhead projector:

Then have each of the other students line up their chips next to those of the first student:

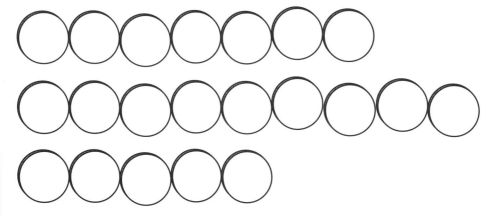

Monitor understanding. Watch the students' faces. At this point most of them will already see the answer. See if you can identify those who don't.

Ask if they can tell now who picked up the most chips. Who picked up the fewest? **Monitor understanding.** Do the students whom you earlier identified as not yet seeing the answer now understand? Have someone count the chips to see how many each student picked up. Write the numbers on the board. Ask which number indicates the most chips. Which number indicates the fewest chips? Ask if we got the right answers when we looked at the rows.

Development

Ask the students if they like to wear shirts with buttons or shirts without buttons. When someone describes a type of shirt, ask who else likes that kind of shirt. Point out that some students are wearing shirts that have buttons and some are wearing shirts without buttons.

Have all the students who are wearing a shirt with buttons stand up; then have them sit down. Have all the students who are wearing a shirt without buttons stand up; then have them sit down. Ask how many have shirts with buttons. How many have shirts without buttons? Ask if there are more with buttons or more without buttons. If the students try to guess, accept their guesses, but then ask if they are absolutely sure their answers are correct. **Monitor understanding.** Take note of students whose guesses indicate a lack of understanding.

Tell the students that we will look again to see who has buttons and who does not, but this time we will do it differently. Have all the students wearing shirts with buttons line up in a straight line. Then have those wearing shirts without buttons line up next to the first line. Be sure that the students are spread out evenly in both lines.

Ask which line has the most students. Ask what that tells us about the shirts. [The longest line tells us there are more shirts of that kind.] **Monitor understanding.** At this point, nearly everyone should understand. Provide further explanation if it is needed.

Have the students count to see how many there are of each kind of shirt.

Explain that instead of lining up people, we sometimes use objects to represent the people. Write "Buttons" on a card, and write "No buttons" on another card. Show the cards to the class and have someone read each of the cards. Place them on the table with one card directly above the other. Give everyone a square of paper. Have each student come forward one at a time and place her or his paper square in line by the cards:

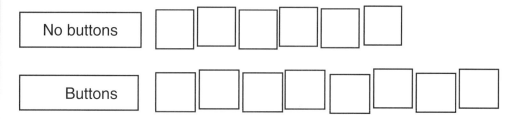

When all the squares are lined up in place, have the students gather around the table to see the result. Explain that what we have made is called a *graph*. Graphs like this help us to see how many are in each group and help us to compare the groups to see which has more or which has fewer. **Monitor understanding.** As before, observe the children's reactions to see who understands and who does not. Provide further explanations or additional examples as needed.

Explain that a graph makes it easier to see the answers to questions. Tell the students to suppose we noticed that shirts come in many colors. Ask what questions we might have about the colors of shirts. Let the students suggest different questions, but lead them to questions about numbers of shirts in different colors.

Have the students look at the picture on the first lesson page. Ask what is pictured. [Shirts on hangers] Ask how they are different. [The colors are different.] Tell them that we are going to make a graph showing the numbers of shirts in the different colors.

Ask the students how many red shirts there are. [Six] Ask how they can find out. [Count them.] Tell them to look at the columns of boxes below the picture. Ask how we can use those boxes to show how many red shirts there are. Have them use a red crayon to color the bottom six boxes in the first column—one for each red shirt. Tell the students to work with partners to figure out how many green shirts there are. When the partners are sure, have them color that many green boxes. Have the partners do the same for the blue shirts and the brown shirts. **Monitor understanding.**

Move around the class, observing to be sure that the shirts are being counted correctly and that the correct number of boxes are colored for each category:

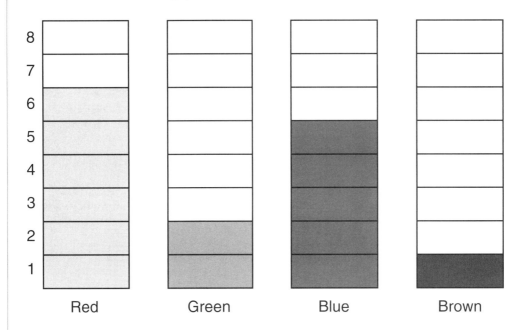

Ask the students what they can see from the graph. Which color has the most shirts? Which color has the fewest?

Direct their attention to the numbers next to the first column. Ask what those numbers tell us. [How many of each color] Explain that if we look at those numbers, we can tell how many without counting the boxes.

Show this graph with a paper covering the bottoms of the columns:

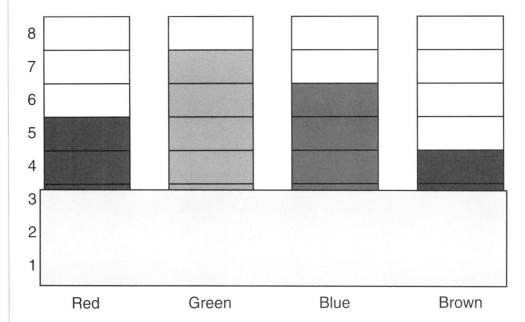

Ask how many red boxes there are. How many brown boxes? How many blue boxes? How many green boxes? **Monitor understanding.** Pay attention to the students who do not volunteer answers. They may need more explanation.

Point out to the students that they are able to see how many without counting.

Using Data Analysis to Solve Problems

Data (information) are used to solve problems in all the grades. Sometimes the students will gather that data from some appropriate source, but at other times, the data are provided in tables or graphs. In general, a problem is posed in the form of a question that is of interest to the students. The strategy used to solve the problem (answer the question) is to use or make a table or graph. And, of course, the strategy may also include gathering appropriate data. Older students may choose the questions that should be asked to produce the needed information, or they might even design a survey instrument to gather appropriate data.

Students in early grades should have been introduced to different kinds of graphs, each of which is used with a particular type of data. The problem-solving process may then include the use of, or selection of, an appropriate graph. For students, the organization of the data or the representation of the data in an appropriate graph may make the solution obvious. Middle grade students may be required to infer answers from the existing information, the tables, or the graphs.

By grades 7 and 8, students may use information gathered from a representative group to infer answers to questions about other similar groups. They may use tables, bar graphs, broken-line graphs, circle graphs, line graphs, stem-and-leaf plots, box-and-whisker plots, scattergrams, histograms, or other kinds of graphs to help them make those inferences. The problems are typically not about data analysis. Rather, data analysis is a tool that can be used to solve problems that arise naturally in many different circumstances.

Probability

Emphasizing the Big Ideas of Probability

As with data analysis, probability has several big ideas. They are big ideas because they are constantly recurring. They are big ideas because they form the basis for other probability concepts. The big ideas also provide a useful framework for the study and understanding of probability in the elementary grades.

One big idea of probability is the notion of *likelihood: Some events (things that happen) are more likely than other events. Some things are very likely to happen, and some may be sure to happen. Some events are very unlikely to happen, and some cannot happen— they are impossible.* The awareness of *likelihood* is the beginning of the understanding of probability.

Another big idea of probability is: *Likelihood can be estimated.* Through observation of events that occur naturally and observation of the outcomes of experiments, we can estimate how likely particular events are to occur. *Estimates of likelihood* can be improved by such observation, particularly if the data gathered are well organized.

A third big idea of probability is: *Likelihood (the probability that an event will occur) can be measured.* Measurement of probability requires a formal definition of probability. After students have learned to measure the probability of a particular event, the study of probability becomes more formal. The language and notation become more precise. The study of the probability of more complex events becomes possible.

Probability in Fifth Grade.
By fourth grade, children should have begun to think about likelihood more formally, by making estimates of likelihood by first considering all the possibilities. They may have conducted experiments where the possibilities are obvious (for example, flip coins or spin spinners). They may have formally defined probability as *m* chances out of *n* possibilities. They may have begun to consider pairs of events, like flipping a penny and flipping a quarter.

By grade 5, students may have formally defined *probability.* They may have used the definition to determine the probability of events. They may have used experimentation to verify probabilities.

In fifth grade, some students may need remediation. The following activities demonstrate how a teacher might remediate some of these ideas of probability.

Activity 10.14   Possibilities I

For this activity, you will need a small paper bag and counting chips in four colors, such as red, blue, yellow, and green.

Show the students that the paper bag is empty by turning it upside down and shaking it. While they watch, place five red chips in the bag. Ask what is in the bag. [Some red chips] Place five blue chips in the bag. Ask what is in the bag. [Some red chips and some blue chips] Continue in the same way until there are five chips of each color in the bag.

Tell the class that you are going to take a chip out of the bag. Ask what color it will be. As each color is suggested, write that color on the board and ask if there are any other possibilities. Continue until all four possibilities have been named and they are listed on the board. Ask if it would be possible to get a white chip. [No.] Why not? [There are no white chips in the bag.]

Point out that all the possibilities have been listed. Any of those colors might be taken from the bag. Have children come to the front, one at a time, to take a chip out of the bag. In each case, say, "Yes. That is one of the possibilities." Then replace the chip that was drawn. Continue until every color has been selected at least once. Ask why no one got a black chip. [That's not possible.] Ask why it is not possible to get a black chip. [No black chips are in the bag.]

Activity 10.15   Possibilities II

For this activity, you will need a cube with 1 written on two faces, 3 written on three faces, and 4 written on one face.

Pass the cube around so everyone can see what is on each face. Tell the class that the cube will be tossed, and we want to see what number will be on top. Ask what the possibilities are. [1, 3, or 4]

Have students take turns tossing the cube. Record the outcomes. After each number has come up, point out that every possibility has happened. Ask why no one got a 2. [That's not possible.] Ask why it is not possible. [There are no 2s on the cube.]

Point out that some numbers came up more often than others. Ask why that happened. [There were more 3s and only one 4.]

Activity 10.16   Probabilities I

This activity is a follow-up to Activity 10.15.

Have the students look at the cube and list the possibilities. [1, 3, and 4] Ask if these possibilities are equally likely. [No.] Why? [There are not the same number of 1s, 3s, and 4s.]

Ask how many faces a cube has. [Six] Ask if each of these faces could end up on top. [Yes.] Ask how many of the six faces have a 1 written on them. [Two] Write on the board "2 chances out of 6 possibilities will be 1." Ask how many faces have a 3 written on them. [Three] Write on the board "3 chances out of 6 possibilities will be 3." Ask how many faces have a 4 written on them. [Only one] Write on the board "1 chance out of 6 possibilities will be 4."

Explain that we would say that the *probability* that we will get a 1 is 2 out of 6. The probability that we will get a 3 is 3 out of 6. Ask what the probability that we will get a 4 is. [1 out of 6] What is the probability that we would get a 5? [0 out of 6]

Activity 10.17   Probabilities II

This activity is a follow-up to Activity 10.16. You will need enough cubes for each set of partners. On all of the cubes, four faces will show a 2, one face will show a 5, and one face will show a 6.

Form groups of two or three partners. Give each group of partners a cube. Have them look at the cube, list the possibilities, and then write the probability for each possibility.

Discuss the results and check to be sure that everyone understands how to find the probabilities. Ask what the probability that you would get an 8 would be. [0 out of 6]

Activity 10.18   Predicting and Checking

Form groups of two or three partners. Give each group of partners a blank cube. Tell them that you want them to write either an 8 or a 10 on each face of the cube. They must decide how many of each number there will be.

After all the partner groups have finished writing a number on each face of their cubes, tell them to write the probability for each possibility.

Tell the class that you want each set of partners to think about the probabilities and predict how many times each possibility will happen if the cube is tossed 25 times. They should write down their predictions, then toss their cube 25 times and keep a record of the outcomes.

When everyone is finished, discuss the results. How accurate were the predictions? Why were they not exactly correct?

Probability in Grades 6 through 8.   In sixth through eighth grades, students will study probability more formally and will learn to use appropriate vocabulary and notation as they determine and use probabilities. They will estimate probabilities from existing graphs and tables, and they will gather data that will be used to estimate probabilities. They will use probabilities to make predictions.

By grade 6, they will have defined the *probability of an event* to be the number of favorable outcomes divided by the number of possible outcomes (when all the possible outcomes are equally likely). They will use tree diagrams and the fundamental counting principle to determine the number of favorable outcomes and the number of possible outcomes.

In grades 7 and 8, students should learn to determine the probability of compound events, including independent and dependent events. They will use the fundamental counting principle and compute the number of permutations and combinations to determine the number of favorable outcomes and the number of possible outcomes.

The following sequence of activities illustrates how a teacher might develop some of these probability concepts.

Activity 10.19 Writing Probabilities I

For this activity, you will need a plastic cup that you cannot see through and counting chips of different colors, such as red, yellow, and green.

Show the students that the cup is empty. Let them see you place a red chip, a yellow chip, and a green chip in the cup. Ask how many chips are in the cup. [Three] Ask how many out of three are yellow. [1 out of 3] Ask what fraction of the chips is yellow. [$\frac{1}{3}$]

Explain that the probability that the chip will be yellow is *one third*. Say, "This is how we write that probability."

On the board, write "P(yellow) $= [\frac{1}{3}]$."

Ask, "What is the probability that the chip will be green?" [$\frac{1}{3}$]

Write "P(green) $= [\frac{1}{3}]$."

Ask, "What is the probability that the chip will be red?"

Call on someone to come to the board and write that probability.

Repeat the activity with four red chips, three green chips, and one yellow chip in the cup.

Activity 10.20 Writing Probabilities II

As a follow-up to Activity 10.19, show the class five pennies, one nickel, and two quarters, then put them in your pocket. Ask them to recall what you put in your pocket. How many coins? How many pennies, nickels, and quarters?

Tell them that you are going to take a coin out of your pocket. Have them write the probability that it will be a quarter, the probability that it will be a penny, and the probability that it will be a nickel. Ask what the probability is that it will not be a quarter. [You may need to point out that this probability is the same as getting either a penny or a nickel.]

Activity 10.21   Estimating Probabilities

For this activity, you will need a small box, 3 red counting chips, and 7 blue counting chips. Place the chips in the box.

Show the box to the class. Tell the students that there are 10 chips in the box. Some of them are red, and some of them are blue. Explain that we are going to estimate the probability that a chip taken from the box will be red. We will experiment by drawing chips from the box to help us make the estimate.

Start by having 10 students come forward, one at a time, to draw a chip from the box without looking. Record each result and have each student place the chip back in the box before the next student takes a turn. Use the results from the 10 drawings to make the first estimate. For example, if a red chip was drawn 4 out of 10 tries, then the best estimate would be $P(\text{red}) = \frac{4}{10}$.

Explain that we can usually improve the estimate by increasing the number of tries. Have another 10 students draw a chip from the box, and add those results to the earlier ones. Use the results from all 20 drawings to estimate the probability that a red chip will be drawn. For example, if this time only one person drew a red chip, then, altogether, 5 out of 20 were red. So, the best estimate would be $P(\text{red}) = \frac{5}{20}$.

Repeat this process until a total of 50 drawings have been made. After writing the estimated probability, point out that this is not the exact probability. Have a student open the box and count the red and blue chips. Write the actual probability of drawing a red chip with the latest estimate of the probability. Ask why they are not the same. [One is just an estimate.] Ask how the estimate might have been improved. [Use even more trials.]

Activity 10.22   Possibility Trees

Tell the students that you are going to flip a penny and a nickel. Point out that you will show them an easy way to figure out every possible outcome. It is called a *tree diagram*.

Ask what the possible outcomes are if you flip only the penny. [Heads or tails] Draw the first branches of the *tree diagram:*

Penny Heads

Penny Tails

Ask what the possible outcomes are if you flip the nickel. [Heads or tails] Draw the next branches of the tree diagram:

Penny Heads — Nickel Heads

Nickel Tails

Penny Tails — Nickel Heads

Nickel Tails

Show the class that to identify a possible outcome for flipping both coins, you can trace that possibility from the beginning point to the end of a branch. For example, if you trace the possibility from the beginning to the end of the second branch, you would have one of the four possibilities: *penny heads and nickel tails.*

Have students come to the board and identify the other possibilities by tracing them from the beginning to the end of a branch.

Ask how you can tell how many possibilities there are. [Count the branches.]

Activity 10.23   More Possibility Trees

Tell the class that you are going to flip a penny, a nickel, and a quarter. Ask how many possible outcomes there would be. Allow only about 5 seconds for the students to answer. Then tell them that you can use a tree diagram to see the possibilities. Lead the class to develop the tree diagram:

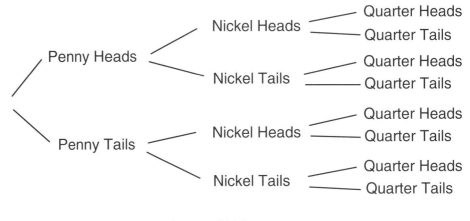

Ask how many possible outcomes there are. [eight]

Activity 10.24   Probability Trees

Form groups of two or three partners. Tell them that you are going to flip a coin and then toss a cube with the numbers 1 to 6 on the faces. Have the partners work together to draw a tree diagram that shows all the possible outcomes.

Ask how many possibilities there are. [12] How many of those possibilities are a tail and a 5? [Just 1] What is the probability that the result will be tails and 5? [$\frac{1}{12}$] How many of those possibilities are heads with a number less than 3? [2: H&1, H&2] What is the probability that the result will be a heads and a number less than 3? [$\frac{2}{12}$ or $\frac{1}{6}$] What is the probability that the result will be tails and an odd number? [$\frac{3}{12}$ or $\frac{1}{4}$]

Activity 10.25   The Counting Principle

Draw a tree diagram for the experiment of tossing a coin and then spinning the spinner pictured at the right.

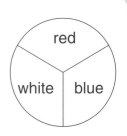

Call attention to the ends of the branches in the tree diagram. Three colors appear two times, so there are 2 × 3, or 6, branches:

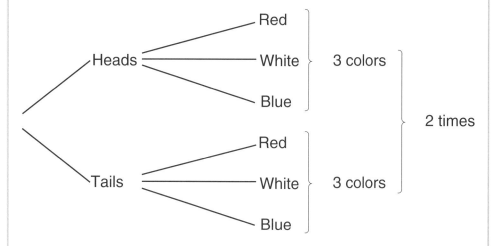

Point out that the first part of the experiment could turn out two ways, and the second part of the experiment could turn out three ways. So, the full experiment could turn out 2 × 3, or 6, ways.

Tell the class that the experiment will be changed so that a penny will be tossed, the spinner spun, and a nickel tossed. Extend the tree diagram to show the possibilities for this new experiment:

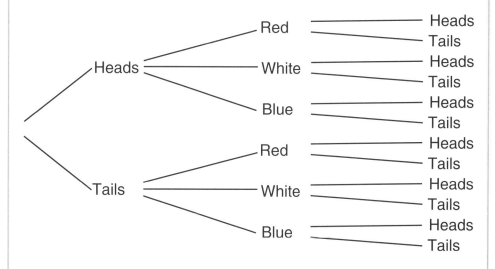

The first part of the experiment could turn out two ways, the second part three ways, and the third part two ways. Altogether, then, there are 2 × 3 × 2, or 12, possible outcomes.

Adapting a Probability Lesson

The following lesson plan is based on a probability lesson that we could expect to find in a middle grade mathematics textbook. The plan will incorporate teaching suggestions that are typical of those that are suggested in published teacher's editions.

LESSON OBJECTIVE

The learner will record and interpret data gathered in probability experiments.

Lesson Opener

Prepare two number cubes with the numbers 1 to 6 on the faces. Show the cubes to the students. Ask them what the greatest possible sum would be if the two cubes were tossed. [12] What would be the least possible sum? [2]

Development

Explain that the cubes will be tossed in an experiment. Point out that the class has already found two of the possible outcomes—the greatest possible outcome and the least possible outcome. [12 and 2] Ask what the other possible outcomes are. [3, 4, 5, 6, 7, 8, 9,10, and 11]

Make a vertical list of the possible outcomes, from least to greatest, on an overhead transparency. Ask a student to tally the outcomes of the experiment. Have the rest of the students take turns coming forward and tossing the cubes twice. Have the recorder tally both tosses for every student. Ask which of the possible outcomes occurred most often. Which occurred least often? Did any possibilities occur the same number of times?

While the class is watching, use a red marker to circle the numbers on one of the cubes. Show the number 5 on both cubes. Point out that now we can tell the difference between the outcome on one cube and the outcome on the other cube. Show the red 2 and the plain 4. Ask what the sum is. [6] Next, show the plain 2 and the red 4. Ask what the sum is. [6] Point out that these two outcomes are different even though we have added the same two numbers to get the same sum.

Tell the students that you want them to list all the possibilities again. Use leading questions to complete the list:

R1, 1	R2, 1	R3, 1	R4, 1	R5, 1	R6, 1
R1, 2	R2, 2	R3, 2	R4, 2	R5, 2	R6, 2
R1, 3	R2, 3	R3, 3	R4, 3	R5, 3	R6, 3
R1, 4	R2, 4	R3, 4	R4, 4	R5, 4	R6, 4
R1, 5	R2, 5	R3, 5	R4, 5	R5, 5	R6, 5
R1, 6	R2, 6	R3, 6	R4, 6	R5, 6	R6, 6

Ask how many possibilities there are altogether. [36] Ask how many ways you could get a sum of 7. [Six ways] Ask how many ways you could get a sum of 6. [Five ways] Ask whether you are more likely to get a 7 or a 6. [7 is more likely.] Ask if there is another sum that is just as likely as a sum of 3. [Yes, 3 and 11 are equally likely.] Using the list of possible outcomes, lead the students to list the possibilities from most likely to least likely.

Practice

Have each student choose and complete two of the experiments on the second page of the lesson.

Closure

Ask the students how a complete list of the possible outcomes of an experiment can help you to predict the outcome.

This is a good lesson plan. There is a step-by-step development of the relationship between understanding of possible outcomes and the ability to predict outcomes. However, as good as it is, the plan can be strengthened. We will do this by providing more development so that generalizations can be based on broader experiences, and by providing more visual representations of the concepts. We will provide for varied learning needs by including more kinesthetic activity and by planning for more student communication about the probability concepts. In order to identify learning difficulties as early as possible so that adjustments to instruction can be made as they are needed, we will plan for continual monitoring of learning.

LESSON OBJECTIVE

The learner will record and interpret data gathered in probability experiments.

Lesson Opener

Prepare enough number cubes with the numbers 1 to 6 on the six faces so that every student in the class has one. Have all the students work with one or two partners. Ask them what the greatest possible sum would be if the two cubes were tossed. [12] How could you get a sum of 12? [6 on both cubes] What would be the least possible sum? [2] How could you get 2? [1 on both cubes]

Development

Explain that the cubes will be tossed in an experiment. Point out that the students have already found two of the possible outcomes—the greatest possible outcome and the least possible outcome. [12 and 2] Have each group of partners figure out what the other possible outcomes are. [3, 4, 5, 6, 7, 8, 9, 10, and 11] **Monitor learning.** As the students are working, move around the room, observe, and listen as the partners figure out the possibilities. Pay particular attention to those with histories of learning difficulties. Provide help as it is needed.

When enough time has been allowed for the students to find the possibilities, have them tell you what the possibilities are. Make a vertical list of the possible outcomes, from least to greatest, on an overhead transparency. Have each set of partners toss two cubes four times and keep a record of the four sums that were tossed. When all the partners have finished, have the groups report their outcomes. Tally the results on the transparency.

Ask which of the possible outcomes occurred most often. Which occurred least often? Did any possibilities occur the same number of times? **Monitor learning.** During this discussion, pay attention to the students who are having difficulty. Be sure that they understand. Encourage them to respond.

Repeat the experiment, but first have each set of partners write down their prediction of how many times each possibility will occur. Repeat the experiment Discuss the results. Who had the best prediction? How did they decide what they would predict?

Ask the class to think about how many different ways you could get a sum of 7. [The class might suggest three ways: 1 + 6, 2 + 5, and 3 + 4.] Ask them to think about how many ways you could get a sum of 12. [There is only one way: 6 + 6.] Ask if this helps explain why 7 occurred more often than 12.

Explain that there is another way to think about the possible outcomes that can help us make our predictions even more accurate. Take a cube from one set of partners and use a red marker to circle all the numbers on that cube. Then toss that cube with another one without the red circles. For example, the result might be a 2 that is circled in red and a 5 that is not circled. Write this result on the board as R2, 5. **Monitor learning.** Ask why you have written an *R* by the 2. Be sure that everyone understands that the *R* means that number was circled in red.

Turn the cubes so that they show a circled 5 and a 2 that is not circled. Point out that this is a different outcome. **Monitor learning.** Watch the eyes of the students. If there seems to be confusion, ask why this result is different. Write this result on the board as R5, 2.

Pass out red markers so that each group of partners can circle the numbers on one cube in red. Toss the cube again and have a student come to the board and record the result. For example, if the result turns out to be a circled 1 and a 3 that is not circled, it should be recorded as R1, 3. **Monitor learning.** Ask why there is an *R* beside the 1. See if students who have had past difficulties can answer.

Have the partners use one cube with numbers circled in red and one cube with plain numbers to make a list of all the possible outcomes by using this recording system. **Monitor learning.** Move around the room and observe the partners' work. Are they recording the possibilities correctly? Are they using some systematic way to discover those possibilities?

When the partners have completed their work, have them tell you what the possibilities are. Write a master list of possibilities on the board. Use leading questions to help you complete the list in an orderly way. For example, you might list the possibilities as follows:

R1, 1	R2, 1	R3, 1	R4, 1	R5, 1	R6, 1
R1, 2	R2, 2	R3, 2	R4, 2	R5, 2	R6, 2
R1, 3	R2, 3	R3, 3	R4, 3	R5, 3	R6, 3
R1, 4	R2, 4	R3, 4	R4, 4	R5, 4	R6, 4
R1, 5	R2, 5	R3, 5	R4, 5	R5, 5	R6, 5
R1. 6	R2, 6	R3, 6	R4, 6	R5, 6	R6, 6

Ask how many possibilities there are altogether. [36] Ask how many ways you could get a sum of 7. [Six ways] Ask how many ways you could get a sum of 6. [Five ways] Ask whether you are more likely to get a 7 or a 6. [7 is more likely.] Ask if there is another sum that is just as likely as a sum of 3. [Yes, 3 and 11 are equally likely.] Using the list of possible outcomes, lead the students to list the possibilities from most likely to least likely.

Write the letters *N*, *E*, and *W* on three white counting chips, and write the letters *N*, *O*, and *W* on three yellow chips:

Place the yellow chips in one paper bag, and place the white chips in another paper bag. Take a chip from each bag. For example, you might draw the yellow *N* and the white *W*. Ask how the result should be recorded. [One way that the result could be recorded is y*N*, w*W*.] Have the partners list all the possible outcomes of this experiment. **Monitor learning.** Move around the room and observe the partners' work. Are they using some systematic way to discover those possibilities?

Ask how many possible outcomes there are. [Nine] Point out that if the outcome is y*O*, w*W*, the two letters can be used to spell the word *OW*. Ask if the letters in any other outcome could be used to spell a word. Ask how many outcomes can spell a word. [Three outcomes: y*O*, w*N*; y*O*, w*W*; y*W*, w*E*] Write these possibilities on the board. Have the students predict how many times the letters could spell a word if the experiment were done 15 times. Repeat the experiment 15 times to check.

Practice

Have the students work with partners to choose and complete two of the experiments on the second page of the lesson.

Closure

Ask the students to review what was done today. Ask what new thing they learned.

Using Probability to Solve Problems

In the elementary grades, problem solving using probability is focused on predicting future events. With younger students that problem solving typically involves choosing a most likely future outcome. The problem may be to determine whether a future outcome is impossible, possible, or sure to happen. In the middle grades, the problem might be to consider all the possibilities when the students are predicting a future outcome. Or, the problem might be to use probability to predict a future outcome, or to determine whether it is reasonable or unreasonable to expect an outcome to occur.

As students get older, they may use empirical probabilities (probabilities that are estimated from experiments or surveys) to predict future outcomes. On the basis of probabilities, they may determine whether a possible decision would be wise or unwise. They will choose strategies on the basis of probabilities and they will use empirical probabilities to make workplace decisions or to make recreational decisions.

Some of the following exercises parallel problems that students in grades 5 to 8 might be asked to solve.

Exercises and Activities

1. Compare the original and revised versions of the *data analysis* lesson plan presented in this chapter. Identify:
   a. The additional development (if any)
   b. The additional visual representation of ideas (if any)
   c. The additional kinesthetic activity (if any)
   d. The additional student communication (if any)
   e. The additional monitoring of learning (if any)

2. Compare the original and revised versions of the *probability* lesson plan presented in this chapter. Identify:
   a. The additional development (if any)
   b. The additional visual representation of ideas (if any)
   c. The additional kinesthetic activity (if any)
   d. The additional student communication (if any)
   e. The additional monitoring of learning (if any)

3. Find a lesson in a published grade 5–8 mathematics textbook series that teaches students how to organize data.
   a. Follow the suggestions provided in the teacher's edition to prepare a lesson plan. Do *not* be creative. Follow the suggestions as exactly as you can.
   b. Revise the lesson plan by adding more development.

4. Find a lesson in a published grade 5–8 mathematics textbook series that teaches students how to make a bar graph.
   a. Follow the suggestions provided in the teacher's edition to prepare a lesson plan. Do *not* be creative. Follow the suggestions as exactly as you can.
   b. Revise the lesson plan by adding more visual representation of the ideas.

5. Find a lesson in a published grade 5–8 mathematics textbook series that teaches students how to make a circle graph.
   a. Follow the suggestions provided in the teacher's edition to prepare a lesson plan. Do *not* be creative. Follow the suggestions as exactly as you can.
   b. Revise the lesson plan by adding suggestions for continual monitoring of learning.

6. Find a lesson in a published grade 5–8 mathematics textbook series that teaches students how to use data gathered in an experiment to estimate the results if the experiment is repeated.
   a. Follow the suggestions provided in the teacher's edition to prepare a lesson plan. Do *not* be creative. Follow the suggestions as exactly as you can.
   b. Revise the lesson plan by adding more kinesthetic activity.

7. Suppose you have a fifth-grade student who does not understand how to solve the following problem:

> Imagine that you work in a shop that sells caps. The sales history of the shop indicates that about 25% of the caps sold have a humorous saying stitched on the front. About 50% have the logo of a sports team, about 15% have an assortment of other images on them, and the rest have no image at all.
>
> There is room in the shop to display 84 caps. After a busy day, there are 41 caps left on display: 8 plain caps, 18 with sports team logos, 12 with humorous sayings, and 3 with other images.
>
> You need to restock the display area so the shop will be ready for the next day's business. How many additional caps of each kind would you place on display?

Think about the variety of reasons that a student might have difficulty solving this problem. Describe how you would help your student understand how to solve the problem.

8. Suppose you have a group of four seventh-grade students who do not understand how to solve the following problem:

> Imagine that you want to make a set of 50 cards that will be used in a game to spell words. You know that there will be a need for more of some letters and fewer of other letters. How can you use an article from the newspaper to help you know how many of each letter to include in the deck of cards?

Describe how you would help these students understand how to solve the problem.

9. Describe an instructional/learning activity in which students toss a plastic cup to estimate the probability that it will fall right side up, the probability that it will fall upside down, and the probability that it will fall on its side.

References and Related Readings

Bush, S. B. & Karp, K. S. (2012). Hunger games: What are the chances? *Teaching Mathematics in Middle School, 17,* 426–435.

Kabiri, M. S. & Smith, N. L. (2003). Turning traditional textbook problems into open-ended problems. *Teaching Mathematics in Middle School, 9,* 186–192.

McClain, K. (1999). Reflecting on students' understanding of data. *Mathematics Teaching in the Middle School, 4,* 374–380.

National Council of Teachers of Mathematics. (2000). *Principles and standards for school mathematics.* Reston, VA: Author.

Websites

www.corestandards.org/the-standards/mathematics
The Common Core State Standards for Mathematics can be found at this site.

http://illuminations.nctm.org/swr/list.asp?Ref=1&Std=4&Grd=-1
Data analysis and probability activities for grades 5 through 8.

eleven

FOUNDATIONS OF ALGEBRA

Properties of Operations on Integers, Rational Numbers, and Irrational Numbers

CHAPTER OUTLINE

Emphasizing the Big Ideas of Algebra
  The Closure Property
  The Associative Property
  The Commutative Property
  The Distributive Properties
  The Identity Elements
  The Inverse Elements

Computation with Integers
  The Order of Operations
Using Properties of Equality to Solve
  Equations
Exponents
Exercises and Activities

Emphasizing the Big Ideas of Algebra

There are many important ideas in algebra, but there are six really big ideas. Before we look at the big ideas of algebra, we will briefly consider the difference between arithmetic and algebraic notation—the way we write mathematical expressions. In both arithmetic and algebra, addition is indicated by the plus sign and subtraction is indicated by the minus sign.

$$12 + 23 \qquad a + b \qquad 24 - 15 \qquad m - n$$

On the other hand, there are three ways to indicate multiplication. We can use the multiplication sign, we can use a raised dot, or we can use juxtaposition (i.e., write the two numbers side by side). In arithmetic, the multiplication sign is almost always used. In algebra, the raised dot is normally used when the numbers are written as Arabic numerals, and juxtaposition is normally used when the numbers are written as variables.

$$12 \times 47 \qquad a \times b \qquad 12 \cdot 47 \qquad a \cdot b \qquad (12)(47) \qquad ab$$

There are also three ways to indicate division. Division can be written using two different division signs or as a fraction (the numerator divided by the denominator). In arithmetic, we typically use one of the two division signs whereas in algebra, we sometimes use the first of the two division signs, but we typically write division as a fraction.

$$48 \div 3 \qquad d \div f \qquad 3\overline{)48} \qquad f\overline{)d} \qquad \frac{48}{3} \qquad \frac{d}{f}$$

As we examine the big ideas of algebra, you may realize that you have already seen the big ideas when you studied the arithmetic operations. These big ideas are recurring, and they form the basis for the development of the rest of algebra. They are the rules that control how operations behave. The big ideas of algebra are the closure property, the associative property, the commutative property, the distributive property, the existence of identity elements, and the existence of inverse elements.

The Closure Property

A *binary operation* (an operation that is performed with two numbers) has closure or is said to be closed if, whenever the operation is performed on two numbers from your number set, there will always be a unique number (exactly one number) in the set that is the answer. For example, suppose your number set is the set of whole numbers.

$$W = \{0, 1, 2, 3, 4, 5, 6, 7, 8, 9, 10, 11, \ldots\}$$

You can choose to add any two whole numbers, and there will be exactly one whole number that is the answer. *Addition is closed in the set of whole numbers.*

$$2 + 17 = 19$$

Both 2 and 17 are whole numbers, so the answer must be a whole number.

$$264 + 1026 = 1290$$

Both 264 and 1026 are whole numbers, so the answer must be a whole number.

Multiplication is also closed in the set of whole numbers. If we multiply two whole numbers, the answer will always be a whole number. If a and b are both whole numbers, then $a \times b$ will also be a whole number. When we perform an operation, we always like to have an answer, but that is not always the case. When an operation is not closed, we expand the number system in order to get closure. Consider, for example, subtraction. Subtraction is not closed in the set of whole numbers. When we subtract a whole number from another whole number, there is not always a whole-number answer. For example, consider this example.

$$3 - 16 = ???$$

There is no whole-number answer for that subtraction. So, *subtraction is not closed in the set of whole numbers.* In order to get closure for subtraction we expand the number set to include negatives. We call this expanded set of numbers the integers.

$$I = (\ldots -4, -3, -2, -1, 0, 1, 2, 3, 4, 5, \ldots)$$

Now, we have an answer to every subtraction. *Subtraction is closed in the set of integers.*

$$3 - 16 = -13 \qquad -4 - (-5) = 1 \qquad -42 - 6 = -48$$

Division is not closed in the set of whole numbers. When we divide a whole number by another whole number, there is not always a whole-number answer. In this case, we expand the set of numbers to include fractions and decimals. This expanded set of numbers is called the *set of rational numbers. Addition, subtraction, and multiplication are all closed in the set of rational numbers.* Division is closed except for one very important exception. We cannot divide by zero. If you try to divide by zero, there is no answer. The following is the formal definition of division:

$$a \div b = c \text{ if and only if } c \text{ is the unique number such that } c \cdot b = a$$

c is the correct answer if and only if two requirements are met. First, $c \cdot b = a$. Second, the answer must be unique. Let's look at several examples where we try to divide by zero.

$5 \div 0 = n$ n can be the correct answer only if $n \cdot 0 = 5$. Regardless of the value of n, $n \cdot 0 = 0$. So, there is no correct answer.

$0 \div 0 = 0$ Zero can be the answer only if $0 \cdot 0 = 0$. It appears that zero is the correct answer. However, we generally believe that when you divide a number by itself, the answer must be one. Let's check that answer.

$0 \div 0 = 1$ One can be the answer only if $1 \cdot 0 = 0$. It appears that zero is the correct answer. However, the definition of division requires the answer to be unique. There cannot be more than one answer.

Therefore, we say that division by zero is undefined.

Addition, subtraction, multiplication, and division are all binary operations. Binary operations are always performed on a pair of numbers. Another kind of operation is *unary operations*. Unary operations are performed on single numbers. One unary operation is raising a number to a power. In the example, $4^2 = 4 \times 4 = 16$, we have raised 4 to the second power, and the answer is 16. In the example, $3^4 = 3 \times 3 \times 3 \times 3 = 81$, we have raised 3 to the fourth power, and the answer is 81. Notice that when we perform this operation in the set of whole numbers, the answer will always be a whole number. The operation, raising a number to a power, is closed in the set of whole numbers. Similarly, raising a number to a power is also closed in the set of integers and in the set of rational numbers.

Another unary operation is finding a root of a number. For example, the square root of 9 is 3 ($\sqrt{9} = 3$). The cube root of 8 is 2 ($\sqrt[3]{8} = 2$). But, there is no rational number that is the square root of 7 ($\sqrt{7} = ?$). No rational number is the cube root of 101 ($\sqrt{101} = ?$). So, the operation, finding a root of a number, is not closed in the set of rational numbers. However, if we expand the number set to include the irrational numbers, we can find roots of all positive numbers and odd roots ($\sqrt[3]{}, \sqrt[5]{}, \sqrt[7]{} \ldots$) of negative numbers. The explanation of why you cannot find even roots of negative numbers is left for an exercise.

The set of numbers that includes the whole numbers, integers, rational numbers, and irrational numbers is called *the set of real numbers*. In higher mathematics, the number set is expanded even further. But, for our purposes here we will only be interested in the behavior of operations in the set of real numbers.

The Associative Property

Both addition and multiplication are associative. This tells us what we can do when we are adding or multiplying with more than two numbers. Remember that addition and multiplication are binary operations. Suppose we are adding the following three numbers:

We could do the addition in two ways. $6 + 11 + 5$

We could add 6 and 11 first and then add 5 to that sum. $(6 + 11) + 5$

Or we could add 11 and 5 and add 6 to that first sum. $6 + (11 + 5)$

Notice that, whichever way we do it, we get the same answer. In fact, for any three numbers, say a, b, and c, we know that

$$(a + b) + c = a + (b + c)$$

Addition is associative in the set of real numbers.

We get a similar result with multiplication. If we multiply three numbers, say, 17, 13.7, and 84, we find that

$$(17 \times 13.7) \times 84 = 17 \times (13.7 \times 84).$$

The answer will be the same, whichever multiplication you do first. So, it turns out that, like addition, *multiplication is associative in the set of real numbers.* We do not have the same result with subtraction and division.

$$(15 - 9) - 4 = \qquad 15 - (9 - 4) =$$
$$6 - 4 = 2 \qquad 15 - 5 = 10$$
$$(15 - 9) - 4 \neq 15 - (9 - 4)$$

Subtraction is not associative in the set of real numbers.

$$(100 \div 10) \div 5 \qquad 100 \div (100 \div 5) =$$
$$10 \div 5 = 2 \qquad 100 \div 2 = 50$$
$$(100 \div 10) \div 5 \neq 100 \div (10 \div 5)$$

Division is not associative in the set of real numbers.

The Commutative Property

Both addition and multiplication are commutative. This property means that we can rearrange numbers being added or multiplied without affecting the answer. Addition and multiplication are commutative in the set of real numbers, which includes whole numbers, integers, rational numbers, and irrational numbers.

$$6 + 13 = 13 + 6 \qquad\qquad 5 \times 19 = 19 \times 5$$
$$(-7) + (-42) = (-42) + (-7) \qquad (+4) \times (-8) = (-8) \times (+4)$$
$$2.35 + 12.06 = 12.06 + 2.35 \qquad .04 \times .7 = .7 \times .04$$
$$10 + 7 = 7 + 10 \qquad\qquad 6 \times 22 = 22 \times 6$$
$$a + b = b + a \qquad\qquad a \times b = b \times a$$

Notice that we do not have the same result when we are subtracting or dividing.

$$6 - 3 = 3 \qquad \text{and} \qquad 3 - 6 = -3 \qquad \text{so, } 6 - 3 \neq 3 - 6$$
$$12 \div 3 = 4 \qquad \text{and} \qquad 3 \div 12 = .25 \qquad \text{so, } 12 \div 3 \neq 3 \div 12$$

Neither subtraction nor division is commutative in the set of real numbers.

The Distributive Property

The distributive property tells us how multiplication interacts with addition and subtraction. Suppose, for example, you have 4 times the sum of 3 and 7. The obvious solution would be to first add $3 + 7$, and then do the multiplication.

$$4 \times (3 + 7) = 4 \times 10 = 40$$

The distributive property gives us an alternative way to approach the solution. Multiplication distributes over addition. 4 is multiplied times each of the addends. So, by applying the distributive property, we have the following.

$$\underline{4} \times (3 + 7) = \underline{4} \times 3 + \underline{4} \times 7 = 12 + 28 = 40$$

Multiplication also distributes over subtraction. In the following example, we could begin by doing the subtraction and then multiply. Or, we could choose to apply the distributive property.

$$\underline{7} \times (13 - 2) = \underline{7} \times 11 = 77 \qquad \underline{7} \times (13 - 2) = \underline{7} \times 13 - \underline{7} \times 2 = 91 - 14 = 77$$

The distributive property lets us break down a multiplication into easier parts that are sometimes referred to as *partial products*.

$$\underline{13} \times 526 = \underline{13} \times (500 + 20 + 6) = \underline{13} \times 500 + \underline{13} \times 20 + \underline{13} \times 6$$
$$= 6500 + 260 + 78$$
$$= 6838$$

The Identity Elements

There are two numbers in the set of real numbers that play an important role. They are the identity elements—one for addition and one for multiplication. If you choose any real number, say 35, and then add 0 to 35, the result is 35. We get the same result whether we add zero on the right or on the left. Addition of zero works the same no matter what number we start with.

$$35 + 0 = 35 \qquad 0 + 35 = 35 \qquad -7 + 0 = -7 \qquad 0 + -7 = -7$$
$$0.8 + 0 = 0.8 \qquad 0 + 0.8 = 0.8 \qquad \sqrt{2} + 0 = \sqrt{2} \qquad 0 + \sqrt{2} = \sqrt{2}$$

Zero is the identity element for addition in the set of real numbers.

The identity element for multiplication is one. No matter what number we start with, when we multiply that number by one, the result is the number that we started with. Furthermore, we get that result whether we multiply on the left or on the right.

$$8 \times \underline{1} = 8 \qquad \underline{1} \times 8 = 8 \qquad \sqrt{7} \times \underline{1} = \sqrt{7} \qquad 1 \times \sqrt{7} = \sqrt{7}$$
$$-15 \times \underline{1} = -15 \qquad \underline{1} \times -15 = -15 \qquad 638 \times \underline{1} = 638 \qquad \underline{1} \times 638 = 638$$

The number 1 is the identity element for multiplication in the set of real numbers.

The Inverse Elements

If we begin with any real number, there is one other real number, such that when we add the numbers, the result will be the identity element for addition. Those two numbers are called *additive inverse elements*. For example if we start with 49, the additive inverse element for 49 would be −49. The sum of 49 and −49 is zero. *In the set of real numbers, every number has an additive inverse.*

$$\underline{62.3} + \underline{-62.3} = 0 \qquad \underline{62.3} \text{ and } \underline{-62.3} \text{ are additive inverses}$$

$$\underline{17} + \underline{-17} = 0 \qquad \underline{17} \text{ and } \underline{-17} \text{ are additive inverses}$$

We have similar results for multiplication. For each real number, there is a real number such that, when those numbers are multiplied, the result will be the multiplicative identity: 1. *In the set of real numbers, every number has a multiplicative inverse.*

$$14 \times \frac{1}{14} = 1 \qquad 14 \text{ and } \frac{1}{14} \text{ are multiplicative inverses}$$

$$100 \times \frac{1}{100} = 1 \qquad 100 \text{ and } \frac{1}{100} \text{ are multiplicative inverses}$$

$$\frac{1}{7} \times 7 = 1 \qquad \frac{1}{7} \text{ and } 7 \text{ are multiplicative inverses}$$

We can use inverse elements to "undo" operations. For example, if we have added 902 to 261, we can undo that addition by adding the additive inverse of 902.

$$261 \underline{+ 902} = 1163 \qquad 1163 \underline{+ (-902)} = 261$$

If we have multiplied 5 times 19, we can undo that multiplication by 19 if we multiply by the multiplicative inverse of 5.

$$19 \underline{\times 5} = 95 \qquad 95 \times \frac{1}{5} = 19$$

An extension of the notion of inverse elements is the notion of *inverse operations. Addition and subtraction are inverse operations.* If we have added 902 to 261, we can undo that addition by subtraction of 902.

$$261 \underline{+ 902} = 1163 \qquad 1163 \underline{- 902} = 261$$

If we have subtracted 375, we can undo that subtraction by adding 375.

$$2016 \underline{- 375} = 1641 \qquad 1641 \underline{+ 375} = 2016$$

Similarly, multiplication and division are inverse operations. If we have multiplied by 21, we can undo that multiplication by dividing by 21.

$$76 \underline{\times 21} = 1596 \qquad 1596 \underline{\div 21} = 76$$

If we have divided by 65, we can undo that division by multiplying by 65.

$$3185 \underline{\div 65} = 49 \qquad 49 \underline{\times 65} = 3185$$

The ability to undo operations will be important when we study equation solving.

Computation with integers

Typically, computation with integers is taught as a set of unrelated rote rules. For example, to add a positive number to a negative number, you find the difference of the absolute values of the two numbers and keep the sign of the number with the greatest absolute value. This is a very good rule; however, many students, particularly the weaker students, will have difficulty learning the rule and even more difficulty remembering it. Moreover, it is easy to build mental imagery for addition of integers, and students will find it easier to learn and remember how to add integers when they know what it looks like. The teacher might use the following sequence of activities to establish mental imagery for addition of integers.

Activity 11.1   Numbers on the Line

Begin with a short activity locating integers on a number line. Include positive integers, negative integers, and zero. Place zero on the line first. Then for the rest of the examples, start at zero and count to the left for negative integers and start at zero and count to the right for positive integers.

Point out that numbers get greater as you move to the right on the number line, and numbers are less as you move to the left on the number line. Ask which is greater, +7 or +2? −3 or +3? +7 or −3? −5 or + 2?

Activity 11.2 Adding Positive Integers

Draw a number line on the board. Have a student write the numbers on the number line.

–7 –6 –5 –4 –3 –2 –1 0 +1 +2 +3 +4 +5 +6 +7 +8

Explain that you can use the number line to find the answer to +2 + +5. Draw an arrow from 0, counting 2 spaces to the right to +2. Next, draw an arrow, starting at +2, and counting 5 spaces to the right, to +7. Added together, the two numbers equal 7.

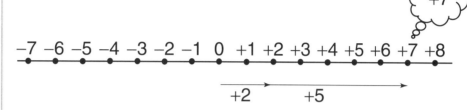

–7 –6 –5 –4 –3 –2 –1 0 +1 +2 +3 +4 +5 +6 +7 +8

+2   +5

Have students come to the board and complete two more examples.

Activity 11.3 Adding Negative Integers

Draw a number line on the board. Have a student write the numbers on the number line.

–7 –6 –5 –4 –3 –2 –1 0 +1 +2 +3 +4 +5 +6 +7 +8

Explain that you can use the number line to find the answer to −4 + −2. Draw an arrow from 0, counting 4 spaces to the left, to −4. Next, draw an arrow, starting at −4, and counting 2 spaces to the left, to −6. Added together, the two numbers equal −6.

–6

–7 –6 –5 –4 –3 –2 –1 0 +1 +2 +3 +4 +5 +6 +7 +8

–2   –4

Have students come to the board and complete two more examples.

Activity 11.4 Adding Positive and Negative Integers

Draw a number line on the board. Have a student write the numbers on the number line.

–7 –6 –5 –4 –3 –2 –1 0 +1 +2 +3 +4 +5 +6 +7 +8

Explain that you can use the number line to find the answer to +5 + −2. Draw an arrow from 0, counting 5 spaces to the right, to +5. Next, draw an arrow, starting at +5, and counting 2 spaces to the left, to +3. Added together, the two numbers equal +3.

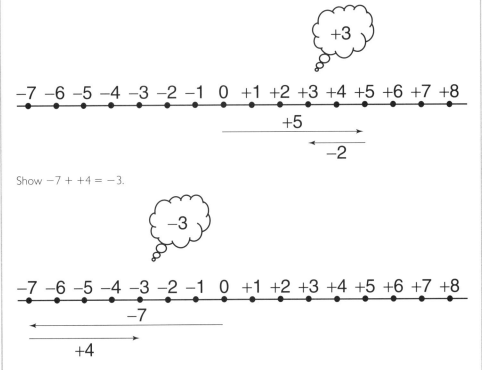

Show −7 + +4 = −3.

Ask a few students to come to the board and complete at least three more examples, but have them "guess" what the answers will be, and use the number line to check the guesses.

Tell the students to "make up" a rule for adding positive and negative integers. Use the rule to find answers, and use the number line to make sure the rule works.

As with addition of integers, subtraction of integers is commonly taught with a rote rule: "Change the sign of the subtrahend and add." This is another very good rule; however, because the rule is typically taught by rote, many students, particularly the weaker students, will have difficulty remembering it. To make the rule more meaningful and therefore easier to remember, we can develop the rule from concepts that the students have already learned. Recall that there is an easy way to check a subtraction. $a − b = c$ if and only if $c + b = a$.

We know that $14 − 6 = 8$ is correct because 8 + 6 equals 14. We know that $16 − 5 = 12$ is not correct because 12 + 5 does not equal 16. We know that $273 − 192 = 81$ is correct because 81 + 192 = 273.

Recall, also, that the answer to a comparison subtraction is called the difference. If we compare 10 and 6, we find that the difference is 4. The following activities illustrate how a teacher might use the number line to compare two numbers.

Activity 11.5 Comparing Positive and Negative Integers

Draw a number line on the board. Write the numbers +10 and +6 on the number line. The difference is 4 spaces.

Ask the students what they think the difference between −8 and −2 would be. Use the number line to check their answers.

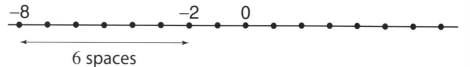

−8   −2   0

← 6 spaces →

Repeat the procedure, finding the difference between +5 and −6. Ask the students predict the outcome and use the number line to check the prediction.

Activity 11.6   Subtracting Positive and Negative Integers

Point out that, in the preceding activity, the difference between numbers turned out to be the number of spaces between the numbers. But, so far, we do not know whether the difference is positive or negative.

Remind the students that, in the first example of Activity 11.5, we found that the difference between +10 and +6 to be 4 spaces. But is that difference positive or negative? If the subtraction is $(+10) − (+6)$, we know that the answer is either +4 or −4.

Help the students recall that, if $(+10) − (+6) = +4$ is true, then $(+4) + (+6)$ must equal +10. $(+4) + (+6)$ does equal +10. The answer checks.

Remind them that, in the second example of Activity 11.5, we found that the difference between −8 and −2 was 6 spaces. But is that difference positive or negative? Point out that, for the subtraction $(−8) − (+6)$, we know that the answer is either +2 or −2.

If $(−8) − (−2) = +6$ is true, then $(+6) + (−2) = +6$. It is *not* true, so +6 is not the correct answer. That answer does not check. That means that the other possibility must be true.

$(−8) − (−2) = −6$ must be true. $(−6) + (−2)$ does equal −8. That answer checks.

Do other examples. Encourage your students to think ahead and predict outcomes.

Activity 11.7   A Relationship between Subtraction and Addition

Write the following subtraction and addition examples on the board.

$(+12) − (+7) =$	$(+12) + (−7) =$	$(−9) − (−3) =$	$(−9) + (+3) =$
$(+9) − (−11) =$	$(+9) + (+11) =$	$(−6) − (−9) =$	$(−6) + (+9) =$

Have the students work in small groups to find all the answers.

When they have finished, ask if anyone noticed the relationship between the subtraction examples and the addition examples. Discuss the relationship. Point out that this relationship offers a simpler way to find subtraction answers.

Ask your students to help you write a rule that uses this relationship to make subtraction easier.

When subtracting, change the sign of the subtrahend and add.

Multiplication of integers also is typically taught using a rote rule: "When multiplying two numbers with the same sign, the answer will be positive. When multiplying two numbers with different signs, the answer will be negative." This is another very good rule. Compared to the rules for addition and subtraction, the rule is relatively easy to remember. However, because the rule is usually taught by rote, many students, particularly the weaker students, will still have some difficulty remembering it. To make the rule more meaningful and therefore easier to remember, we can relate the rule to concepts that the students will have already learned.

Recall that every integer has a multiplicative inverse. When you multiply an integer times its inverse, the answer is one, regardless of what integer you start with. We consider the integer's inverse to be the opposite of the integer.

-21 is the opposite of 21. 3 is the opposite of -3.

$-(72)$ is the opposite of 72. $-(-42)$ is the opposite of -42.

$-1(9) = -9$, the opposite of 9. $-1(-12) = 12$, the opposite of the opposite of 12.

The following activity demonstrates how a teacher can use a variety of examples and the commutative property to develop the rule for multiplication of integers.

Activity 11.8   *The Signs of Integer Multiplication*

Write the following multiplication example on the board.

$(6)(-7) = (6)(-1)(7)$ $(-1)(7)$ is the opposite of 7.
$ = (-1)(6)(7)$ I can rearrange the numbers.
$ = (-1)(42)$
$ = (-42)$ $(6) \bullet (-7) = -42$

The product is negative.

Continue with this example.

$(-9)(-4) = (-1)(9)(-1)(4)$ $(-1)(9)$ is the opposite of 9.
$ = (-1)(-1)(9)(4)$ $(-1)(4)$ is the opposite of 4.
$ = (-1)(-1)(36)$
$ = (36)$ I can rearrange the numbers.
$(-9) \bullet (-4) = 36$

The opposite of the opposite of 36 is positive. The product is positive.

Work other examples but have the students tell you what to do on each step. Finally, ask the students what the sign of the answer will be if the numbers being multiplied have different signs. What will the sign of the answer if both numbers have the same signs?

Have the students work in small groups to find all the answers.

Then ask them to help you write a rule that uses this relationship to make multiplication easier. *If the numbers being multiplied have the same sign, the product will be positive. If the numbers being multiplied have different signs, the product will be negative.*

It turns out that every division example can written as a multiplication.

$$8 \div 4 = 8 \cdot \frac{1}{4} \qquad 5 \div 5 = 25 \cdot \frac{1}{25} \qquad (-56) \div 8 = (-56) \cdot \left(\frac{1}{8}\right)$$

$$32 \div (-4) = 32 \cdot \left(-\frac{1}{4}\right) \qquad (-22) \div (-11) = (-22) \cdot \left(-\frac{1}{11}\right)$$

So, the rule for the signs of division answers is the same as the rule for signs of multiplication answers. *If the dividend and divisor have the same sign, the quotient will be positive. If the dividend and divisor have the different signs, the quotient will be negative.*

The Order of Operations

When there is a sequence of additions and subtractions to complete, we normally complete them in order, working from the left to the right. Consider this example.

$$12 + 5 - 3 + 8 - 9 = 12 + 5 - 3 + 8 - 9 \qquad 12 + 5 = 17$$
$$= 17 - 3 + 8 - 9 \qquad 17 - 3 = 14$$
$$= 14 + 8 - 9 \qquad 14 + 8 = 22$$
$$= 22 - 9 \qquad 22 - 9 = 13$$
$$= 13$$

Notice that if we choose to perform the operations in some other order, the answer would be the same.

$$12 + 5 - 3 + 8 - 9 = 12 + 5 - 3 + 8 - 9 \qquad 5 - 3 = 2$$
$$= 12 + 2 + 8 - 9 \qquad 2 + 8 = 10$$
$$= 12 + 10 - 9 \qquad 10 - 9 = 1$$
$$= 12 + 1 \qquad 12 + 1 = 13$$
$$= 13$$

Even though we may choose another sequence, it is seldom to our advantage to do so.

If we are completing a sequence of operations that includes addition, subtraction, multiplication, or division, it is important to follow a specific sequence. Notice the results when the following example is completed in two ways.

Doing the addition first:

$$4 + 6 \cdot 2 = 10 \cdot 2 \qquad 4 + 6 = 10$$
$$= 20 \qquad 10 \cdot 2 = 20$$

Doing the multiplication first:

$$4 + 6 \cdot 2 = 4 + 12 \qquad 6 \cdot 2 = 12$$
$$= 16 \qquad 4 + 12 = 16$$

Both of these answers cannot be correct. We must have a rule that tells which of these answers is correct—that rule is: *First, complete the multiplication and division, working from left to the right. Then, complete the addition and subtraction, working from left to right.*

The following activities illustrate how a teacher can develop the need for an order-of-operations rule and then introduce the rule for order of operations.

Activity 11.9   *Too Many Answers*

Write the following example on the board: $7 - 2 \cdot 5 + 6 =$

Point out that there is a subtraction, a multiplication, and an addition. Have the class help you do the arithmetic, working from left to right.

First, do the subtraction.	$7 - 2 = 5$	$7 - 2 \cdot 5 + 6 = 5 \cdot 5 + 6$
Next, do the multiplication.	$5 \cdot 5 = 25$	$= 25 + 6$
Finally, do the addition.	$25 + 6 = 31$	$= 31$

Next, tell the class that you want to do the addition, then the multiplication, and finally do the subtraction. Have the class help you to do the arithmetic.

First, do the addition.	$5 + 6 = 11$	$7 - 2 \cdot 5 + 6 = 7 - 2 \cdot 11$
Next, do the multiplication.	$2 \cdot 11 = 22$	$= 7 - 22$
Finally, do the subtraction.	$7 - 22 = -15$	$= -15$

Tell the class that you want to do the multiplication, then the addition, and finally do the subtraction. Have the class help you to do the arithmetic.

First, do the multiplication.	$2 \cdot 5 = 10$	$7 - 2 \cdot 5 + 6 = 7 - 10 + 6$
Next, do the subtraction.	$7 - 10 = -3$	$= -3 + 6$
Finally, do the addition.	$-3 + 6 = 3$	$= 3$

Point out that we need to have a rule that tells us the order in which the operations should be completed. We have such a rule: *First, complete the multiplication and division, working from left to the right. Then, complete the addition and subtraction, working from left to right.*

Activity 11.10   Order of Operations

Write these examples on the board. Have the students work with one or two partners to complete the examples.

$$2 + 6 \div 2 = \qquad 8 \div 4 + 9 \cdot 2 = \qquad 20 - 5 \cdot 3 + 6 =$$

$$2 \cdot 6 - 2 \cdot 3 = \qquad 40 - 4 \cdot 5 \cdot 2 = \qquad 8 + 4 \cdot 3 - 20 =$$

Monitor the students' work. Listen to their conversations. As needed, remind the student groups of the rule. Point out errors and reinforce correct work.

Algebraic expressions may also include exponents. When this occurs, the terms with exponents must be evaluated first. The following examples illustrate this.

$7 \cdot 4 + \underline{3^2} = 7 \cdot 4 + \underline{9}$	*Exponents first.*
$= \quad 28 + 9$	Multiplication next.
$= \quad 37$	Then addition.
$\underline{(-2)^2} - \underline{(-4)^2} + 7 = \underline{4} - \underline{16} + 7$	*Exponents first.*
$= -5$	Addition and subtraction next.
$6 + \underline{4^2} - 5 \cdot 2 = 6 + \underline{16} - 5 \cdot 2$	*Exponents first.*
$= 6 + 16 - 10$	Multiplication next.
$= 12$	Then addition and subtraction.

Algebraic expressions often make use of grouping symbols. There are many different kinds of grouping symbols, but they all have the same basic purpose. They tell you that what is inside the grouping symbol is to be considered a single number. Consider these examples that include grouping symbols.

$2 + 9 - (4 + 2) = 2 + 9 - 6$	In this case, the grouping symbol is a set of parentheses. They tell us that $4 + 2$ is to be treated as a number, 6. The original expression is equivalent to $2 + 9 - 6$.
$56 - 2 \cdot [11 - 4] = 56 - 2 \cdot 7$	In this case, the grouping symbol is a pair of braces. They tell us that $11 - 4$ is to be treated as a number, 7. The original expression is equivalent to $56 - 2 \times 7$.
$40 \div (9 - 4) + 2 = 40 \div 5 + 2$	The parentheses tell us that $9 - 4$ is to be treated as a number, 5. The original expression is equivalent to $40 \div 5 + 2$.

The order-of-operations rule, when it is expanded to include exponents and grouping symbols, is the following.

First, do the computations inside grouping symbols.

Second, expand exponents.

Third, do the multiplication and division, working from left to right.

Fourth, do the addition and subtraction, working from left to right.

Evaluating Algebraic Expressions

Variables are numbers that may vary. For example, the following algebraic expression contains three variables: a, b, and c.

$$a \cdot (b + c)$$

The value of the expression depends on the value of the variables. Suppose $a = 2$, $b = 3$, and $c = 4$. Then the expression becomes $2 \cdot (3 + 4)$.

We use the order-of-operations rule to do the computation.

$$2 \cdot (3 + 4) = 2 \cdot 7$$
$$= 14$$

We say that for $a = 2$, $b = 3$, and $c = 3$, the value of $a \cdot (b + c)$ is 14.

Next, we will evaluate the following expression for $m = 5$, $n = 4$, and $p = 8$.

$$m^2 - (p + n) = 5^2 - (8 + 4)$$
$$= 5^2 - 12$$
$$= 25 - 12$$
$$= 13$$

For $m = 5$, $n = 4$, and $p = 8$, the value of $m^2 - (p + n)$ is 13.

If the value of the variables is changed, the value of the algebraic expression will probably change. To illustrate this, we will evaluate the previous expression for $m = 3$, $n = -4$, and $p = 5$.

$$m^2 - (p + n) = 3^2 - (-4 + 5)$$
$$= 3^2 - 1$$
$$= 9 - 1$$
$$= 8$$

For $m = 3$, $n = -4$, and $p = 5$, the value of $m^2 - (p + n)$ is 8.

To evaluate algebraic expressions, follow these steps: First, substitute the given values for the variables in the algebraic expression. Second, do all the computation, carefully following the order-of-operations rule. The result of the computation is the value of the expression for the given values of the variables.

Using Properties of Equality to Solve Equations

An equation is simply an algebraic statement that two things (numbers) are equal. For example, consider these equations.

$$2 + 3 = 5 \qquad 16 - 5 = 14 + (-3) \qquad x + 2 = 47 \qquad 5^3 + y = 100 - 2y$$

The first two of these equations do not contain variables. The last two of these equations do contain variables. The variables have unknown values. *Equation solving* is the process of finding the values of the variables in the equations. Most equations can be solved by applying one or more of the following properties of equality. The first of these properties is the *addition property of equality*,

If $a = b$, then $a + c = b + c$

Notice that this property allows us to add the same thing to both sides of the equation without losing the equality. The second property is the *subtraction property of equality*.

If $a = b$, then $a - c = b - c$

This property allows us to subtract the same amount from both sides of the equation without losing the equality. The third property is the *multiplication property of equality*.

If $a = b$, then $a \cdot c = b \cdot c$

This property allows us to multiply both sides of the equation by the same amount without losing the equality. The fourth property is the *division property of equality*.

If $a = b$, then $a \div c = b \div c$

This property allows us to divide both sides of the equation by the same amount without losing the equality.

The following examples illustrate how to use the four properties of equality to solve equations.

$$x - 3 = 8$$ To get rid of the subtraction of 3, we can add 3.
$$(x - 3) + 3 = 8 + 3$$ But, we must add 3 to both sides of the equation.
$$x = 11$$ The variable, x, is equal to 11.

$$m + 5 = -2$$ To get rid of the addition of 5, we subtract 5.
$$(m + 5) - 5 = (-2) - 5$$ But, we must subtract 5 from both sides of the equation.
$$m = -7$$ The variable, m, is equal to -7.

$$z \cdot 6 = 24$$ To get rid of the multiplication by 6, we divide by 6.
$$(z \cdot 6) \div 6 = 24 \div 6$$ But, we must divide both sides of the equation by 6.
$$z = 4$$ The variable, z, is equal to 4.

$$a \div 7 = 3$$ To get rid of the division by 7, we multiply by 7.
$$(a \div 7) \cdot 7 = 3 \cdot 7$$ But, we must multiply both sides of the equation by 7.
$$a = 21$$ The variable, a, is equal to 21.

Solutions of the preceding four equations were one-step solutions. Those equations can be solved by taking one step. Notice that in each solution we "undid" a single operation to find the solution. We undid subtraction of 3 by adding 3. We undid addition of 5 by subtracting 5. We undid multiplication by 6 by dividing by 6. We undid division by 7 by multiplying by 7.

Next, we will consider equations that require two-step solutions. These equations contain two operations. Both operations must be undone.

This equation contains two operations, a multiplication and an addition.

$$4 \cdot y + 26 = 2$$

If we were going to perform those two operations, the order-of-operations rule tells us to perform the multiplication first and then perform the addition. However, if you are solving an equation by undoing the indicated operations, you undo the indicated operations in reverse order. So, you would undo the addition first and then undo the multiplication. The following activity illustrates how a teacher might explain why we undo the indicated operations in the reverse order that the operations would be performed.

Activity 11.11 Order of Undoing Operations

Tell the students you are going to tell them a story about a very rich man. Explain that this rich man has a large, beautiful gem. He was afraid that the gem would be stolen. (*As you tell the story, write the steps that he goes through to hide his gem.*)

He: Wrapped the gem in a soft cloth.
Placed it in a box.
Sealed the box inside a resealable plastic bag.

Placed the plastic bag in a hole in the ground.
Filled the hole with dirt, and
Placed a large flat rock on top of the dirt.

Sometime later the man wants to admire his gem. So, he had to undo all the things he had done to protect his gem. *(As you tell the rest of the story, list the things that he has to undo in order to retrieve the gem.)*

He has to: Remove the flat rock,
Dig the dirt from the hole.
Remove the plastic bag from the hole.
Take the box from the plastic bag.
Remove the soft cloth from the box, and
Take the gem out of the soft cloth.

Point out that when you need to undo things that had to be done in a particular order, you must undo them in reverse order. This is true of mathematical operations that are found in equations. The order for undoing those operations is the reverse of the order for performing them.

As we solve the following equations, pay particular attention to the order in which the operations are undone.

$5 \cdot y - 12 = 3$	First we undo the subtraction of 12 by adding 12.
$5 \cdot y - 12 + 12 = 3 + 12$	We must add 12 to both sides of the equation.
$5 \cdot y = 15$	Next, we undo the multiplication by 5 by dividing by 5.
$5 \cdot y \div 5 = 15 \div 5$	We must divide both sides of the equation by 5.
$y = 3$	The variable, y, is equal to 3.
$b \div 2 - 10 = 12$	First, we undo the subtraction of 10 by adding 10.
$b \div 2 - 10 + 10 = 12 + 10$	We must add 10 to both sides of the equation.
$b \div 2 = 22$	Next, we undo the division by 2 by multiplying by 2.
$b \div 2 \cdot 2 = 22 \cdot 2$	We must multiply both sides of the equation by 2.
$b = 44$	The variable, b, is equal to 44.

Exponents

There are several properties of exponents. We will deal here with some of those properties and focus our attention on instructional activities that can help our students to understand them. Before examining the properties, we should be sure that our students understand what an exponent is and what it means. That can be accomplished by using the following activity.

Activity 11.12   What is an Exponent

Write this multiplication example on the board. $3 \cdot 3 \cdot 3 \cdot 3 =$
How many factors are there? [There are 4 factors.]
What do you notice about the factors? [They are all the same.]
Ask someone use a calculator to find the answer. [The product is 81.] $3 \cdot 3 \cdot 3 \cdot 3 = 81$
Explain that there is a "shorthand" way to write this multiplication.
Rewrite the example using an exponent.

$$3^4 = 81$$

The factors all equal 3.   There are 4 factors of 3.

Write this multiplication example. $5 \cdot 5 =$

How many factors are there? [There are 2 factors.]

What are both factors equal to? [Both factors equal 5.]

Ask a student what the product is. [The product is 25.] $5 \cdot 5 = 25$

Explain that this example can also be written using an exponent.

Ask what the factors are equal to. Then write the 5. 5

Ask how many times 5 appears as a factor. Then write the exponent.

$$5^2 = 25$$

The factors all equal 5.   There are 2 factors of 5.

Write $2^5 = ?$ Have the students rewrite the example without using an exponent.

Write $7 \cdot 7 \cdot 7 \cdot 7 = ?$ Have the students rewrite the example using an exponent.

Write $4 \cdot 4 \cdot 4 \cdot 4 \cdot 4 = ?$ Have them write the example using an exponent.

Write $6^9 = ?$ Have them write the example without using an exponent.

Do other examples as needed. Introduce and use the language as in "6 to the fourth power" and "6 raised to the fourth power" when referring to 6^4.

Introduce and use the names for the parts of a power. In 6^4, 6 is called the *base* and 4 is called the *exponent*.

The first property of exponents that we will consider appears when you are multiplying two powers with the same base. For example, in $7^3 \cdot 7^5$ the base is 7 in both powers.

$$7^3 \cdot 7^5 = (7 \cdot 7 \cdot 7) \cdot (7 \cdot 7 \cdot 7 \cdot 7 \cdot 7)$$
$$= 7 \cdot 7 \cdot 7 \cdot 7 \cdot 7 \cdot 7 \cdot 7 \cdot 7$$
$$= 7^{3+5}$$
$$= 7^8$$

Any number except zero can be the base and any integers can be the exponents. In general, we find that for any nonzero number a and any integers m and n:

$$a^m \cdot a^n = a^{m+n}$$

The following activity illustrates how a teacher might develop this property of exponents.

Activity 11.13   Multiplying Powers with the Same Base

Write this example on the board. $3^2 \cdot 3^5 =$

Tell the students that you want to simplify
this expression. Write out all the factors of 3. $3^2 \cdot 3^5 = (3 \cdot 3) \cdot (3 \cdot 3 \cdot 3 \cdot 3 \cdot 3)$

Altogether, how many factors of 3 are there?
[There are 7 factors of 3.] $3^2 \cdot 3^5 = 3^7$

Write another example on the board. $6^3 \cdot 6^3 =$

Ask if anyone would like to guess what the answer will be.
Write guesses on the board, but do not say if guesses are correct.

Write out all the factors of 6. $6^3 \cdot 6^3 = (6 \cdot 6 \cdot 6) \cdot (6 \cdot 6 \cdot 6)$

Ask how many factors of 6 are there. Record the answer. $6^3 \cdot 6^3 = 6^6$

If any students' guesses were correct, ask those students how they got their correct answer.

Ask the students to make up a "rule" that they can use to get correct answers.

Do another example. $8^4 \cdot 8^6 =$

Have the students use their "rule" to get the answer.

Check the answer by writing out the all the factors of 8 and counting them.

Restate the "rule" in your words. $a^m \cdot a^n = a^{m+n}$

If needed, do other examples.

The next property of exponents is an extension of the previous one. In general, we find that for any nonzero number a and any integers m and n:

$$(a^m)^n = a^{m \cdot n}$$

The following activity illustrates how a teacher might develop this property of exponents.

Activity 11.14   Powers of Powers

Write 17^3 on the board. Remind the students what the expression means. $[17 \cdot 17 \cdot 17]$

Write 8^2 on the board and ask the students what the expression means. $[8 \cdot 8]$

Write 504^3. Ask what the expression means. $[504 \cdot 504 \cdot 504]$

Write $(4 + 7)^5$. Ask what it means. $[(4 + 7) \cdot (4 + 7) \cdot (4 + 7) \cdot (4 + 7) \cdot (4 + 7)]$

Write $(5 \cdot 3)^4$. Ask what it means. $[(5 \cdot 3) \cdot (5 \cdot 3) \cdot (5 \cdot 3) \cdot (5 \cdot 3)]$

Write $(5^4)^2$. Ask what this expression means. $[(5^4) \cdot (5^4)]$

Point out that this expression can be simplified further.

$(5^4)^2 = (5^4) \cdot (5^4)$
$= (5 \cdot 5 \cdot 5 \cdot 5) \cdot (5 \cdot 5 \cdot 5 \cdot 5) = 5^8$

Write $(6^3)^4$.

Ask if anyone would like to guess how this one will turn out.
Do not comment on the accuracy of the guesses.

Simplify the expression.

$$(6^3)^4 = 6^3 \cdot 6^3 \cdot 6^3 \cdot 6^3$$
$$= (6 \cdot 6 \cdot 6) \cdot (6 \cdot 6 \cdot 6) \cdot (6 \cdot 6 \cdot 6) \cdot (6 \cdot 6 \cdot 6)$$
$$= 6^{12}$$

Tell the students to look for a pattern that will let them predict the outcome.

Repeat the process with other examples until the students are able to predict the outcome.

Ask them to make a rule that will produce correct outcomes. $[(a^m)^n = a^{m \cdot n}]$

The next property of exponents appears when you are finding the quotient of powers with the same base. In general, we find that for any nonzero number a and any integers m and n:

$$a^m \div a^n = \frac{a^m}{a^n} = a^{m-n}$$

The following activity illustrates how a teacher might develop this property of exponents.

Write $\frac{6}{8}$ on the board. Ask a student to reduce the fraction.

Point out that reducing a fraction is equivalent to eliminating a factor that is in both the numerator and the denominator. In this example, the common factor is 2.

Write $\frac{5}{15}$ on the board. Ask the students what the common factor is in the numerator and denominator of this fraction. Reduce the fraction.

Write $\frac{3^6}{3^4}$. Ask students to predict the answer.

Reduce the fraction.

Write $\frac{6^9}{6^5}$. Ask students to predict the answer.

Reduce the fraction.

Do other examples until the students are able to consistently predict the correct answer. Have them develop a rule that will produce correct results.

Point out that $\frac{6^9}{6^5} = 6^4$ is equivalent to $6^9 \div 6^5 = 6^4$.
Restate other examples as division.

Help the students state the rule for division of powers with the same base.
$[a^m \div a^n = a^{m-n}]$

There are other properties of exponents that would be examined if this were a complete treatment of algebra. We will not consider the rest of the properties of exponents. However, the instructional activities described here illustrate an approach that is useful in the study of foundations of algebra and other mathematics topics in the middle grades. That approach includes exploration, looking for patterns, prediction of outcomes, generalization, and testing of those generalizations. A lesson on simplification of fractions follows.

LESSON OBJECTIVE

The learner will simplify algebraic fractions.

Lesson Opener

Prepare groups of cards with equivalent fractions such as the ones shown here. Prepare enough cards so that every student in the class will have a card. Prepare one extra card for yourself.

$$\frac{1}{2} \quad \frac{2}{4} \quad \frac{3}{6} \quad \frac{4}{8} \qquad \frac{2}{3} \quad \frac{4}{6} \quad \frac{6}{9} \quad \frac{8}{12} \quad \frac{10}{15} \qquad \frac{3}{5} \quad \frac{6}{10} \quad \frac{9}{15}$$

$$\frac{1}{4} \quad \frac{2}{8} \quad \frac{3}{12} \quad \frac{4}{16} \quad \frac{5}{20} \qquad \frac{5}{7} \quad \frac{10}{14} \quad \frac{15}{21} \qquad \frac{3}{4} \quad \frac{6}{8} \quad \frac{9}{12} \quad \frac{12}{16}$$

Shuffle the cards and give every student a card. Explain that you want them to form six groups so the all the fractions in each group are equivalent. Tell them to work together and help others to get in the correct groups. **Monitor understanding.** Watch for students who are having difficulty. Ask leading questions that will remind them of previously learned concepts related to equivalent fractions and procedures used for reducing fractions.

After sufficient time has been allowed for students to find their groups, show them the card that you kept for yourself. Have them help you find what group you belong to. Monitor understanding. If some students are still having difficulty, write another fraction on the board, and ask them to help you work through the process of finding which group that fraction belongs to.

Development

Review the process of reducing a fraction.

Write the fraction $\frac{4}{6}$ on the board.

Factor the numerator and the denominator.

Point out that the common factor is 2.

Remind the class that to reduce a fraction, you merely eliminate factors that appear in both the numerator and the denominator. Write $\frac{10}{15}$ on the board. Have the students independently reduce that fraction. Have a student show the class how to reduce that fraction. **Monitor understanding.** Take note of any students who are having difficulty. Remember to provide additional instruction for them.

Explain that when we *simplify* an algebraic fraction, we are merely reducing the fraction. You simplify an algebraic fraction by eliminating factors that are common to both the numerator and denominator. An algebraic fraction is *simplified* if it has no common factor in the numerator and denominator.

Write the fraction b^2/bc on the board.
Expand the factors.
Eliminate the common factors.
The simplified fraction is b/c.
Write the fraction $6x^2y/4xy^2$ on the board.
Expand the factors.
Eliminate the common factors.

The simplified fraction is $\frac{3x}{2y}$.

Do other examples as needed.

Practice

For practice, have the students work in small groups to complete exercises 3, 4, 5, 8, 9, 12, and 14 in the student book. **Monitor understanding.** While the class is working, move about the room. Pay particular attention to those students who earlier had difficulties.

Closure

Ask the students what they learned today. Ask how simplifying fractions and reducing fraction are alike. Tell the class that their homework assignment is to explain to someone at home how to do exercise number 10 in the student textbook.

Exercises and Activities

1. Examine the preceding lesson plan on simplification of fractions. Identify the parts of the lesson (if any) that involve
   a. kinesthetic activity
   b. visual imagery
   c. student communication about the material being learned
   d. monitoring by the teacher of student learning
2. Develop a step-by-step instructional activity that will help a teacher determine whether a group of students has mastered subtraction of integers.

3. Earlier, in the discussion of closure properties, it was indicated that there are no even roots of negative numbers. Why is this the case?

4. When evaluating algebraic expressions, a student had the following answers:

For $x = 3$, $y = 4$, and $z = 7$, evaluate the following expressions.

$$4 + 3y - 1 = 15 \qquad x + z^2 = 52 \qquad x^2 + y^2 - 3 = 22$$

$$y \cdot z \div 2 + 5 = 19 \qquad 6 + x^3 - 10 = 4$$

Find the correct answers, evaluate the student's answers, and identify the error pattern that he or she is following.

References and Related Readings

Tillema, E. S. (2012). What is the difference? Using contextualized problems. *Mathematics Teaching in the Middle School, 17*, 472–478.

Townsend, B. E. & Barker, D. D. (2009). Promoting efficient strategy use. *Mathematics Teaching in the Middle School, 14*, 542–547.

Websites

www.corestandards.org/the-standards/mathematics
The Common Core State Standards for Mathematics can be found at this site.

twelve

EFFECTIVE PRACTICE

Games and Activities
for Practice and Fun

CHAPTER OUTLINE

Matching Activities
Ordering Activities

Answer or Example Construction
Activities

Because of the importance of the development phase of lessons—that part of the lessons during which the students are learning things that they do not already know and developing skills that they do not already have—the learning activities found in the earlier chapters are predominantly developmental activities.

The purpose of practice activities is to help students become proficient in the use of concepts and skills that have already been developed. Whereas the emphasis of developmental activities is on comprehension and understanding, the emphasis of practice activities is to develop greater proficiency with what the students have learned. As a general rule, students do not learn new things from practice. However, through practice they develop higher levels of skill in what they have already learned. Practice may also help that learning to be more permanent. Furthermore, the use of practice activities provides opportunities for the teacher to observe and identify students who need remediation.

Think-time practice is preferred over other practice activities. Students have enough time to carefully think about concepts and connections, enough time to think carefully through each step of a procedure, and enough time to look up things they do not fully understand. In think-time practice, the emphasis is on accuracy, not on speed.

In this chapter, we see activities that by their very nature can make practice interesting and even fun. We show activities that provide a lot of practice, even more than the students get by completing a practice page from the textbook. In addition, there are practice activities that require students to cooperate with each other as they consider, discuss, question, and explain mathematical concepts and skills. There are also practice activities that fully engage the students' attention by requiring physical (kinesthetic) involvement.

The reader should be cautious, though. Remember that a practice activity, even one that is really neat, cute, exciting, and engaging, cannot be truly effective until after the students have achieved understanding. *No practice activity can take the place of good, solid concept and skill development.*

We begin with a class of activities that require the students to match two or more things. These things might match because they are equal; they might match because they have the same answer; they might match because they share some geometric characteristic; they might match for any number of different reasons. The important thing to remember is that, regardless of what is being matched and regardless of the matching criterion, the activity can easily be adapted to any other things that match. So, if the students enjoy a particular matching activity, that activity can be used repeatedly with other content. In this chapter, we have also included some activities that involve low-level mathematics. These activities can easily be adapted for any level of mathematics. For example, in Activity 12.01 below, instead of matching the number of dots, the activity might involve evaluation of algebraic expressions.

Matching Activities

One effective matching activity is *Match Me*. The basic procedure for this activity is illustrated in the following two activities. The procedures for activities 12.01 and 12.02 are identical, but the level of content is different.

Activity 12.01   Match Me (variation 1)

Prepare pairs of cards like the ones illustrated. Both cards in each pair should have the same number of dots, but the dots should be arranged differently:

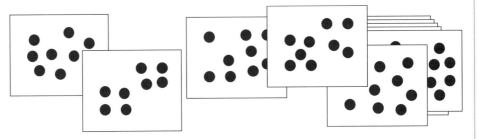

Mix the cards and pass one out to each student. Have the students find partners so that the partners have cards with the same number of dots. If there is an odd number of children, the teacher should take a card and participate so everyone has a partner.

When all the children have found a partner, have the partners show their cards to the class and tell how many dots they have.

Activity 12.02   Match Me (variation 2)

Prepare pairs of cards like the ones illustrated. The cards in each pair should picture different rectangles with the same area:

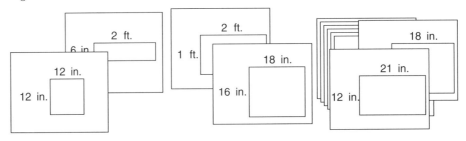

Mix the cards and pass one out to each student. Have the students find partners so that the partners have cards with rectangles with the same area. If there is an odd number of students, include one set of three cards with the same area and tell the students that there will be either two or three partners.

When all the children have found their partners, have the partners show their cards to the class and tell what their area is.

Match Me has an excellent level of kinesthetic activity. The children must get up and move about the room in order to complete the activity. But, because the movement is purposeful, this activity seldom results in behavior problems. Another advantage of Match Me is that it takes little time. This makes it a good choice for inclusion in a lesson opener, when the children's attention should be focused on particular content but the time that needs to be spent on developing concepts or skills being taught in the lesson is not being used up.

Another nice use of Match Me is to form pairs of students for a partner activity. This activity can be used if random pairings of students are acceptable. A variation of March Me can also be used to form small groups or teams for a group or team activity. To do this, you must construct the cards so that groups of students (however many are to be in each group) will have matching cards. Activities 12.03 and 12.04 are examples of activities that would accomplish forming groups.

Activity 12.03   Match Me (variation 3)

Prepare sets of four cards like the ones illustrated. The cards in each set should show subtraction examples with the same answer:

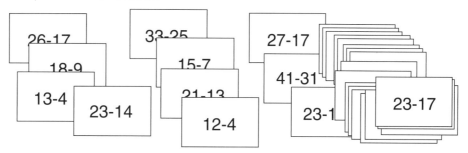

Mix the cards and pass them out to the children. Have the children find others with cards with problems that have the same answer as theirs. Tell them to check the answers for the cards of everyone in the group to be sure that they match.

When all the students have found their groups, have the groups show their cards to the class and tell what their answer is.

Activity 12.04   Match Me (variation 4)

Place bundles of sticks with unbundled sticks into paper bags so that numbers are represented in several ways. For example, you might include three bundles and 1 stick, two bundles and 11 sticks, and one bundle with 21 sticks in three of the bags. Prepare enough bags so that each student will have one.

Have the students look in their bags to see what numbers of sticks are there. Then have them get into a group with all the other children who have the same number of sticks represented in different ways.

All the preceding examples of Match Me use equality as the matching criterion, but other matching criteria can easily be used. For example, the students could match money amounts that add up to one dollar, numbers that have a sum of 10, angles that are complementary, metric lengths that have a sum of 1 meter, or shapes that can be combined to form a rectangle. But, whichever variation of Match Me is used, and whichever matching criterion is used, *remember that Match Me is a practice activity, and concepts and skills must be developed before they can be practiced.*

The next matching activity is called *Piles*. Again, we see two variations of the activity demonstrating how it can be used for different content. Note that although the content is different in the two activities, the procedures are identical. For example, the content of this activity could be adapted to equal area of congruent figures, or to sets of numbers with the same means.

Activity 12.05   Piles (variation 1)

Prepare cards showing addition examples. Include many sets of examples with the same answers:

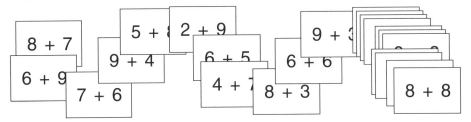

Mix the cards. Place one in the board tray, and pass the rest out to the students. Have the children come, one at a time, to place their cards in the board tray. If there is already a card in the tray with the same answer as is on a child's card, the card is placed on top of the one with the same answer. If there is not a card in the tray with the same answer as a child's card, the child should start a new pile.

When all the cards have been placed in the board tray, go through the cards in each pile with the students to check whether the answers are all the same.

Activity 12.06   Piles (variation 2)

Prepare cards showing geometric shapes. Include many squares, circles, rectangles, and triangles, all of different sizes:

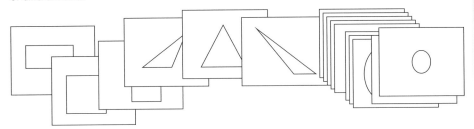

Mix the cards, place one in the board tray, and pass the rest out to the students. One at a time, have the children place their cards in the board tray. If there is already a card in the tray with the same shape as a student's card, the card is placed on top of the one with the same shape. If there is not a card in the tray with the same shape as is on a student's card, he or she should start a new pile.

When all the cards have been placed in the board tray, go through the cards in each pile with the students to check whether the shapes are all the same.

Piles is another activity that is very kinesthetic, and students usually enjoy it while getting to think about many examples. However, the involvement level is not high in this activity. Only one student is actively involved at a time, while all the rest of the children are either waiting for their turns or they are finished. If the activity is used too often, the students will get tired of it and misbehaviors could occur during the time that they are uninvolved. Piles can be an effective practice activity if it is not overused. The children will stay mentally involved even when it is not their turn. *Remember, though, that it is practice and should be used only after sufficient concept development has taken place.*

Still another kinesthetic matching activity is *Scavenger Hunt*. This activity also has the advantage of encouraging a lot of student cooperation and communication. In activities 12.07 and 12.08, we see two variations that demonstrate the variety of content for which it can be used.

Activity 12.07 Scavenger Hunt (variation 1)

Prepare four different lists of answers like the ones illustrated next. Also prepare large cards with problems on them. Every answer on a list must have a matching problem card. Several problem cards that do not match any answers should also be included.

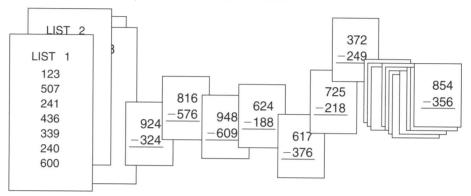

Tape the problem cards to the walls of the classroom.

Form four teams and give each team one of the answer lists. Tell the students that each team is to find a problem that matches each of the answers on their list. They are to collect the problems that match their answers, and when they have all of them, bring them to the teacher. The first team to finish correctly wins.

Activity 12.08 Scavenger Hunt (variation 2)

Prepare four different lists of names of shapes like the ones illustrated next. Also prepare large cards with geometric shapes on them. Every shape name on a list must have a matching shape card. Several shape cards that do not match any shape names should also be included.

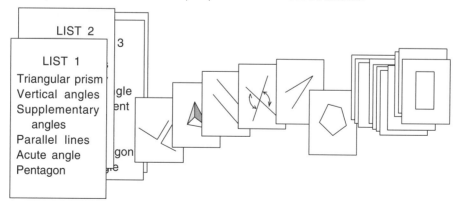

Tape the shape cards to the walls of the classroom.

Form four teams and give each team one of the shape-name lists. Tell the students that each team is to find a shape that matches each of the shape names on their list. They are to collect the shapes that match their shape names, and when they have all of them, bring them to the teacher. The first team to finish correctly wins.

There are many matching activities involving cards that are effective with small groups of two to four students. These small-group activities offer opportunities for students to talk about the mathematical concepts or skills that they use when they participate. One such activity is *Concentration*. We include three variations of Concentration to demonstrate how it can be used to practice a wide variety of content.

Activity 12.09   Concentration (variation 1)

Prepare 12 pairs of matching cards. Each pair of cards should have one showing the picture of a shape and the other showing the name of that shape:

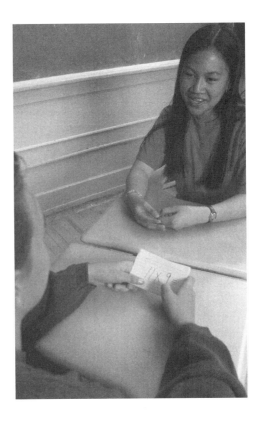

Form a group of two to four players. Shuffle the cards and place them facedown in six rows of four cards.

Players take turns. The player turns two cards over. If the cards match, the player takes them and the play is finished. If the cards do not match, the player returns the cards to their facedown positions, and the play is finished. Play continues until all the cards have been taken. The player with the most cards wins.

Activity 12.10 Concentration (variation 2)

Prepare 12 pairs of cards. Each pair of cards should have both cards picturing coins that are less than 10 cents, and the amounts on the coins in each pair should add up to 10 cents.

Form a group of two to four players. Shuffle the cards and place them facedown in six rows of four cards.

Players take turns. The player turns two cards over. If the money on the cards adds up to 10 cents, the player takes them and the play is finished. If the money on the cards does not add up to 10 cents, the player returns the cards to their facedown positions, and the play is finished. Play continues until all the cards have been taken. The player with the most cards wins.

Activity 12.11 Concentration (variation 3)

Prepare 30 cards showing one-digit numbers. There should be 3 cards showing each of the numbers 0 through 9:

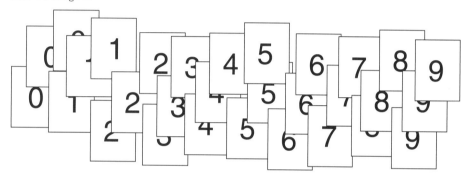

Form a group of two to four players. Shuffle the cards and place them facedown in six rows of 5 cards. Players take turns.

The player turns two cards over. If the cards have a sum of 9, the player takes them and the play is finished. If the cards do not have a sum of 9, the player returns the cards to their facedown positions, and the play is finished. Play continues until all the cards have been taken. The player with the most cards wins.

The procedures described in these concentration activities are different from those that are usually followed (Tucker, 1981). In most concentration games, if a player finds a match, he or she gets to try to find another one and can continue to pick up cards as long as he or she finds matches. In the procedures recommended here, the player is allowed to pick up only one match in each turn. The reason this is recommended is that we want to reduce the amount of time the other players have to wait for their turns (the time when they are not directly involved). This helps to maintain interest for a longer time and to reduce disruptive off-task behavior.

Another small-group card game that is a matching activity is *Pairs*. This game has simple procedures that can be quickly taught, as is true of the other activities presented in this chapter. The Pairs activity can be used to provide practice with a great variety of content. Activities 12.12, 12.13, and 12.14 demonstrate this variety.

Activity 12.12 Pairs (variation 1)

Prepare 25 pairs of cards showing division examples with one-digit divisors and two-digit dividends. The cards in each pair should have the same remainder. Remember that the remainder could be 0. You may use the same remainder in more than one pair.

Form a group of two to four players. Shuffle the cards and place them facedown on the table. Spread 3 starter cards faceup around the deck.

Players take turns. The player takes 1 card from the deck and turns it over, placing it with the other starter cards. If the player sees 2 cards that have the same remainder, the player takes those cards and the turn is over. If no 2 cards have the same remainder, the turn is over.

Play continues until all the cards have been turned faceup and all possible matching pairs have been taken. The player with the most cards wins.

Activity 12.13 Pairs (variation 2)

Prepare 25 pairs of cards showing lengths expressed in standard units. The cards in each pair should have equal lengths (for example, 24 inches and 2 feet).

Form a group of two to four players. Shuffle the cards and place them facedown on the table. Spread 3 starter cards faceup around the deck.

Players take turns. The player takes 1 card from the deck and turns it over, placing it with the other starter cards. If the player sees 2 cards that have equal lengths, the player takes those cards and the turn is over. If no 2 cards have equal lengths, the turn is over.

Play continues until all the cards have been turned faceup and all possible matching pairs have been taken. The player with the most cards wins.

Activity 12.14 Pairs (variation 3)

Prepare 25 pairs of cards showing pictures of combinations of coins. The cards in each pair should show the same amount of money (for example, 2 nickels and 1 dime, or 1 dime, 1 nickel, and 5 pennies).

Form a group of two to four players. Shuffle the cards and place them facedown on the table. Spread 3 starter cards faceup around the deck.

Players take turns. The player takes 1 card from the deck and turns it over, placing it with the other starter cards. If the player sees 2 cards that have equal amounts of money, the player takes those cards and the turn is over. If no 2 cards have equal amounts of money, the turn is over.

Play continues until all the cards have been turned faceup and all possible matching pairs have been taken. The player with the most cards wins.

Another small-group card game that can be an effective way to provide practice is a simplified variation of *Rummy*. The procedures for playing Rummy are more complex than the ones that we have seen so far. The added complexity means that Rummy is probably not appropriate for children younger than third- or fourth-graders. In activities 12.15 and 12.16, we demonstrate that Rummy can be used with a wide variety of content.

Activity 12.15 Rummy (variation 1)

Prepare 48 cards showing multiplication facts without answers. There should be 4 cards for each answer.

Form a group of two to four players. Shuffle the cards. Deal each player 6 cards, and place the rest of the deck facedown. Turn over the top card and place it next to the deck to start a discard pile.

Players take turns. On each play, the player may draw either the top card from the deck or the top card from the discard pile. If the player holds 2 or more cards that have the same answer, the matching cards are laid faceup on the table. If the player has cards with the same answer as cards that have been laid down by other players, those cards may be laid down with the others having the same answer. When the player is unable to lay down any more cards, he or she places 1 card on the discard deck, and the play is finished.

Play continues in this fashion until a player has used all the cards in his or her hand. That player is the winner. If no one has won when the deck has been played, then there is no winner.

Activity 12.16   Rummy (variation 2)

Prepare 48 cards showing metric lengths. There should be 4 cards for each length:

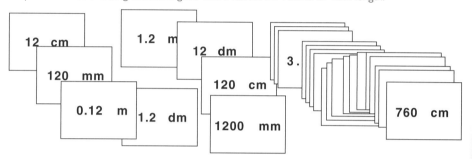

Form a group of two to four players. Shuffle the cards. Deal each player 6 cards, and place the rest of the deck facedown. Turn over the top card and place it next to the deck to start a discard pile.

Players take turns. On each play, the player may draw either the top card from the deck or the top card from the discard pile. If the player holds 2 or more cards that have equal lengths, the matching cards are laid faceup on the table. If the player has cards with the same length as cards that have been laid down by other players, those cards may be laid down with the others having the same length. When the player is unable to lay down any more cards, he or she places 1 card on the discard deck, and the play is finished.

Play continues in this fashion until a player has used all the cards in his or her hand. That player is the winner. If no one has won when the deck has been played, then there is no winner.

Ordering Activities

Another category of activities requires the participant to make comparisons or to arrange things in order. There are multiple uses for these activities also, since many things that we study in mathematics can be arranged in order. The first activity from this category that we consider is *Line Up A*. It is kinesthetic, requiring the students to get up and move about in order to complete the required tasks. To demonstrate the flexibility of this activity, we show three variations in activities 12.17, 12.18, and 12.19.

Activity 12.17   Line Up A (variation 1)

Prepare large cards showing lengths in standard units. There should be enough cards for each participating student to have one. The cards should be big enough so that they can be read from a distance. There should not be cards with equal lengths.

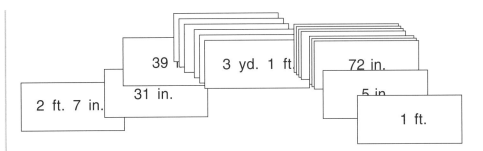

Shuffle the cards, and give one to each student. Separate the class into two teams. Have the teams go to opposite sides of the room.

Tell them to line up along the wall so that the lengths are in order from shortest to longest. When both teams are lined up, have them hold their cards in front of them so the other team can read them.

Have each team check the other to see if the members are lined up exactly right. Discuss the line-ups. Why are they correct, or why are they not correct?

Activity 12.18 Line Up A (variation 2)

Prepare large cards showing multiplication facts. There should be enough cards for each participating student to have one. The cards should be big enough so that they can be read from a distance.

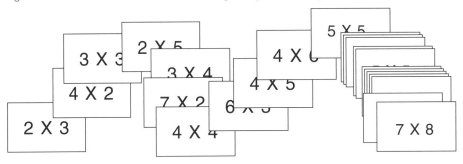

Shuffle the cards, and give one to each student. Separate the class into two teams. Have the teams go to opposite sides of the room.

Tell them to line up along the wall so that their answers are in order from smallest to largest. When both teams are lined up, have them hold their cards in front of them so the other team can read them.

Have each team check the other to see if the members are lined up exactly right. Discuss the line-ups. Why are they correct, or why are they not correct?

Activity 12.19 Line Up A (variation 3)

Prepare large cards showing mixed computation examples without answers. There should be enough cards for each participating student to have one. The cards should be big enough so that they can be read from a distance. Avoid having two cards with the same answer.

Shuffle the cards, and give one to each student. Separate the class into two teams. Have the teams go to opposite sides of the room.

Tell them to line up along the wall so that their answers are in order from smallest to largest. When both teams are lined up, have them hold their cards in front of them so the other team can read them.

Have each team check the other to see if the members are lined up exactly right. Discuss the line-ups. Why are they correct, or why are they not correct?

The second activity in this category, *Line Up B*, is another good kinesthetic activity. It is a version of Line Up A, but it uses alternative procedures. Whereas Line Up A encourages the students to help their team members get lined up correctly, Line Up B minimizes a student's opportunities to get help from classmates. Line Up B is just as flexible as Line Up A and can be used with a wide variety of content topics.

Activity 12.20   Line Up B

Prepare large cards like the ones described in activities 12.17, 12.18, or 12.19.

Shuffle the cards, and give one to each child. Choose two students to come to the front of the room and hold their cards so that the other students can read them.

Have other students come forward, one at a time, and stand in line with the others so that their answers are in order from smallest to largest. If a student has difficulty deciding where to stand, have the other students help.

There are several small-group activities that are based on comparisons or ordering. One of these activities is a game called *Shuffle*. Shuffle emphasizes arranging problems in order quickly. As students play Shuffle, they quickly realize that they do not need to know the exact answers but, rather, just which answers are bigger or smaller. As a result, the game naturally becomes an estimation activity. Although only one variation is included here, Shuffle can also be used to provide practice with a variety of content topics.

Activity 12.21   Shuffle

Prepare a deck of 40 cards showing two-digit addition examples. Avoid having 2 cards with the same answer.

Form a group of two to four students. They take turns dealing the cards.

On each play, the dealer shuffles the cards and gives each player 4 cards facedown. When the dealer says "Go," the players race to arrange their cards in order from smallest answer to largest answer.

The first player to correctly arrange the cards in order scores 1 point. The first player to get 5 points is the winner.

Compare is another small-group comparison activity. Activities 12.22, 12.23, and 12.24 are three versions of this game. The content variations that are illustrated can be used in all three versions.

Activity 12.22   Compare: Big Wins

Prepare a deck of 40 cards showing two-digit addition examples. Avoid having 2 cards with the same answer.

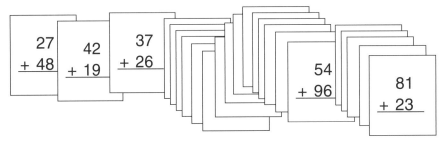

Form a group of two to four students. They take turns dealing the cards.

On each play, the dealer gives 1 card to each player. The players compare their cards, and the player with the largest answer takes the cards used in that play.

When there are not enough cards for another play, the player with the most cards is the winner.

Activity 12.23   Compare: Small Wins

Prepare a deck of 40 cards showing rectangles labeled with their dimensions. Avoid having 2 cards with the same area.

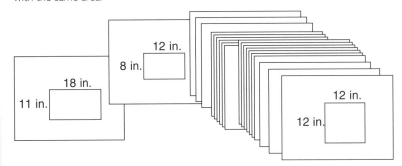

Form a group of two to four students. They take turns dealing the cards.

On each play, the dealer gives 1 card to each player. The players compare their cards, and the player with the smallest area takes the cards used in that play.

When there are not enough cards for another play, the-player with the most cards is the winner.

Activity 12.24   Compare: Dealer's Choice

Prepare a deck of 40 cards showing multiplication facts without answers. Avoid having 2 cards with the same product.

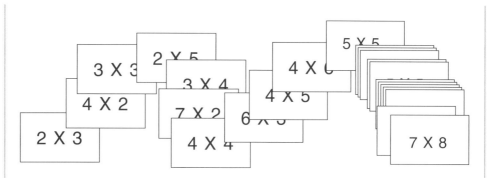

Form a group of two to four students. They take turns dealing the cards.

On each play, the dealer gives 1 card, facedown, to each player. Before anyone looks at his or her card, the dealer indicates whether the big answer or the small answer will win. Then, the players compare their cards, and the player with the winning card takes the cards used in that play. If there is a tie, all the cards from that play stay on the table, and the winner of the next play takes them also.

When there are not enough cards for another play, the player with the most cards wins the game.

Answer or Example Construction Activities

Many excellent practice activities require the students to construct their own examples or answers, rather than select from examples or answers that are given to them. We now show a selection of activities of this type. The answer or example construction activities range from small-group to whole-class activities. Many of them are flexible and can be used for a wide variety of content.

Century Mark is an interesting small-group game that provides practice with two-digit addition and subtraction. Activity 12.25 is appropriate for children in grades 3 through 5.

Activity 12.25 Century Mark

Prepare a deck of 50 cards showing the digits 0 through 9. There should be 5 cards for each digit:

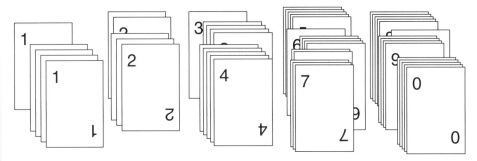

Form a group of two to four children. Shuffle the cards and place the deck facedown on the table. Each player writes a beginning score of 0 on a sheet of paper. On each play, each player takes 2 cards from the deck and forms a two-digit number. (For example, if a player draws 7 and 4, that player could form either 74 or 47. If a player draws 3 and 0, the player could form 30 or 03.) The players then either add their numbers to their current score, or they may subtract their numbers from their current score.

Play continues until a player's score is exactly 100. That player wins the game. If play continues without a winner until there are not enough cards for another play, the game ends, and the player whose score is closest to 100 is the winner.

Another excellent small-group practice activity is *Target Practice*. Activities 12.26 through 12.31 illustrate the flexibility of this activity.

Activity 12.26 Target Practice (variation 1)

Prepare a deck of 50 cards like those illustrated in Activity 12.25, showing the digits 0 through 9.

Form a group of two to four students. They take turns dealing the cards.

On each play, the dealer shuffles the cards and gives each player 2 cards. The players add the numbers on their cards. The player with the sum closest to 10 takes all the cards used in that play.

If there is a tie, the cards from that play are left on the table. The winner of the next play gets those cards also.

When there are not enough cards for another play, the player who has taken the most cards is the winner.

Activity 12.27 Target Practice (variation 2)

Prepare a deck of 50 cards like those illustrated in Activity 12.25, showing the digits 0 through 9.

Form a group of two to four students. They take turns dealing the cards.

On each play, the dealer shuffles the cards and gives each player 2 cards. The players use their cards to form two-digit numbers. The player whose two-digit number is closest to 50 takes all the cards used in that play.

If there is a tie, cards from that play are left on the table. The winner of the next play gets those cards also.

When there are not enough cards for another play, the player who has taken the most cards is the winner.

Activity 12.28 Target Practice (variation 3)

Prepare a deck of 50 cards like those illustrated in Activity 12.25, showing the digits 0 through 9.

Form a group of two to four students. They take turns dealing the cards.

On each play, the dealer shuffles the cards and gives each player 3 cards. Each player uses 2 of the 3 cards to form a two-digit number. The player whose two-digit number is closest to 50 takes all the cards used in that play.

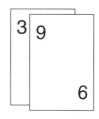
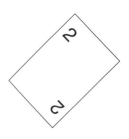

If there is a tie, the cards from that play are left on the table. The winner of the next play gets those cards also.

When there are not enough cards for another play, the player who has taken the most cards is the winner.

Activity 12.29 Target Practice (variation 4)

Prepare a deck of 50 cards like those illustrated in Activity 12.25, showing the digits 0 through 9. Form a group of two to four students. They take turns dealing the cards.

On each play, the dealer shuffles the cards and gives each player 4 cards. Each player uses the cards to form 2 two-digit numbers whose sum is as close to 100 as possible. The player whose sum is closest to 100 takes all the cards used in that play.

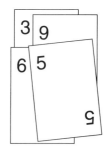

If there is a tie, the cards from that play are left on the table. The winner of the next play gets those cards also.

When there are not enough cards for another play, the player who has taken the most cards is the winner.

Activity 12.30 Target Practice (variation 5)

Prepare a deck of 50 cards like those illustrated in Activity 12.25, showing the digits 0 through 9. Form a group of two to four students. They take turns dealing the cards.

On each play, the dealer shuffles the cards and gives each player 3 cards. Each player uses the cards to form a two-digit number and a one-digit number whose product is as close to 200 as possible. The player whose product is closest to 200 takes all the cards used in that play.

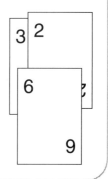

If there is a tie, the cards from that play are left on the table. The winner of the next play gets those cards also.

When there are not enough cards for another play, the player who has taken the most cards is the winner.

Activity 12.31   Target Practice (variation 6)

Prepare a deck of 50 cards like those illustrated in Activity 12.25, showing the digits 0 through 9. Form a group of two to four students. They take turns dealing the cards.

On each play, the dealer shuffles the cards and gives each player 5 cards. Each player uses the cards to form a three-digit number and a two-digit number whose difference is as close to 500 as possible. The player whose difference is closest to 500 takes all the cards used in that play.

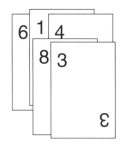

If there is a tie, the cards from that play are left on the table. The winner of the next play gets those cards also.

When there are not enough cards for another play, the player who has taken the most cards is the winner.

The final answer or example construction activity that we present in this chapter is *Shape Makers*. In this activity, students create shapes by stretching a loop of rope.

Activity 12.32   Shape Makers

Make a loop of rope by tying the ends of a rope that is about 25 feet long.

Give the rope to a group of four students. Have them stretch the rope loop out to make a rectangle. Have them also make a square. Have them try to make a circle. Ask why this is not possible.

Form a group of 3 students. Have them stretch the rope into the shape of a triangle. Have them make a triangle with all three sides equal. Have them make a right triangle. Then have them try to make a rectangle. Ask why this is not possible.

Have 6 students try to make a circle. Have 10 students try to make a circle. Can 20 students make a circle?

Summary

There are many activities that provide interesting—even fun—practice. Good practice activities are widely varied. Some of these activities are games, where there are winners. Others can be just as engaging even though they are not games. Good practice activities have varying levels of active involvement. They range from small-group to whole-class activities. Good practice activities range from very kinesthetic to moderately kinesthetic to fairly sedate. Good practice activities nearly always allow interaction among the students about the concepts or skills being practiced.

Most effective teachers of middle-grade students in mathematics develop and use a wide repertoire of non-pencil-and-paper practice activities. But even though those activities are neat and lots of fun, the effective teacher must remember that *practice activities can be effective only after the concepts and skills have been adequately developed.* They know that *mathematical concepts and skills must be learned before they can be practiced.* And, of course, they know that *before we can expect those concepts and skills to be learned, they must be taught.*

References and Related Readings

National Council of Teachers of Mathematics. (2000). *Principles and standards for school mathematics.* Reston, VA: Author.

Tucker, B. F. (1981). Variations on concentration. *The Arithmetic Teacher, 29*(3), 22–23.

Activities to Take to Your Classroom

Index